REAL ESTATE INVESTMENT STRATEGY

REAL ESTATE INVESTMENT STRATEGY

SECOND EDITION

MAURY SELDIN
Professor of Finance and Real Estate
School of Business Administration
The American University
Washington, D.C.

RICHARD H. SWESNIK
Chairman of the Board
Swesnik and Blum Companies,
Washington, D.C.

JOHN WILEY & SONS
New York•Chichester
Brisbane•Toronto

Library of Congress Cataloging in Publication Data:

Seldin/Maury, 1931
    Real Estate 2nd Ed.

    Investment Strategy 1st Ed. published under title: Real Estate
    Investment Strategy.

    "A Wiley publication."
    Includes index.
    Real Estate Investment   I   Swesnik, Richard H., joint
    author.   II   Title.

HD 1375.535   1979   332.6   324   78-26734
ISBN   0-471-05012-1

Printed in the United States of America

10   9   8   7   6   5   4   3   2   1

To Rachel and Sylvia

PREFACE
TO THE FIRST EDITION

How many times have you asked someone in real estate investments, "Do you have anything good coming up soon that I may be interested in?" Have you ever wondered, "What is best to invest in—vacant land or an apartment house)" You have probably often wished that you could obtain answers to such questions in a brief statement or two.

Unfortunaltely no simple answer is possible. The real estate investment process is a complex one. Its risks and rewards vary by kind of property and financing; timing and location also make a big difference. An understanding of the fundamentals is necessary for intelligent real estate decisions.

There is no better way to invest money, provided you seriously wish to make a profitable investment (rather than play a money game) and are willing to accept the risks inherent in real estate investment. This type of investing is for you only if you are an investor seeking profits, not a saver seeking interest. To decide whether to invest in real estate, you must understand the economic benefits of such investment—cash flow, tax shelter, and proceeds of sale. You should know that your profit potential depends, among other factors, on *when* you enter the investment process. You should also know the cast of characters in the investment process.

The method of financing your investment can increase or decrease the risk and rewards. Hency you should know who provides the money and how and why money markets change, as well as which type of real estate presents the greatest risks and rewards, and which is the safest though probably the least profitable.

When investing in real estate you have a choice among land, houses, garden apartments, high-rise apartment buildings, stores and shopping centers, office buildings, and such special-purpose structures as gas stations, industrial sites, warehouses, hotels, and motels. You must decide which type of real estate is the best for you.

You must also choose the method of taking title— whether alone, in partnership with others, or as stockholder in real estate corporations and real estate investment trusts, and if so, what *kind* of corporations and trusts.

How do you go about "getting in" and, more importantly, when and how do you "get out?" Is it necessary to develop an investment strategy or can you analyze each opportunity as it arises and evaluate it on the spot?

This book is inteded to fill a void in the literature. It serves as a guide to the real estate investor in developing his investment strategy, hence in making profitable investment decisions. Much of the material is of necessity based on personal observation and experience because sufficient data on investment results simply are not available. The book is pragmatic in approach. it represents hundreds of converstsations with the Who's Who of the real estate industry and incorporates their actual investing experiences, drawing lessons from the mistakes of those among them who "flew by the seat of their pants" and are no longer flying. The book also makes full use of the body of knowledge that has been developed in the field of real estate investment. It makes no sense for an investor to learn the hard way, through error. This is too expensive a way. A better approach is to do the learning, analyzing, evaluating, and drawing up of a general strategy *before* you part with your money.

Maury Seldin
Richard H. Swesnik

October 1978

PREFACE

This second edition of *Real Estate Investment Strategy*, published approximately nine years later than the first edition, contains five significant factors that could have a major impact on anyone's real estate investment strategy.

First: The federal income tax laws have been changed by the acts of 1976 and 1978, and these changes relate, in the main, to the postponement of construction real estate tax and interest write-offs gradually until 1982, when the write-offs commencing the year the property is placed in service must be spread over a ten year period. Additionally, the capital gains rate has been reduced so that sales of income-producing properties are no longer as heavily taxed as before. All these changes have been introduced in this new edition. Since Congress seems to be forever tinkering with out tax laws, new changes will probably be made. Happily, we have never been overly enamored with tax losses, and we have stressed the importance of avoiding "taxation gymnastics" while concentrating on the economic and pragmatic factors that influence the risks and rewards of real estate investing. (We express our gratitiude to Elliot H. Cole, Esquire, a partner in the law firm of Patton, Boggs and Blow, Washington, D.C., who assisted us in conforming the manuscript with the Tax Reform Act of 1976, and the 1978 revisions.)

Second: The marketing of major properties in desirable locations used to require a good deal of thought and negotiations over a rather extended period of time. Because of the influx into the United States of Canadian, Western European, and Arab monies, this is no longer true. Canadians leaving the French sections of Canada emigrated (with their capital) mainly to the United States because of our ethnic and language similarities. Many were investors and developers in Canada

The Western Europeans viewed the drop in the value of the United States Dollar (1976-1978) as compared to their respective currencies as a bargain too compelling to overlook. The creeping socialism of Western European governments is also viewed as anathema to the financial future of well-off Western Europeans. They sought and found income-producing real estate in our major cities.

Because of the steadily increasing prices of crude oil, an entire select generation of Arabs has become wealthy and as a consequence feels a need to invest. Many are acquiring income-producing properties in our major cities.

These three investment-conscious groups have been in competition to acquire quality income-producing properties. Cash on the down payment returns (cash-on-cash) have dropped from approximately 10% in 1969 to as little as 4% in 1978. The future will depend on the aforementioned demand factors and inflation.

The rate of inflation accelerated during the past nine years. This has not only brought in new investors looking for the protection we discuss, but it has caused investments in prime properties to have massive increases in their net worths. Some investors have quadrupled their net worth *without additional* investing, simply by having a strategy utilizing the principles outlined in the first edition. They took advantage of the timing and location.

Third: There has been a major increase in consumer political activity, which became evident when California's Proposition 13 was enacted into law. We have residential rent controls in two major cities: Los Angeles, and Washington, D.C., both enacted during the past five years. Although the information relating to residential rental properties in the first edition is still valid, a new and significant risk may affect future investments in residential rental properties. We call this risk a "political risk" which now must be weighed together with other economic risks: financial, purchasing power, and liquidity when evaluating the risks and rewards extant in every income-producing investment. It is axiomatic that *the greater the risk, the greater the rewards.* To cover the new political risk involved, higher cash flows must be generated from residential rental property. Many astute real estate investors feel that local rent control laws are virtually confiscatory. One possibility is that they will seek federal government *insurance* against what they view as confiscatory rent controls enacted by local governments. American businesses currently may obtain federal insurance from having their foreign properties and businesses confiscated by a foreign government without fair compensation. The reasoning for having federal insurance against local rent controls for investors owning residential rental properties appears to have merit. But that is for our congress to decide.

Fourth: As a practical matter, it is no longer economically feasible in most areas to build a high-rise apartment building for rental as an investment. Most apartment construction has some subsidy. Current building costs (1978) in Washington, D.C., are such that in order to "break even" an ennual rental of at least $13,000 a square foot is necessary. A fairly snug two-bedroom, two-bath apartment (1,000 square feet) would rent for about $1,100 monthly, not including garage space, just to bring the owner enough money to allow the owner merely to break even! Very few families can allocate this much of their monthly income solely for rent. This means that aal new high-rise apartments must be offered for sale as condominiums rather than held for rental income. The discussion of rental properties is expanded to include condominimum investments.

Fifth: Financing has changed dramatically during the last decade. Swings in the cost of money have become wider. Thus financial strategy has become more important than ever before. The elements discussed in the first edition still hold, but the discussion has been expanded to include wrap around mortgages as a way of holding on to the benefits of olden, lower-rate mortgages. In making an investment choice between common stocks and income-producing properties, and examination of real returns over the last decade leaves stocks a poor, poor second choice. The Dow-Jones index was at about 1000 in December 1968. The index was at about 800 in December 1978. How it will fare over the next decade is open. But, people are flocking to real estate. If you want to capture the mood, ask anyone who bought a home in the late 1960s and sold it in the late 1970's how well they did. There is no guarantee that the next decade will be as good for real estate as the last. But if you are an investor or would be investor, you would be well advised to develop a strategy and revise it with the times. This second edition is designed to help you in developing your strategy for the early 1980s.

MAURY SELDIN
RICHARD H. SWESNIK

February 1979

CONTENTS

PART TWO
REAL ESTATE DEVELOPMENT PROCESS   53

PART THREE
FINANCING REAL ESTATE INVESTMENTS   105

LIST OF TABLES

REAL ESTATE INVESTMENT STRATEGY

PART ONE

Introduction

1 THE IMPOSSIBLE DREAM

In our culture it is almost impossible to escape the "Horatio Alger" syndrome. There is nothing wrong in setting high professional or even personal goals, but it is sheer madness to speculate wildly in real estate investments. When we learn of small fortunes made in real estate, we feel it can happen to us. Because you may be very astute and highly imaginative and may have had good fortune in a small investment or two, you may be mesmerized into seeking higher rewards than prudence dictates.

Consider that the value of any real estate is not enhanced simply because *you* are going to invest in it. No matter what management techniques you develop, what imagination you bring to bear, or how you handle the financing, the ultimate success of the investment will depend on its timing, its location, and the quality built into the structure. *You* cannot make a loser into a winner. It is possible however to make a mediocre investment produce satisfactory results by your own skills. That is the best you can do, aside from putting yourself in a position where timing and location will help you.

We hereby imply a conservative strategy—pick an investment with which you can live. You may wind up with a fantastic winner if you only play long shots, but the risks will be way out of line with the rewards.

WHAT TO EXPECT

Compared to other investments, it is not unreasonable to assume you can do *very* well in real estate investments. Published data on the broad spectrum of real estate investment results are not available. However some generalizations, based on our experience and observation, are possible, which may serve as a guide for your investment decision-making.

It is not unreasonable to expect the following:

1. Tripling your money in three years in land investment (speculation) using 80% leverage.
2. Tripling your money in 8 to 12 years in garden apartments using 75 to 80% leverage.
3. Quadrupling your money in 8 to 12 years in high-rise apartments using 75 to 80% leverage.
4. Quintupling your money in 8 to 12 years in office- building investment using 80 to 90% leverage.
5. Quadrupling your money in 5 to 7 years in shopping-center investment using 80 to 90% leverage.

Investment Strategy

With these economic benefits accruing to winners, why not develop an investment strategy that will put you in the winner's circle? Such a strategy demands that you *put in writing* your own investment policies. Your stated objectives will include what type of real estate investment you will consider, what kind of financing you will accept, how much you will invest, how much liability you will assume, where in the pyramid (the owning cycle) you will invest, whether you will go it alone or invest with others, and how long you will remain with the investment, You might also *put in writing* what you will *not* do under any circumstances. For example: you may not want an investment so risky as to jeopardize your entire investment, and possibly more; you may want to avoid an investment that could have a negative cash flow; you may not want any single investment to be so large that your needs for capital could force a sale at an unpropitious time; you may not want an investment that will take up much of your time. The things you do not want are also objectives.

Your investment strategy will develop after you have determined the risks you are willing to assume and the probable resulting rewards. Make no mistake—the risks and the rewards are inexorably related. You alone must decide how much cash you are willing to invest, realizing that your investment is not liquid.

As an example of what goes into the development of an investment strategy, note a statement of purchasing policy developed by two fulltime investor-developers in 1956. At that time they had a combined net worth of $60,000. In 1969 their combined net worth was in excess of $2 million and by 1979 it had zoomed to over $10 million. See Figure 1.

A. Large properties only

1. Office buildings having a minimum net rental area of 80,000 square feet.
2. Shopping centers in excess of 80,000 square feet of net rentable space or prime leasebacks.
3. Industrial leasebacks such as warehouses and research laboratories to AAA-1 tenants.
4. Apartment buildings having a minimum of 100 rental units.
5. Vacant ground to accommodate any of the structures listed above.

B. New or relatively new properties only

1. To ensure an attractive property for loan purposes at the outset and for refinancing purposes after acquisition. This policy recognizes that many lenders, especially insurance companies, avoid making loans on older properties.

2. To ensure that amortization exceeds depreciation (*actual* wear and tear), so that the investor's equity is constantly increasing.

3. To provide a desirable property for sale after depreciation is no longer attractive enough in its tax consequences to produce tax-sheltered income. (This policy should not rule out properties that have been or may be completely restored through the installation of new mechanical, electrical, and air-conditioning equipment.)

C. Large equities, never thin

The payment of sufficient equity capital above a conservative first deed of trust (mortgage) to ensure servicing of nonfluctuating debt service even in periods of economic recession.

D. Limited to Washington, D. C., and surrounding area

With the heavy concentration of federal and local governmental employment, we believe that Washington provides an atmosphere of economic stability enjoyed by extremely few metropolitan areas.

Only very impressive factors concerning other metropolitan areas may dictate a variance from this policy.

E. No speculative-type business properties

We do not buy any real property whose major source of income is derived from the operation of speculative-type business ventures such as hotels, motels, swimming pools, golf links, or country clubs, amusement parks, bowling alleys, or stadiums; nor single-purpose buildings, such as funeral homes, garages, or automobile retail locations.

Figure 1 Statement of Purchasing Policy

Other investment policies will better suit other investors. The important thing is to get the right policies to suit your objectives and your willingness to take on risks. In addition you want the right kinds of property and ownership forms to match your ability and willingness to manage your investments.

You cannot expect to reap all of the projected benefits if you invest in a joint venture or limited partnership.

Understand how much "load" you will be paying for someone else (a builder, a developer, or a syndicator) to acquire or develop the investment project for you and others and deduct this "load" from your potential benefits. Some practitioners charge more of a "load" than others—and they are not necessarily better than those who charge less.

If you select a real estate investment trust as an investing vehicle, analyze what you are paying (in terms of less benefits) for such an investment. Remember that there may be no tax shelter in such an investment. You may reasonably expect capital gains distributions from an equity trust as well as increases in the value of the certificates of beneficial interests from both types of trusts.

Experienced investors do not deviate from their written objectives. They review their objectives frequently to determine, in the light of changing tax laws and changing personal net worths, whether their investing policies still have validity for them. Although many subjective investors have done well (especially in a booming market), without an investment strategy, you are up against formidable forces mitigating against economic gain. In the high-risk ventures there are more losers than winners. You just do not hear about them. Unfortunately subjectivity in real estate investment decisions is more prevalent than objectivity, many important decisions are made on the basis of emotions, rather than fact. We are swayed by such subjective conclusion statements as, "it is bound to go up," "when the beltway goes near this parcel of land, your investment return can be fantastic," "this location will *always* be great," and "you'll *never* have a vacancy." Learn to identify conclusion statements and separate them from fact. Just because you *want* them to be true, it does not follow that conclusion statements *are* true. The kind of wishful thinking that propels people into unwise investments cannot happen to you if you have an investment strategy and if you remain objective. Make sure however that your strategy is realistic.

Selecting an Investment

You will not find property that is ideal in view of your objectives. You may want more in benefits and less in risks than you can realistically expect to get. And, even if you are not overly optimistic on rewards relative to risks, you probably will not find property that exactly fits your investment ideal.

Each parcel of real estate is unique. None is perfect. Its location may be imperfect because of some adverse land use nearby. It may be a little too old. It may be too big. It may seem to miss the path of development. The design may not suit your taste. You will see some mistakes that could have been easily prevented. In short it is not perfect.

The questions should be whether the proposed investment meets your objectives *reasonably* well. You may have to compromise a little to obtain a satisfactory relationship between rewards and risks. In making such a compromise your realistic and objective judgment can make the difference between a good and a bad investment. If you are not discriminating enough, you will make investments that are ill suited to your needs. If you are too choosy, you will not make any investent.

THE INVESTMENT DECISION

By the time you reach the point of decision, the decision itself should be relatively easy. You have started with your general investment objectives and an assessment of your liquidity needs. You have decided to seek some protection from inflation and to risk some of your capital. At this point you know how much you have to invest.

You now want to know how best to invest your money, rather than do nothing with it. Having decided to give up liquidity, you need only to select the type of real estate investment.

Your range of choice is not very wide. It is narrowed

through the process by which you select the particular property. The process varies with individual circumstances, but you can expect that you will either look for the right people to get you into an investment, or look for a general type of investment, or do both at the same time.

If you have already invested in real estate without much success, do not blame the broker, the developer, or the market. Chances are that you did not apply the technique of starting with a written investment strategy or that you failed to stay objective. Do not fret about it—after all most of us have made even more important decisions on a highly subjective basis. Isn't that how most of us got married?

This book provides you with the *basic knowledge necessary to decide on the type of real estate investment that meets your needs* and to obtain the information to make that decision. Technical experts can be consulted for answers to the technical questions. You alone however bear the responsibility, and therefore you alone should judge what risks you will take and what rewards you will seek.

Obtaining information about a specific parcel of real estate can be a chore, but if it leads to the right kind of investment, it will pay off in the long run. By buying the service necessary to protect yourself on the technical questions and by selecting properties that are basically sound and that you can afford to hold, you will wind up with a winner even if you pay a bit too much or make some minor mistakes.

DEVELOPING AN INVESTMENT STRATEGY

Developing an investment strategy requires choosing risks in order to get rewards. The next chapter discusses the selection of risks and Chapter 3 explains the rewards.

2 SELECTING RISKS

An investment strategy is a plan for making investment decisions—how much money to put into real estate, what kind of real estate to buy, where to invest, and how to get into a real estate investment. The guidelines in the plan are called policies.

Policies oriented toward making the most money call for taking substantial risks. For example if you took all your cash and borrowed heavily for a down payment on land, you would be pursuing an aggressive policy.

Policies that are designed to protect the investor from loss are defensive policies. Diversifying your investments is a defensive policy. It provides some protection against loss because the chance of all the investments turning out to be losers is smaller than that of one investment turning out to be a loser. In addition the winning investments may compensate for the occasional losing investment. Another defensive policy is to limit real estate investments to properties that are well leased for a long period of time to tenants who are sure to pay, such as a post office leased to the United States Postal Service for 15 years or longer. While such a policy limits risks, it also reduces the potential profit.

The idea of making the most money with the least risk is sheer nonsense. Making more money implies taking more risk of some sort. The risk could be that of not getting all or some of your money back, or that any money recovered would not buy as much as when originally invested. The risk could also be that of taking a loss in order to get your money back quickly. You can make more money by taking more of one or a combination of such risks.

A sensible approach is to attempt to make the most money within the limits imposed by the amount of risk you are prepared to take. Some of the money you save is not available for investment. Its purpose is to provide ready cash for unexpected needs. You will not invest it in stocks or real estate and take the chance of not getting it back because of having selected a losing investment. You might avoid putting it into an investment, such as a long-term bond or mortgage that you could not quickly convert to cash without taking too much loss. You will keep it in cash or in something quickly convertible to cash.

You probably have a policy of keeping some amount of cash readily available. An old rule of thumb is to have available enough money for six months' living expenses. It may be available in the form of cash, savings deposits, and short-term highly liquid assets, such as United States government bills or other high-quality short term paper. Many investors will hold much higher amounts of cash and near-cash assets to meet investment as well as personal needs. Other investors will hold much smaller amounts of cash because the potential emergencies may be covered by insurance, high-quality credit, or assets that are good collateral for a loan. Some investors count on family or friends as a source of cash for emergency needs. The amount of cash anyone should hold is a highly personal matter, just as is the way in which one chooses to spend it.

Developing an investment strategy starts with the policy decision of how much cash to hold. The strategy also requires policies on how much to invest in the various kinds of assets that will go to make up the investment portfolio. Such policy decisions call for understanding the kind of risks associated with the various kinds of investments. This chapter discusses the type of risks that should be considered in developing a real estate investment strategy.

THE THREE BIG RISKS

Of the numerous risks in any investment, the following three are the most important:

1. *Financial risk*—The risk that you will not recover your money:
2. *Purchasing power risk*—The risk that when you get your money back, it will buy less than when you invested it (because of inflation).
3. *Liquidity risk*—The risk that you will lose some of your money by the process of converting to cash quickly.

No investment can be free of all three risks. Just holding cash exposes you to the purchasing power risk. Thus if you do nothing with your money and prices are rising, your money will buy less the longer you hold it. Inflation, which is a general rise in the price level, causes loss of money because the purchasing power of the money declines.

You can get some protection from the loss of purchasing power by putting your money out at interest and using some of the interest to compensate you for any loss due to inflation. But the more interest you get, the greater the chance of not getting all of the money back (financial risk) and the greater the chance that converting to cash will cost you some of your money (liquidity risk).

Understanding the effects of inflation will help you to determine how much of the purchasing power risk you are prepared to accept.

EFFECTS OF INFLATION

Holding cash or money in a checking account may bring you some real losses. Of course you will always have the same amount of dollars if you keep your money in cash. But, will the money buy as much next year as it does today? If not, you will have lost some of your money just as surely as if it had been stolen. Inflation has been a thief to holders of cash for the past quarter of a century. The economic facts of life show that all persons who hold cash and those who receive fixed incomes from retirement have suffered because of the purchasing power of the dollar.

The problem became especially severe in the latter part of the 1970s. Inflation, which had hovered at about 2% per year in the 1950s was up to 4% at times during the 60's. Then in the 70's it was up to 6%, 8% and even more. Such changes in the rate of inflation influence not only what you will do with your money, but also the investment results of what you have already done with it.

You must therefore concern yourself with how much inflation to expect. If you purchase a bond that produces a 6% annual rate of interest, you should be aware that with a 2% annual inflation you are earning only 4% on your money. The *nominal* yield is 6%. The *real* yield is 4%. You can thus compare your yield from interest-income assets with your yield from profit- seeking assets by first converting the nominal yield on these assets to a real yield. What is the real yield on a bond that pays 5% per year? If inflation is 2%, the real yield is 3%.

You may also wish to look at the amount remaining after federal income taxes have been paid. If you pay taxes at the rate of 40% of your taxable income, then on a 6% bond you have in taxes an amount equivalent to 2.4% of the amount of the bond, or $24 out of the $60 income on a $1000 bond. This would leave you with a nominal after-tax yield of 3.6%, or $36 per $1000. If inflation were also at work at the rate of 2% per year, the purchasing power of the $1000 due you would decline by 2% per year or $20. Your real after-tax yield would be 1.6% or $16 per 1000. To recapitulate:

$1000 bond at 6% interest produces income of $60

Less income taxes at 40% rate
   (0.40 × $60) $24

Loss in purchasing power at 2%
   (0.02 × $1000)   20   44

Real after-tax earnings $16

$$\text{or } \frac{\$16}{\$1000} = 1.6\%$$

To obtain an idea of the impact of inflation and rising interest rates in recent years, assume you had bought a $1000 government bond in August 1962. At the time the rate of interest was much lower than in the late 1960s. The rate of interest at that time was 4.25%, which amounts to $42.50 per year. You would over the span of seven years collect about $300 in interest (42.50 × 7 = $297.50). But seven years after you bought, investors could buy the same bond with a 6.25% yield. In August 1969 the price was about $750, which would yield about 6.25%.

If you sold that bond at the prevailing price of $750 (quoted at 75 to mean 75% of face value), which would be the best price you could get with rates at 6.25%, you would have lost $250 of your original investment. If you offset the $250 against $300 interest you receive, your interest income was $50 for the seven years you held the bond. No matter how you measure inflation you will have a loss because the $750 that you get back seven years later buys less. Inflation has not been at an even rate, but obviously those who bought bonds in the early sixties have in reality lost part of their capital when measured in purchasing power. The interest income has not been sufficient to compensate for that loss in capital. Furthermore the federal income taxes paid on the earned interest were also irrevocably lost.

Since lenders know about inflation, the rates of interest that they charge will include some compensation for an expected rate of inflation. When the rate of inflation is generally expected to rise, the lender will expect and get higher interest rates. If you own a bond, a mortgage, or any other asset that has a fixed rate of interest, the rise in interest rates will make your asset less valuable. That is, if rates rise to 7% when you have invested in an asset bearing 6% interest, you would have to sell it at a discount if you wanted to convert the asset to cash. Note that inflation and rising interest rates go together.

Since 1969 there has been a resurgence of inflation. Thus the higher interest rates further depressed bond prices. Some authors call the loss in value of the bond attributed to rising interest rates an "interest-rate" risk. Thus the bondholder might wait until maturity, reclaim the full $1000, and earn something less than 4.25% depending on the rate of inflation.

Stocks or real estate as classes of investment provide protection against inflation. The long term value of any specific share of stock or parcel of real estate is influenced by a variety of factors, the prime factor being the *ability of these assets to produce income*. Real estate income is produced by rents, which are prices, and these prices generally rise with other prices. The increase in rents actually contributes to inflation. This emphasizes the fact that real estate rental prices act as other prices in causing inflation. Thus well-located properties that have the potential for rent increases are an effective hedge against inflation.

EARNING INTEREST

If you elect to earn interest on some or all of your loanable or investable funds and take your chances on inflation, you have many choices available. You may deposit money in any one of a number of savings-type institutions. Savings and loan associations, commercial banks, savings banks, and credit unions will be delighted to accept deposits. They pay interest and permit withdrawal virtually on demand. Or you could purchase United States Savings Bonds or other government bonds that pay interest and give ample assurance that you will be repaid in full. Sometimes, as in the case of Series E, United States Savings Bonds, the price you pay for the bond is less than its face amount, which you receive if you hold the bond until maturity. Such investments have little financial risk and little liquidity risk. The rates of interest are low compared to other investments.

Governments and many major business corporations issue long-term bonds on which interest is paid semi-annually. You can buy these bonds at the time of issue for a price that is very close to the face amount and be reasonably certain that you will collect the interest when it becomes due as well as principal in 10, 20, 30, or more years. These bonds are also resold from time to time, so that the owners can obtain cash before the bonds become due. Generally long-term bonds have higher interest rates than short-term obligations, reflecting the degree of liquidity risk. The financial risk also influences the rate of interest.

The federal government has programs for guaranteeing and insuring loans made by mortgage lenders to individuals who wish to borrow by pledging real estate as security for the loan. Such loans are made by savings and loan associations, insurance companies and banks. An agency of the federal government insures these mortgages. The result is that the lender gets his money back, even if the borrower is unwilling or unable to repay and even if the property turns out to be inadequate security for the loan.

If the individual does not pay promptly and the loans are thus in default, the lender may institute foreclosure proceedings. As a result the loans are paid in full at the foreclosure sale. The government becomes the new buyer or makes up the loss. Sometimes the government issues its own bonds to replace the mortgages in default, as in the case of mortgages insured by the Federal Housing Administration (FHA). The lender cannot lose, except perhaps for some expenses or by accepting a lower rate of interest from an FHA bond. The protection varies under different programs, such as the FHA insurance programs (commonly called FHA loans) or the Veterans Administration guarantee programs (commonly called VA loans).

Arrangements have been made to enable individuals to purchase FHA-insured mortgages or participation interests in pools of such mortgages. Such investments ordinarily return considerably higher interest to the purchaser than he can obtain by depositing funds directly in banks or savings and loan institutions. But the mortgages cannot be cashed or called on demand, which is why the interest earned on them is so much better than can ordinarily be obtained in deposits that can be withdrawn virtually on demand.

If you, as an investor, want to invest in real estate mortgages in order to earn interest, you could make money by investing in mortgages that carry no insurance or guarantee. You could earn a higher interest rate, but there would be some risk of loss not present under an insured or guaranteed loan.

Since most mortgages on homes call for a monthly payment combining both interest and principal, their owner receives a portion of his capital back each month. The mortgages vary in term, but they are very long-term, usually from 20 to 30 years. On the *average* however the loan is paid off in about 12 years. This is because the houses are frequently resold or refinanced. Refinancing causes the loans to be paid off in full from the proceeds of the new financing. The difficulty with individuals buying these loans is that averages do not mean much to the individual buying a *single* loan since one may be owning such a loan for up to 30 years.

Mortgage loans as a type of investment are not very liquid. FHA-insured or VA-guaranteed loans are more liquid than conventional loans (those without insurance or guarantees). They also carry less financial risk than conventional loans.

In general, the greater the financial risk, the higher the rate of interest. Also the greater the liquidity risk, the higher the rate of interest. But even if you were to minimize the financial risk and the interest-rate risk, you would still have the risk of inflation.

Lenders get compensated for the risk of inflation by charging a higher rate of interest. For example at a 2% rate of inflation, a lender may charge 6% interest. The lender then earns a 4% *real* rate of return. If inflation moves up to 5%, the interest rate is likely to be 9%, so that the lender can still earn a *real* rate of return of 4%. Similarly a 6% rate of inflation will bring *nominal* rates of return up to 10%.

As compensation for inflation, individuals who lend money at the higher rates illustrated do not do very well because of income taxes. Way back when inflation was 2% per year or less, it was said that if you can't make 6% on your money, drink it up. Actually, the real after-tax rate of return for most such individuals was only 2%, which was the bare minimum as an incentive to lend. They earned 6% interest and paid one-third of it in income taxes. This left 4% after taxes. There was also a 2% loss in purchasing power, thus the real after-tax rate of return was only 2%.

With inflation at about 6% instead of 2%, the interest rate would be 10% instead of 6%. But at a 10% interest rate and a progressive income tax, the lender is paying about 40% of the interest in income taxes, thus the after-tax return is 6%. And that 6% is being eroded. Thus at 10% interest there is no real rate of return after taxes. One is staying even. Some people "drink it up." Others buy goods, any goods. In countries with hyperinflation people flee monetary assets for holdings of physical goods.

A lender would need to get over 12% interest to earn a real after-tax return of about 2% if the marginal tax rate were 40% and if inflation were 6%. At 12% interest less 4.8% loss from the 40% marginal tax rate, there would be an after-tax return of 7.2%. With inflation at 6%, the real rate of return would be only 1.2%. That's better than nothing, but not easy to get without taking the substantial financial risk of not getting the money back. Clearly, putting money out at interest has become less and less attractive over the last decade.

INTEREST OR PROFIT

Savings deposits may be called *monetary assets* because they are assets in the form of a money claim against someone. Bonds and mortgages are also monetary assets. Other assets, such as real estate and stocks, are called *non-monetary assets.* The distinction between monetary assets and non-monetary assets is that in the former, one owns a money claim. Somebody owes the owner of the asset money and the owner of the asset is paid interest for use of the money. Investors in real estate or common stock are not owed any money and do not have a money claim. There is no borrower-debtor relationship. There is no ownership of a monetary asset. Investors have a non-monetary asset on which they may earn a profit.

The profit you can obtain by investing in a non-monetary asset is generally greater than you would have received as interest. If you select a common stock, the amount of money you will be able to make will depend on: (1) the dividends that the stock pays, if any, and (2) the price you get when you sell the stock. These benefits are related to the current and anticipated earnings of the company in which the stock is owned. Any money you receive over and above your original investment constitutes your profit.

Real estate investments also provide profit opportunities, rather than interest. The ways in which you, as a real estate investor, receive profits from real estate are explained in chapter 3.

LIQUIDITY

There is no due date on which the investment is to be returned to the investor in real estate or any other non-monetary asset. The ability to "cash in" an investment is dependent on the salability of the asset without sacrificing price. This is an important characteristic of any investment and is called liquidity. The more liquid the asset, the quicker it may be converted to cash without sacrificing price.

Monetary assets are generally more liquid than non-monetary ones. Money in a checking account is the next thing to cash and is obviously a very liquid monetary asset. The saver may obtain his money by simply withdrawing it from his account.

Aside from cash or demand deposits, the most liquid monetary assets are federal government obligations that are nearing maturity. Short-term obligations of state and local governmental bodies are also relatively liquid because the owner of the monetary assets may wait for redemption at maturity or sell the asset quickly and easily in a stable market.

Non-monetary assets as a group are less liquid than monetary assets because the investor may not withdraw the investment. No one owes the investor money. There is no borrower-debtor relationship and there is no due date. Non-monetary assets can be sold of course. Well-known stocks of good reputation are relatively liquid as compared to other non-monetary assets because they can be readily sold even though the price is subject to some fluctuation. But, even well known, widely held stocks are less liquid than short-term high-grade bonds and most other monetary assets.

The majority of real estate investments are less liquid than publicly held common stock. The sale of real estate is cumbersome and time-consuming. Borrowing on real estate, which is a way to get some liquidity, is much more complicated than borrowing on common stock.

One way of making more money is to give up liquidity. You can do so by buying monetary assets, such as mortgages or bonds, that have due dates in the distant future. Or you can buy non-monetary assets; these have no due dates. Investing in common stocks is an investment in non-monetary assets and there is some measure of liquidity when the stocks are widely held. *But you can get the most profit by investing in an illiquid asset, such as real estate. You can be very handsomely compensated for giving up liquidity.*

You should meet your needs for liquidity by keeping some of your money in monetary assets. The rest should be available for investment in illiquid assets. If you are overly enamored with the idea of liquidity, you will not be interested in real estate at all.

SUMMARY

As part of your strategy, you may have determined what part of your funds will be placed in savings accounts for liquidity and what part in widely held stocks for some protection from inflation. This allocation helps take care of liquidity and inflation. Now you must decide whether there are substantial benefits available to you that you cannot find in savings accounts or stocks.

Many investors think that such benefits are available in real estate. Real estate investors have illiquid investments and they know it. But the profitability of an investment in real estate is frequently a great deal more than is necessary to compensate investors for their lack of liquidity. In other words real estate investments may provide rewards far in excess of those that would be necessary to compensate investors for giving up their liquidity.

By understanding the effects of inflation, you will have correctly concluded that having *all* your surplus cash in savings or in any other monetary asset is not part of a rewarding investment strategy. You will not be deceived about your return on such monetary assets as bonds or savings because you know the difference between real yield and nominal yield.

As part of your developing investment strategy, you will tend to emphasize the profit aspect of investing, rather than the receiving of interest income. You know that this involves the giving up of some liquidity, and yet the rewards seem to favor the allocation of the majority of your investment funds in non-monetary assets, such as stocks or real estate.

You will want to consider real estate investments because if real estate is that illiquid, you are wondering about the benefits that surely must compensate for such lack of liquidity. You have probably heard of some benefits, at least vaguely, that seem to be intrinsic in real estate investments. Tax shelter, cash flow, and proceeds of sale are all intriguing terms to any investor. We shall, in the next chapter, explore the benefits of investing in real estate.

3 BENEFITS OF INVESTING

The benefits of investing in real estate come in three major forms: (1) cash flow while you own the real estate, (2) tax shelter, and (3) the proceeds of sale.

There are variations within the three major forms, such as receiving cash proceeds from refinancing; receiving cash income after selling the property; and, sometimes, deferring the payment of income taxes well beyond the time of sale. Variations of benefits also include trading one real estate investment for another.

Since the three major benefits (cash flow, tax shelter, and proceeds of sale) may be received in various combinations, you should look for an investment that has the right combination of benefits and risks to meet your objective. You can change the benefits and risks associated with an investment by changing the financing, but any investment has an inherent set of risks and rewards. This chapter discusses the rewards.

To help you understand the arithmetic used to calculate the benefits of investing (and the logic), we have developed a simple formula. The formula sets up the basis for understanding tax shelter and the tax consequences of the ultimate sale:

Cash Flow + Amortization − Depreciation = Taxable Income

CASH FLOW

In any income-producing real estate, rents are received and all expenses of operating the real estate are paid out of the rental income. If there is a mortgage, and there usually is, both the interest and the principal payments are also paid out of the rental income. Whatever cash is left over is called the cash flow. Thus cash flow is the cash left over from rents after all *cash* expenditures of every kind have been disbursed, including payments on the mortgage.

The term "cash flow" is part of the jargon used by real estate specialists and investors to express what is left over and is, in essence, "spendable" after all expenses have been paid and the mortgage payments have been made. Cash flow is *not* the same as taxable income, earnings, yield, or profit. Such terms as return on investment, net profit, earnings, net income, monies s ibject to federal taxation, and taxable income have been used by many persons in an endeavor to explain the results of real estate investing. Disregard these terms, for in the context of our immediate discussion the only term you need acquaint yourself with is cash flow.

Cash flow is determined by three major considerations. The first is the amount of rent received, the second is the amount of expenses paid out to operate the property, and the third is the amount and method of repaying the debt. Cash flow is usually calculated for the period of a year, although other than annual periods may be used.

Rent

The amount of rent a given property will produce depends on its location and physical characteristics. The more desirable the location and the physical characteristics, the higher the rent.

Leasing the property for a long period of time to a tenant with a high credit rating will assure the investor of rental income. For example an office building under a long- term lease to General Motors Corporation will most assuredly produce rental income. Poor-quality tenants or ill-conceived leases detract from stable rents, hence

reduce cash flow. Property that is poorly located, shoddily built, or badly planned cannot produce a satisfactory
cash flow. Generally high-quality tenants prefer high-
quality properties. It would be unrealistic to expect a
high-quality tenant to "bail out" a property that is visual-
ly unattractive or is cheaply, hence badly, built.

If the income from rents is not high enough to cover the
expense of operating the property and the mortgage
payments, the resultant effect will be a *negative cash
flow*. Some real estate specialists and accountants have
recently begun calling the gross rental income the *"gross
cash flow."* We prefer the term "gross income." This can
be defined as all the rents received and all other monies
received from vending machines, coin-operated laundry
equipment, garage income, and any other monies collected in connection with the property from any source.

Appraisers use the term "scheduled gross income" to
refer to the maximum potential rent at current rental
rates. The scheduled gross income, less allowances for
vacancy and collection loss, is the effective gross income.
We are here concerned with effective gross income. Cash
flow starts with the cash collected, which is the effective
gross income.

Operating Expenses

Property that is built for long-term investment by the
developer frequently differs from property that is built
for sale on completion. Some of the principal differences
are found in such surface characteristics as unevenly
laid brick. Other quality characteristics may not be so obvious, such as poorly designed room layouts or cheap
heating equipment. The quality of workmanship,
materials, and design is an important determinant of the
level of occupancy and the level of operating expenses.
The better-quality properties have lower vacancies and
lower operating expenses. Astute developers know the
kind of maintenance costs they are building into the struc-

ture. If they are not going to sell the property on completion, they will certainly be very careful about the quality of air-conditioning and heating systems for example. The building's mechanical system has a direct bearing on the cost of operating the building. If they are planning to sell immediately on completion, they will frequently stint on quality, usually on components that are not visible, in order to maximize profits.

The expenses are affected by the extent and kind of services included in the rent, such as nursery facilities or switchboard service.

An objective evaluation of the cash flow of a property must therefore consider the realistic analysis of the expenses necessary to produce the gross income. Such an analysis begins with a review of the historical expenses. In new projects without an expense history, it is essential to obtain comparisons with operating expenses of relatively new properties. The significance of a study of expenses is indicated by the Securities and Exchange Commission's (SEC's) policy of requiring a five-year historical expense analysis when making a public offering of partial interests in income-producing property.

In evaluating the expenses, the "owning cost" is an important concept. For example asphalt tile used in the entrance level of an apartment buliding costs less to install than vinyl tile, and it has a higher "owning cost." In the long run the vinyl looks better and is cheaper. Its total "first cost equivalent" is lower. Consider another case. It costs more to install good-quality wool carpeting than asphalt or vinyl tile; however in upper levels of high-quality office buildings, the maintenance costs are less for carpeting than for asphalt or vinyl tile. If one considers the worth of the savings in maintenance, the carpeting is less expensive and, as most people would agree, looks better.

Any materials used in an office building, an apartment house, or a shopping center could have had a better and more expensive substitute. Investors are not looking for "the best". They are looking for something that will keep their expenses in line with the rental income they can reasonably expect to receive. Investors would be short-sighted to look for the cheapest-quality items because in the long run these materials will either lower gross income or increase expenses, or do both.

An important construction concept is to make quality concordant with location and the proposed rental structure.

Repayment of Debt

Real estate investors frequently have a debt against the property. This debt, whether in the form of a mortgage or a deed of trust, is usually paid out of the income that the property produces. The amount of debt obviously influences the amount of income to be used to service the debt. The rate of interest will also determine how much income must be employed to pay for the use of the borrowed funds. The time in which investors have to repay the debt will also influence how much of their income they have to use in servicing the debt. Thus the cash flow is affected by the amount of payment on the mortgage, and the amount of these payments is determined by how much is being paid off on the debt and how much interest is being paid on the debt.

Manipulating Cash Flow

The cash flow is a very important consideration to the real estate investor. It is therefore subject to manipulation for the purpose of enhancing the superficial attractiveness of the investment. It may be manipulated or altered through the use of various management techniques, such as obtaining high and temporary rents by offering leases on very short terms. Forcing lower expenses, by postponing needed painting or other maintenance, will also produce a high cash flow for a short period of time. The use of large amounts of borrowed money, very little of which is repaid out of gross income, will also provide a high cash flow relative to down payment. It is not sufficient merely to look at the dollars that constitute the cash flow. You must look behind the cash flow to see what has been done to produce it.

AMORTIZATION

Most investors in real estate borrow a portion of the purchase price and pledge the property as security for the repayment of the debt. This security instrument is generally a mortgage or a deed of trust. The details of the contract vary from state to state. Some investors buy property that is already encumbered with a mortgage or a deed of trust (commonly called "trust deed"). In some cases the borrowers or purchasers are personally liable. In all cases the property may be sold or taken over by the lender if the debt is not repaid.

There are three general plans for repaying the debt. The first is to pay the money back to the lender in a lump sum when the mortgage becomes due. The interest could be paid periodically or at the same time the principal is paid. The second method is to make periodic payments that include principal and interest, thus eventually repaying the entire loan. This method of gradually reducing the principal amount of the loan is the most popular. It is called *amortizing* the loan, and the mortgage is called an *amortizing* mortgage. The third method is a combination of the two—the mortgage is amortized for a period of time, say five years, and then the unpaid balance becomes due and payable in one lump sum. The lump-sum payment is called a balloon payment. Its size depends on how much of the loan has been amortized.

The discussion here is concerned with the second plan for repaying the debt—amortization. Generally the mortgage calls for monthly payments, but occasionally quarterly or semiannual payments are used.

The periodic payment, say monthly, is generally fixed. This means that the borrower pays the same amount each month. The interest due has first claim on the payment; whatever remains is credited toward repayment of the debt. The debt is thus reduced each month.

Since each month the debt is less than it was the previous month, the amount of money paid each month on interest declines. The amount going to principal increases. In this way the debt is eventually paid off.

It is important to note that although the payment combines both interest and principal, the payment of the interest is not amortization. *Only the payment of principal is the amortization.*

From the standpoint of accounting for income tax purposes, there is no allowable deduction as an expense for the amount of amortization that goes on each month. The interest however is a deductable expense.When investors borrow money for any reason, they do not have income for federal income tax purposes, nor do lenders have a deductible expense. When the loan is being amortized, lenders have income in the form of interest, and investors have an expense in the form of interest. It is essential to remember that borrowed money is not subject to federal income taxes, and repaying borrowed money is not a tax deduction.

The amount of money and the terms under which it may be borrowed generally depend on the type of property, the lender, the condition of the money market, and the credit of the borrower. Most mortgage money comes from institutional lenders, such as savings and loan associations, savings banks, commercial banks, and life insurance companies. These regulated institutions have ceilings on the amount of the loan that they can make in relation to the value of the property.

The period of repayment also varies. Commercial banks prefer shorter-term loans of say 10 to 15 years. Savings and loan associations (also known as building and loan associations) lend for terms of from 20 to 30 years. Insurance companies may occasionally lend for even longer periods of time. The time over which the loan is to be amortized depends in part on the kind of property. Investors frequently get longer terms on high-rise buildings than on garden apartment developments because of the longer economic life of the high-rise building.

Annual Constants

Interest rates also vary. The riskiest properties have the highest interest rates. Yet some lenders accept the risky loans because they need higher interest income. The rate of interest, the amount borrowed, and the period of time to repay determine the payment of a loan. The amount of money to be repaid annually for each $1000 borrowed, including both interest and principal, is expressed as a *percentage* that is called the *annual constant.* For example an annual constant of 9% with a 6% interest rate would fully amortize a loan in 18 years 5 months. The loan balance would be zero at that time, fully paid. It would require an annual payment of $90 for each $1000 borrowed to amortize the loan over the term of 18 years 5 months. The ratio of the $90 annual payment to each $1000 borrowed is the *annual constant,* in this case 9%.

A portion of each $90 per $1000 per annum goes to the payment of interest. The remaining portion is for amortization. If the annual constant were 8.5, then the annual payment per $1000 would be $85. Assuming the same interest rate of 6%, the amount going toward amortization would be less than under the 9% annual constant. In this instance it would require 20 years 6 months to amortize fully the 8.5% annual constant loan.

The time required to repay a loan is governed by the annual constant. Most investors want low annual constants, which means that they repay more slowly. High annual constants mean speedier repayments.

The constant annual percent is vital to a quick calculation of monies required for annual payments of interest and principal of a debt. The annual payments of any loan can be calculated by multiplying the amount of the loan by the constant annual percent. Table 1 shows the number of years necessary to amortize loans of varying interest rates and constant annual percents.

Investors most interested in cash flow try to get the lowest constant annual percent on their mortgages. Frequently they will pay a higher interest rate in order to get a lower constant annual percent. For example an 8.75% constant annual with a 6% interest rate might not be as desirable as an 8.5% constant annual with a 6.25% interest rate. Even though lower interest is desirable, given a choice most investors would rather pay a higher interest rate if the annual constant were kept low. Paying back a loan more slowly lets the investor keep more cash.

Amortization, as you recall, is the second part of the three-part formula that real estate investors can use in determining the results of their investments. Cash flow is the first part of the same formula. The cash flow is directly related to the annual constant, hence the interrelationship of the cash flow and amortization is a vitally important consideration in making a real estate investment. The more you have to pay back in any one year, the less cash you get to keep that year.

Patterns of Principal Reduction

Chapters 7 and 8 are devoted to the financing of real estate and will review a portion of this material in some detail. For present purposes however it should be noted that the first payment made by the invester to a lender consists mainly of interest; the small balance of the payment is credited to principal. The second payment will consist of a little less interest and a little more principal. This constant reducing of interest payments and increasing of principal payments is a pattern that is readily

Table 1   Constant Annual Percents and Amoritization of Loan[a]

Constant Annual	Interest Rate	Percentage of Original Loan Not Paid After			Time Required to Amortize Loan Fully	
		5 Years	10 Years	15 Years	Years	Months
8.5	6.0	85.6	66.1	39.9	20	6
	6.5	88.2	71.9	49.4	22	4
	7.0	91.1	78.4	60.4	24	11
	7.5	94.0	85.2	72.4	28	8
9	6.5	85.3	64.9	36.8	19	10
	7.0	89.1	71.1	47.2	21	7
	7.5	90.9	77.8	58.6	24	0
	8.0	93.9	84.8	71.2	27	7
9.5	7.0	85.1	63.9	34.0	19	2
	7.5	87.9	70.3	44.8	20	11
	8.0	90.8	77.1	56.7	23	7
	8.5	93.8	84.3	69.9	26	7
10	7.5	84.9	62.9	31.0	18	7
	8.0	87.8	69.5	42.3	20	3
	8.5	90.7	76.5	54.8	22	5
	9.0	93.7	83.9	68.5	25	9
10.5	8.0	84.7	62.9	27.9	18	0
	8.5	87.6	68.6	39.7	19	7
	9.0	90.6	75.8	52.7	21	9
	9.5	93.6	83.4	67.0	24	11
11.0	8.5	84.5	60.8	24.6	17	6
	9.0	87.4	67.7	36.9	19	1
	9.5	90.4	75.1	50.5	21	1
	10.0	93.5	82.9	65.5	24	1
11.5	9.0	84.3	59.7	21.2	17	1
	9.5	87.3	66.8	24.0	18	6
	10.0	90.3	74.4	48.2	20	6
	10.5	93.5	82.4	63.8	23	5
12.0	9.5	84.1	58.5	17.5	16	7
	10.0	87.1	65.9	30.9	18	0
	10.5	90.2	73.6	45.7	19	11
	11.0	93.4	81.9	62.1	22	9

[a] Table based on monthly payments.

**Table 2   Allocation of Principal and Interest for
the First Year on a 20-Year, 6% Interest, $10,000 Loan** [a]

Month	Payment	Interest	principal	Loan Balance
1	$71.64	$50.00	$21.64	$9,978.36
2	71.64	49.89	21.75	9,956.61
3	71.64	49.78	21.86	9,934.75
4	71.64	49.67	21.97	9,912.78
5	71.64	49.56	22.08	9,890.70
6	71.64	49.45	22.19	9,868.51
7	71.64	49.34	22.30	9,846.21
8	71.64	49.23	22.41	9,823.80
9	71.64	49.12	22.52	9,801.28
10	71.64	49.01	22.63	9,778.65
11	71.64	48.89	22.75	9,755.90
12	71.64	48.78	22.86	9,733.04

[a] Interest is calculated on unpaid balance. Annual rate of 0.06 divided by 12 months equals monthly rate of 0.005. Each month the interest cost is deducted from the payment, the balance goes to reduction of principal. the next month the interest is charged on the reduced principal.

determinable. Each time a payment is made, a certain amount of principal is credited on the loan on behalf of the borrower. Since mortgage interest is always computed on the *unpaid* balance, there is a curtailment in the amount of debt and therefore a reduction in the amount of interest. Since the monthly or quarterly payments remain level (as determined by the annual constant), the interest portion of the repayment is on a constantly descending scale as each month goes by, while the amortization is on a constantly ascending scale. This pattern of principal reduction (which is useful to the investor as well as to his accountant in preparing his annual tax returns) usually may be obtained from the lender on request and is called an amortization schedule. Tables 2 and 3 are examples of an amortization schedule.

Some institutions do not make a practice of issuing such schedules since the loan amounts vary with each loan, but investors usually can find them through a mortgage banker in the area where they live. If such a schedule is not available in your area, you can purchase one from the Financial Publishing Company, Boston, Massachusetts.

Table 3   Annual Summary of Monthly Amortization: 20 years, 6% Interest, $10,000 Loan, 240 Monthly Payments of $71.64

Year	Balance	Principal	Interest
1	$9,733	$266	$593
2	9,450	283	576
3	9,149	301	559
4	8,829	319	540
5	8,490	339	521
6	8,130	360	500
7	7,748	382	477
8	7,342	406	454
9	6,911	431	429
10	6,453	457	402
11	5,967	486	374
12	5,452	516	344
13	4,904	548	312
14	4,323	581	278
15	3,706	617	243
16	3,051	655	205
17	2,355	695	164
18	1,616	739	121
19	832	784	76
20	0,000	832	27

DEPRECIATION

In time every mechanical item, every manufactured item, even brick, wears out or deteriorates. Unless it has historical significance, any improvement eventually is demolished or abandoned because it can no longer serve the function for which it was originally built. In time any income-producing property, such as an office building, apartment house, or shopping facility, is incapable of producing a cash flow because of physical deterioration. By reason of the wearing out process, no one would invest in capital improvements if there were no method by which the capital could ultimately be returned. In some cases investment capital is not returned fast enough because the improvements become obsolete before physical deterioration would appear to call for demolition.

For example we recently saw a beautiful but small motel bypassed in constructing a new interstate route. Nothing was done to enable the motorists traveling along his route to use the facilities of the motel since the closest cloverleaf was placed approximately seven miles from it. Thus the motel has become obsolete because it is now in an isolated section with no access from what has become the main route for motorists.

Professionals in the real estate industry call this loss in value "economic obsolescence." It is a classic example of a real estate investment being incapable of producing a positive cash flow even though it is virtually new and modern in every respect.

Those of middle age among us will remember when bathtubs stood on legs and so did stoves. These examples of obsolescence can be traced to design. The higher costs of labor following the post-World War II period virtually rendered obsolete in most high-rise apartment buildings and office buildings manually operated elevators. The automatic elevator, a postwar development, points up a form of functional obsolescence brought about by the replacement of a component part of a building, which could do the job better at less cost.

Because of these varying forms of obsolescence, both standard principles of accounting and federal tax laws are designed to allow the investors, on an annual basis, to provide for the return of their capital over the life expectancy of the improvement in which they have invested. Depreciation is the *accounting* term for this provision of return of capital.

The accounting entry made each year for depreciation does not affect the cash flow because depreciation is not a cash item. That is it is not paid out to anyone. Because of this it is quite often called a "paper deduction." Every owner of a building, old or new, is entitled to deduct each year a certain portion of the capital that is attributed to the cost of the building only.

Since land does not wear out, its cost may not be depreciated, Thus it is necessary for the real estate investors to separate the cost of their improvements from the cost of the land. Let us assume that an investor purchases a property (land and building) for $250,000. The value of the land is say $50,000. This would be subtracted from the purchase price of $250,000. The resulting $200,000 would be subject to depreciation, and an annual amount of depreciation would be allowed for federal income tax purposes. The accounting records of the purchase would always reflect the $50,000 attributable to the cost of the land and would not be subject to change as long as the investor owned the property. For purposes of our discussion we shall assume that the method of depreciation used for accounting purposes is the same as the method used for federal income tax purposes.

Straight-Line Depreciation

For purposes of federal income tax, an accountant would

be making an entry each year for a portion of the $200,000 in improvements as depreciation to allow for the recovery of the capital invested. The amount of the depreciation reported each year would depend on the method of depreciation selected by the investor together with either an accountant or tax counsel. The simplest form of depreciation is the straight- line method. the accountant or tax counsel could rely on published federal criteria in determining the estimated useful life of the building. *The Monthly Trader* has prepared a table of useful life for various kinds of property (Table 4). If the building is new and the straight-line method of depreciation is used and it is determined that the property has a useful life of 40 years, the investor would be allowed an annual charge-off for depreciation purposes of one- fortieth of the cost each year for 40 years. This amounts to 2.5% of the $200,000 (or $5000) each year for the next 40 years. Under this straight-line method of depreciation, the annual allowance for depreciation would be $5000, which multiplied by the 40 years would provide for the recovery of the $200,000 investment.

The accountant treats this depreciation allowance of $5000 annually as an expense item, although the investor would not actually pay out this "expense" to anyone. The expense comes in because the investor has purchased an asset that is depreciating both physically and functionally. In this case it is *presumably* at the rate of $5000 per year.

In our example an estimated 40-year life was used because the building was new. If the building were older, a shorter useful life expectancy would be employed for depreciation purposes. If a real estate appraiser concluded that the property had a useful remaining life of approximately 20 years, an annual depreciation allowance of 5% could be used. (5% × 20 years = 100%.) Therefore a depreciation allowance of $10,000 per an-

Table 4 Useful Life in Years for Various Properties

Type of Building	Formerly Allowed by Bulletin "F" and Commission	Presently Allowed by Revenue Procedure 62–21	Allowed by Courts
Apartments	50	40	33
Banks	67	50	40
Dwellings	60	45	20
Factories	50	45	30
Farm buildings	60	25	20
Garages	60	45	33⅓
Grain elevators	75	60	25
Hotels	50	40	30
Loft buildings	67	50	33⅓
Machine shops	60	45	50
Stores	67	50	25
Theaters	50	40	25
Warehouses	75	60	40

Source: Howard M. Benedict, "Factors in Depreciation," *The Monthly Trader* (International Traders Club, Exchange Division, National Institute of Real Estate Brokers, February 1967).

num could be deducted as an expense item in computing federal income taxes. $10,000 annually for 20 years equals $200,000. These examples provide for recovering 100% of the cost of the improvements over the useful life of the property. If there were a salvage value to the building at the end of its useful life, this would be taken into account in calculating the amount that is subject to depreciation. For our purposes we can ignore salvage value.

Declining Balance Method of Depreciation

Depreciation methods that provide for more depreciation in the earlier years of ownership and less depreciation in the later years are also available. Such methods simply permit the depreciation allowance to be taken earlier. But no matter which technique of depreciation allowance is employed, it is not possible to deduct an amount that would exceed the cost of the improvements, which, in our example, is $200,000.

The method of taking more depreciation in the early years is called *accelerated depreciation.* the declining balance method is one form of accelerated depreciation. It comes in two popular forms. One is called the "150% declining balance" and the other the "200% declining balance."

Under the 150% declining balance method, a depreciation allowance of 1½ times the straight-line rate would be allowed. The amount of depreciation is 50% more than the straight-line rate during the first year of ownership. In the second year the same rate (1.5 times the straight- line rate) would be applied against the declining balance. In our $200,000 example, depreciation is computed for the first year at 150% of 2.5%, for a first-year charge-off on the improvements of 3.75%. Thus instead of $5000 the first year's charge-off is $7500. The second year's charge-off would be 3.75% of the unrecovered balance—$200,000 less the $7500 that was charged off the prior year is the unrecovered balance. The remaining $192,500 is called the *book value* or the adjusted basis. The second year the amount of allowable depreciation would be 3.75% of $192,500 (book value). Each year, while the *percentage* of depreciation remains the same (in this case 150% of the straight-line rate), the *amount* is declining because the book value is declining. In time the *annual* charge-off is less than if the straight-line method had been employed. Table 5 shows a comparison of straight-line depreciation with 150% declining balance and 200% declining balance methods of depreciation.

The 200% declining balance method allows a charge-off of twice the rate used in the straight-line method, but since it is also computed on the remaining book value each year, the annual charge-off is constantly diminishing. The 200% declining balance method gives high depreciation charges in the early years. Of course the depreciation charge in late years is much less than with the straight-line method. The 200% declining balance method is also illustrated in Table 5.

Any method of depreciation that gives higher depreciation in early years than the straight-line method is called "accelerated depreciation." All forms of accelerated depreciation produce a greater amount of depreciation the first year; this amount declines from year to year until the amount of depreciation in the later years is less than if the straight-line rate were used from the beginning.

At this writing only new residential rental property is eligible for the 200% declining balance method. Other new property is, at best, eligible for the 150% declining balance method. Used residential property with a remaining economic life of 20 years or more is eligible for the 125% declining balance method.

The Sum of the Year's Digits

The sum of the year's digits is another form of accelerated depreciation that produces an early charge-off greater than the 150% declining balance method, but less than the 200% declining balance method. While it has not been a very popular form of depreciation, its concept is relatively simple. In arithmetical progression the accountant adds the number of years of useful life of the building. In the case of a 40-year life expectancy, he would add $1 + 2 + 3 + 4 + 5$ and so on through the number 40 for a total of 820. This total is used as the denominator. The first year the depreciation charge-off would be computed at $^{40}/_{820}$, of the original cost, the second year at $^{39}/_{820}$, the third year at $^{38}/_{820}$, and so on through each year. The denominator (820) always remains the same, while the numerator becomes less; thus the percentage is higher for the first year and becomes progressively less over the useful life of the property.

**Table 5   Depreciation Schedule—Annual and
Cumulative Allowance (dollars per thousand assuming 25-year life)**

Year	Straight-line		150% Declining Balance		200% Declining Balance	
	Annual Write-off	Cumulative Write-off	Annual Write-off	Cumulative Write-off	Annual Write-off	Cumulative Write-off
1	$40.0	$ 40.0	6.%	6.0%	8.%	8.0%
2	40.0	80.0	5.6	11.6	7.4	15.4
3	40.0	120.0	5.3	16.9	6.8	22.2
4	40.0	160.0	5.0	21.9	6.2	28.4
5	40.0	200.0	4.7	26.6	5.7	34.1
6	40.0	240.0	4.4	31.0	5.3	39.4
7	40.0	280.0	4.1	35.1	4.9	44.3
8	40.0	320.0	3.9	39.0	4.5	48.8
9	40.0	360.0	3.7	42.7	4.1	52.9
10	40.0	400.0	3.4	46.1	3.8	56.7
11	40.0	440.0	3.2	49.4	3.5	60.2
12	40.0	480.0	3.0	52.4	3.2	63.4
13	40.0	520.0	2.9	55.2	2.9	66.3
14	40.0	560.0	2.7	57.9	2.7	68.0
15	40.0	600.0	2.5	60.4	2.5	71.5
16	40.0	640.0	2.4	62.9	2.3	73.8
17	40.0	680.0	2.2	65.0	2.1	75.9
18	40.0	720.0	2.1	67.1	1.9	77.8
19	40.0	760.0	2.0	69.1	1.8	79.6
20	40.0	800.0	1.9	71.0	1.6	81.2
21	40.0	840.0	1.7	74.3	1.4	84.1
22	40.0	880.0	1.6	74.3	1.4	84.1
23	40.0	920.0	1.5	75.9	1.3	85.4
24	40.0	960.0	1.5	77.3	1.2	86.6
25	40.0	1000.0	1.4	78.7	1.1	87.7

To simplify the mathematics, a property with a useful life of 4 years would have the following annual depreciation:

Sum of the digits 4 + 3 + 2 + 1 = 10	
1st year 4/10	= 40%
2nd year 3/10	= 30%
3rd year 2/10	= 20%
4th year 1/10	= 10%
Total	100%

Total 10/10 = 100%
This method is only for new residential property.

The Component-Parts Method

The builder-investor, or the investor who has a building constructed for him, frequently uses a depreciation method known as the "component-parts method." This is a technique that is usually combined with one of the forms of accelerated depreciation just discussed. It is based on separating the building into all of its component parts: bricks, other masonry, air-conditioning and heating equipment, elevators, refrigerators, stoves, dishwashers, disposals, venetian blinds, and so on. Each such component part is assigned a useful life. For example refrigerators may be assigned a realistic useful life of 15 years and venetian blinds a life of 5 years. Each component part is then separately computed (usually) on the 200% declining balance method. All computations are added together, and the total of the composites produces a much higher depreciation allowance in the earliest years of ownership than any other method. This method is not allowed to subsequent investor-owners of the same property.

All of the methods of depreciation, and obviously there are more choices if the improvement is built by the investor, will produce an annual deduction for depreciation on the books of the investor. If the straight-line method is used it is the same amount each year. If a form of accelerated depreciation is used it is a varying amount each year, the depreciation allowances being greater in the earlier years and lesser in the later years. The factor of great significance is that the depreciation, which is charged as an expense against the property, is not being paid out in cash as are all other expenses. This is of great significance because the *choice of depreciation methods affects your taxable income, but not your cash flow.*

Understanding the concept of cash flow, amortization, and depreciation provides the basis for understanding the important tax aspects of real estate investment. The formula that we stated earlier simplifies the tax picture for investing in real estate and is therefore worth repeating:

Cash Flow + Amortization − *Depreciation* = Taxable Income
or

$$CF + A - D = TI$$

The formula may also be represented with the symbols:

$$C_f + A - D = I_t$$

Where C_f still represents cash flow, A represents amortization, D represents depreciation, and I_t represents income taxable, which is the same as taxable income. The former and simpler but nontraditional notations will be used in this book.

The federal government taxes the income you receive from your investments. Cash flow is obviously income that may be subject to taxation. The property generated cash and you received it. The amount of amortization is also taxable because it is simply your repayment of the money you borrowed. There was no tax when the money was borrowed, so it is not a deduction when it is repaid. However some of the cash that has been received is a return of your investment, which is the depreciation we have been discussing. The depreciation is the allowance for a loss in value. Thus you can count part of the cash you receive as a return of a portion of your original investment. Hence the cash flow plus the amortization minus the depreciation is the *taxable income.*

FEDERAL INCOME TAX RULES

For federal income tax purposes, the methods of depreciation available to the real estate investor vary depending on whether the property is residential or commercial. New residential rental property may use the 200% declining balance or the sum of the year's-digits methods of depreciation. Used residential property having a useful life of 20 years or more may be depreciated under a 125% declining balance method. All other new property (office buildings, shopping centers, and so on) is limited to 150% declining balance. Other used real estate property is limited to straight-line depreciation. Residential rental property is a building from which 80% or more of the gross rental income during the year is derived from dwelling units. If any portion of the building is occupied by the owner, the gross rental income will include the rental value of the portion so occupied. Apparently the owner of a duplex, living in one of the two apartments, will qualify for 200% declining balance or sum of the year's-digits depreciation in the case of a new building and for 125% for a used building having a useful life of 20 years or more. A dwelling unit is a house or apartment used to provide living accomodations. The term does not include hotels, motels, inns, or other establishments in which more than one-half of the units are occupied on a transient basis.

A special five-year straight-line depreciation deduction (without salvage value) was provided in the case of expenditures for rehabilitation of low-income rental housing. Since capital improvements of this nature should have a useful life of much longer than five years, this is a method of accelerated depreciation. For this purpose not more than expenditures exceeding $3,000 in any two-year period can be taken into account. This provision, originally set to expire January 1, 1976, was modified changing the original $15,000 maximum to $20,000 and extended to January 1, 1978. At this writing these provisions were again extended and are now set to expire January 1, 1979.

Another limitation on tax shelter from accelerated depreciation is in the minimum tax for tax preferences. Beginning with 1976 the tax on certain items of tax preference, one of which is the amount by which any deduction for depreciation of real property under an accelerated method exceeds the deduction that would have been allowed under the straight-line method was increased to 15%. The excess of all items of tax preference over $10,000 or one-half the regular tax liability, whichever is greater, is taxed at a 15% rate, and this tax is then added to the regular tax liability.

TAX-SHELTERED INCOME

If the amortization and the depreciation are equal, the taxable income equals the cash flow. (You reduce your debt by the same amount as the depreciation). Thus whatever you get in cash is your income. Some, all, or more than all of the cash flow is *not* subject to federal income tax to the extent that depreciation *exceeds* amortization. An examination of our formula reveals this fact.

If cash flow is $9000 and amortization is $4000, the total is $13,000. When a depreciation allowance of $7500 is deducted, the taxable income is $5500. The $3500 of the cash flow that was not taxable is *tax-sheltered*. For the present it is not taxed.

It will be taxed later because when the property is sold the taxes will be computed by deducting the book value from the sales price. The depreciation that has been providing the tax shelter has been reducing the book value. The taxation of the proceeds of sale is discussed in the next section. For the present it is sufficient to note that one of the economic benefits of investing in real estate is receiving tax-sheltered income, that is income on which the investor does not immediately have to pay taxes. Frequently when the taxes are paid their amount is substantially reduced because of long-term capital-gain rates. Thus one benefit of investing in real estate is deferring the payment of income taxes and reducing the amount of taxes ultimately paid.

Using the formula $CF + A - D = TI$, it can be seen that whenever D is greater than A, some of the income is tax-sheltered. It will also be noted that if D is greater than the sum of $CF + A$, some taxable loss will occur. For example if the cash flow is $9000 and the amortization is $4000, the sum of the two would be $13,000. If the depreciation allowance was $14,000, a loss of $1,000 would occur. In this example all of the cash flow ($9000) would be tax- sheltered. The excess $1000 loss could be used as a deduction against your income from any other source.

Theoretically if your tax losses from owning income-producing property were high enough, you could eliminate all your tax liability from your other income. You could do this if your tax loss from income property was larger than your taxable income from your salary, business, or profession: when you added the two, your taxable income would be zero. As a practical matter there are relatively few investors who are able to get that much tax shelter. But there are many investors who are able to get some relief from the burden of high taxes when they invest in a property that ultimately proves to be profitable to them.

There are two valid, but opposing, arguments as to the speed with which to depreciate a property. Some experts argue that property that is going to be held for a long time should be depreciated very slowly. They point out that amortization increases, so that in time the amortization will exceed even straight-line depreciation, leaving all of the cash flow taxable; then amortization continues to increase, so that the investor may have taxable income in excess of cash flow. In most cases this would not occur until the loan was quite old and would present no problem. But if accelerated depreciation techniques are used, the time of its happening is moved up considerably, generally when about one-third of the loan is paid off. The consequence is a pressure to sell or refinance a good investment that cannot readily be replaced.

Opposing experts hold that you should take all the depreciation as fast as you can, thus paying less taxes during the initial years of ownership. They also used to argue that you will pay lower taxes when you sell because you can then pay on the basis of favorable long-term capital gains. The tax law has been changed however and now all accelerated depreciation is subject to recapture provisions. This means that the gain attributable to depreciation in excess of straight-line depreciation is taxed as ordinary income, not long-term capital gains. This excess depreciation is a tax preference item and this may be the subject of a minimum tax. The tax rules are further discussed in the following section on proceeds of sale. But, in brief, much of the benefit from accelerated depreciation is now gone so that accelerated depreciation is much less popular.

The choice should not be made by your accountant or attorney, because only you should decide your strategy. You may decide on the basis of your present total tax picture, your best guess as to what the future holds for you, and how long you intend to hold the property. But before you   decide how to use the depreciation to obtain tax-sheltered income, you will want to know more about the capital-gains tax and the characteristics of real estate investment.

Some persons erroneously refer to tax shelter in real estate as "tax-free" income. There is no "tax- free" income in real estate. There is tax-sheltered income. This postpones payment of taxes and may reduce the ultimate burden by taxing the profits at capital-gains rates, rather than at ordinary income-tax rates. The postponement is an advantage because you get to use the money without charge (unless your tax rate rises). The capital gains rate is an advantage because the tax rate is usually lower. thus the benefit of tax shelter is the free use of tax money and the reduction of taxes by using long-term capital-gains rates where applicable.

PROCEEDS OF SALE

Proceeds of sale can only be realized by selling your property. When you sell and realize your profit you can be sure that it is time to pay your income taxes. You will have earned a taxable profit, some of which may qualify for treatment of long-term capital gains, which means that you pay less tax than if you made ordinary income. Whether you own vacant land, an apartment house, a warehouse, a hotel, office building, or a house that you have been renting, the formula for determining the *taxable profit* (taxable gain) is the same.

The taxable profit is based on the excess of the *sales price* over the book value (adjusted basis). The sales price is what you get for the property. The book value is the original cost of the property to you, less the depreciation taken prior to the sale. Thus the taxable profit formula is: sales plus price minus book value equals taxable profit.[1]

$$S P - B V = T P.$$

If you paid $100,000 for a property, held it for 10 years, and had taken a total of $25,000 depreciation, your book value would be $75,000. If you sold it for $150,000 and paid a real estate broker a commission of $7500, the sales price net to you would be $142,500. (In this discussion sales price means *after* expenses of the sale.)

The difference between your book value of $75,000 and the sales price of $142,500 is the taxable profit: $67,500. Part of this taxable profit may be taxable as ordinary income under the depreciation recapture rules discussed below; the balance will be taxed at long-term capital-gains rates.

Under the capital-gains rule the tax attributable to long-term gains cannot exceed an amount computed under an alternative tax schedule. However the effective long-term capital-gains rates are generally much lower than ordinary income rates. Until the 1978 tax law changes, one-half of the long term capital gains was in-

---

[1] Some tax experts will argue with the oversimplification of not only this formula, but also the basic formula of $C F + A - D = T I$. They will correctly point out that we have omitted the costs for possible capital improvements, such as additions or alterations to the structures. This is true, but in the formula relating to cash flow, capital improvements are *just that* and as such should be paid out of *new capital,* not out of normal building operations as an expense item. If handled in the correct manner, the formula stands up.

In the formula for computation of taxable profit, $S P - B V = T P$, the book value becomes greater because of any additions that are capital improvements. By definition book value is cost less depreciation. New costs for capital improvements are added to the book value and depreciated along with the original improvements.

cluded as taxable income. At this writing, as of the 1978 tax change, only forty percent of the long term capital gains are included in ordinary income.

Ordinarily the gain realized from the sale of investment real estate held for more than one year is taxed as long-term capital gain. However, since deductions for depreciation are allowed against the rental income, the effect of these rules is to change what would have been ordinary income into long-term capital gain. To correct this situation the federal tax rules provide for "recapture" of some or all of the *excess* of acclerated depreciation over straight-line depreciation at the time of the sale.

With respect to depreciation for periods after 1969, but before 1976, that part of the gain from the sale of the property representing *excess* depreciation is taxable as ordinary income under the following rules:

1. In the case of residential rental property, if the property is sold in less than 1 year after acquisition or construction, all depreciation (including straight-line) is recaptured as ordinary income to the extent of the gain.

2. If the property has been held more than 1 year, only the *excess* of accelerated over straight-line depreciation is recaptured, and this amount is reduced 1% per month after 8 years 4 months and nothing is recapturable after 16 years and 8 months.

3. In the case of limited rental housing projects under FHA 221 (d) (3) or FHA 236, and certain similar state-assisted projects, the 1% per month phaseout begins after the property is held 20 months, so that after 10 years nothing is recaptured. (This is the rule that applied to all classes of real property for periods before 1970.)

4. In the case of all other real property, after 1 year, all *excess* of depreciation is recapturable without any phaseout.

5. With respect to accelerated depreciation after 1975, all accelerated depreciation on normal residential rental property held more than 1 year is subject to recapture. Computation form 4797 is available from the Internal Revenue Service (IRS).

With regard to depreciation for periods after 1976, all of the gain representing *excess depreciation* (depreciation in excess of straight line) is subject to recapture. Recapture means that it is treated as ordinary income and may be a tax preference item.

The advantages of long-term capital gains also may be reduced for some investors by the minium tax for tax preferences described earlier, which applies to one-half of capital gains.

The IRS will deny long-term capital gains to persons they classify as "dealers," that is those who consistently buy and sell rather than invest.

In view of our tax laws, if you are seeking maximum tax shelter, obviously you are consequently going to become a long-term investor. Many developers of income-producing properties intend to hold their investments for about 10 years. Such investors generally say they will hold their properties from 8 to 12 years before selling them.

SUMMARY AND CONCLUSIONS

The benefit of investing are cash flow, tax shelter, and proceeds of sale. The cash flow is the cash you get while you own the property. The tax shelter is the benefit you get by deferring some of your taxes until you sell. Proceeds of sale is what you get after you sell and pay your taxes.

When you sell, it will be to someone who also wants benefits from investing. The combination of benefits may change, but the property must have the ability or potential for producing a cash flow in order to bring a price in the market. In the long run it is this ability to produce income, by way of cash flow, that makes the difference between losers and winners.

Inflation brings about rising rents. The growth of a community brings about the need for more real estate, and some real estate increases in relative desirability, hence in rents. The continued ability of the property to produce rents make it valuable, and when there are rents that are rising faster than expenses, there is a real winner.

Depreciation is an allowance for the building that is wearing out—which any building does—given enough time. The fact that occasionally, as in the late sixties and early seventies, construction costs rose rapidly for a short period of time means only that the *rate of* depreciation varies over time. The question is, what you can get for it when you sell.

You need that allowance for the depreciation because some of it does occur. For those who wind up with a loser, the depreciation that was taken will not be enough. But those who wind up with a winner—hopefully you—get to keep a large portion of the profits.

When you have a big winner, the greatest benefit is the proceeds of sale, which will be accompanied by good cash flow and tax benefits. When you have an average good investment, it is this cash flow that counts. You can manipulate the financing to increase the tax shelter (which is discussed later), but it will not turn a loser into a winner; those who have losers—and there are some— derive no net benefits because the tax losses are real losses.

Picking the winning investments requires an understanding of who is trying to do what. If you know what the people involved in the real estate development and investment processes are doing, you will be able to decide when in the life cycle of a real estate project you want to get in—and out. You need to know who you have to work with and how you can work with them. The next chapter tells you who does what, and how.

PART TWO

Real Estate Development Process

4 UNDERSTANDING THE DEVELOPMENT PROCESS

The investment process has a variety of risks. In the case of new construction, the risks are most dependent on the stage of development at which the investor makes his commitment. In the case of existing construction, the risks depend on the stage of the life cycle at which the investor buys. In either event, it is important to understand who does what. This chapter explains the process of development, including a discussion of the cast of characters involved.

Chapter 5 explains the risks and rewards of each *step* in the process of creating an income-producing property—bringing it to the point where it is a new building producing a cash flow. Chapter 6 discusses the risks and rewards of investing at any point after the depreciation forces have started to use up the income-producing ability of the building. The present chapter focuses on the *people* who are involved in creating the investment opportunity.

We shall follow an entrepreneur through the development process. The entrepreneur does business with many specialists and supporting professionals in getting the building built and occupied and later refinanced, sold, remodeled, and torn down.

In the process of getting the project developed, each specialist performs a function that, when accomplished, reduces the investment risk. There are three broad categories of such specialists: entrepreneurs, agents, and lenders. The development process starts with an entrepreneur who wants to do something with land. Owners, developers, builders, investors, and speculators are among those who become entrepreneurs by taking the initial risks of putting cash (or promising to put up cash) in the acquisition of land.

Agents are real estate brokers who usually represent sellers of land, and mortgage brokers (or correspondents) who represent mortgage lenders. Sometimes many functions are performed by different people in the same firm; sometimes one person performs various functions.

Many of the most successful real estate brokers achieve their competence by specializing. In addition to specializing in selling houses, brokers may specialize in income-producing properties and have a following of investors who buy apartments, office buildings, or shopping centers. Some specialize in selling only motels or hotels, others only industrial land and warehouses, or only apartments, stores, or offices. Still others specialize in property management, earning a percentage of gross income from property owners as compensation. Property managers are also agents, but they rent or lease space, rather than sell ownership interests.

Traditionally the seller pays the broker any commission earned on real property. By special arrangement the buyer can pay the commission. It is unethical and generally illegal for the broker to receive commission from both seller and buyer, unless both are aware of, and agree to, this arrangement. The broker who is paid by the seller has a responsibility to the seller to endeavor to obtain the highest price for the property, inasmuch as the seller is paying a fee. Thus there is an inherent conflict if the broker is to be paid by the buyer as well as the seller.

In using the services of an agent to borrow money on real estate, the commission is generally paid by the *borrower*. The agents for loans fall into two broad classifications. The first are mortgage brokers who survey the entire market for money from institutional lenders, mostly savings and loan associations, mutual savings banks, life insurance companies, and commercial banks. Their job is to know what lender has money available for what kind of projects, the current rate of interest, and other pertinent aspects of the mortgage loan. The second category is mortgage loan correspondents who represent one or several companies on a more or less exclusive basis in a given geographical area. They frequently work (and share commissions) with active mortgage brokers in the same community.

Since *most* of the money in a typical real estate investment comes from a lender and not from the entrepreneur, mortgage agents obviously play a vital role in the development and total investment process. Some of the lenders, especially large insurance companies, maintain local offices in major metropolitan areas. Although they represent themselves, they frequently charge commissions for the money they lend. These fees are designed to cover the expenses incurred in establishing and maintaining local offices. They also work with mortgage brokers in making loans and have various commission arrangements with such brokers.

Local lenders may also lend directly to the borrowers, as is frequently the case with savings and loan associations and commercial banks. There are mortgage bankers as well who, in addition to acting as correspondents or brokers, function as dealers, that is they commit to a loan, make the loan, and later sell it to a lender. The institutional structure of lenders varies by local area.

There are other specialized personnel active in the real estate investment and development process who are paid a fee or salary for services performed. For example appraisers are paid for their services—regardless of whether their appraisal is higher or lower than that of their client or employer. Real estate counselors act on a fee basis irrespective of their recommendations. Other supporting professional services include market research, advertising specialists, attorneys, accountants, architects, and land planners; these people are paid a fee for providing answers to questions that arise in reaching investment decisions.

IT STARTS WITH THE LAND

The development process starts with the land. Whether one knows what one wants to develop and seeks land for a specific purpose of first acquires land and later decides what to build on it, one does need land.

Real estate brokers (agents) seek to make a match between the desires of the developer (entrepreneur) for land and the wish of a land investor for a sale. The landowner usually pays a commission to the broker for arranging the sale. The entrepreneur, who could be a developer, investor, or builder, needs an inventory of land in order to have something to develop. Without land the entrepreneur is out of business. It is mostly for this reason that the entrepreneur who is not engaged full time in the development business has difficulty in acquiring a choice parcel of land. The brokers know that professional entrepreneurs must eventually buy and that it is merely a question of finding what they want. Part-time investors however are not in this *must* position since they can meet their financial obligations from their regular work. Many top flight real estate brokers rarely bother with anyone other than full-time entrepreneurs. In addition full-time entrepreneurs are knowledgable. They have an inventory—they pay the going price. Highly regarded full- time entrepreneurs are suspicious of prices that are seemingly lower than the market price. They are interested in finding property with which they can do something, not property that is "real cheap."

The acquisiton of land for development is a complex business transaction requiring more than a surface knowledge of land-use regulation, mortgage finance, building costs, designs, and real estate markets. Because the facts needed to reach decisions are not easy to identify, collect, and analyze, part-time entrepreneurs are at a significant disadvantage when among the professionals.

Once entrepreneurs are satisfied that the available parcel of land is suited to their purposes, they must proceed to get control of it. They do this by an option—a contract stipulating that, having paid a fee, they have the right to buy at an agreed upon price and terms, but they do not have the obligation to buy. An alternative method of acquiring control is to put up a deposit on the land under an agreement to purchase. Naturally the conditions of the agreement should provide an opportunity to withdraw if the entrepreneur cannot use the land for development—otherwise an entrepreneur becomes an unwilling land investor or a former entrepreneur. In any case some financing of the purchase is usually necessary.

FINANCING THE LAND

Land that is purchased for development is usually purchased with some borrowed money. A source of financing is the seller. The broker usually knows what financing the seller will provide. The terms on which land financing from the seller can be obtained vary widely. In some cases very generous provisions may be obtained—a low down payment, a long term, and even a subordination of the loan to a long-term first mortgage from an institutional lender—but they are usually reflected in a higher price than would be paid on an all-cash basis.

The purchase of land is rarely financed by the traditional institutional lenders—life insurance companies, savings and loan associations, savings banks, and commercial banks. However other institutional lenders and some private lenders, who are part of the development process, occasionally make land loans.

Loans can be obtained only through four avenues: through the seller; through the lender directly, such as a direct loan from a bank or savings and loan association; through a mortgage banker (mortgage loan correspondent) who represents a lending institution; or through a mortgage broker who can place such a loan with an institution or private investor. Institutional lenders usually make land loans as a start on providing construction and long-term financing. Private investors do so because they like the high rates they can and do obtain.

CONSULTING SPECIALISTS

Assume that the entrepreneur buys a parce of land to be developed into a project capable of producing income. This can be accomplished by combining a building with the land. To do so the entrepreneur-developer needs a lawyer to help draw up the original contract and to make certain that the land being bought can be used. Next the entrepreneur-developer needs a title attorney or title company to provide adequate assurance or insurance that the necessary ownership rights are forthcoming. Entrepreneur-developers need some kind of financing help. They must know the maximum use to which they can put the land (usually subject to the control of some zoning authority) and to be certain that they are paying a fair price. And they must know how they should design the project, so that it will produce an adequate return on their investment.

In making design decisions, the developer needs the help of an architect, a land planner, or both. Hopefully, the developer has been acquiring as much of the pertinent data as possible before actually taking title to the land—an expensive procedure because the required expertise must be obtained from a variety of specialized personnel. Usually it is not feasible to get all of the information prior to acquiring title to the land, and this makes the risks inherent in land acquisition extremely high. The risk or cost is especially great for expensive land on which a large project will be built. Professional developers learn to weigh the variety of risks that can be reduced by the use of professional services. They make their commitment to the land in the face of a multitude of unknown facts. Land development is not the place for an amateur, nor for some of the so-called pros.

AN EXAMPLE OF A PROJECT

Assume that our developer believes that a market exists for luxury apartments, but somewhat below the purely luxury level with very high rents. Our developer asks several commercial and land brokers to look out for a parcel of land large enough for a project of about 200 apartments, designates which areas in the community are acceptable, and indicates an approximate price. Our developer can make these preliminary decisions because of a knowledge of the city, the general rental market, the general costs, and enough rules of thumb or experience to be in the ball park.

The brokers employed are eager tigers and submit a number of parcels of land. The developer chooses one of these as the best available location for what is planned, calls a lawyer, and starts spending money. Eventually a contract to purchase the land is signed. A small deposit is put up and an agreement to take title to the land in 6 months is made. The contract may stipulate an agreement to withdraw within 2 months if the developer cannot obtain zoning permission, if the soil turns out to be incapable of supporting a high-rise structure, or if some other contingency occurs.

The contract will call for the balance of the down payment at the time of settlement or the close of escrow. The terms "take title" "settle," or "close escrow" all refer to the same result: to formally "close" a transaction and pass title from seller to buyer. The settlement may take place at a title company or a lawyers office, and the title company or the lawyer records the transaction in the county courthouse or similar place within which the real estate is located. The recording of the deed then is a matter of "public record."

Assume that in this case the seller provides financing by taking back a mortgage that is due and payable one year after settlement. This amount of time was agreed on under the terms of the contract because the developer felt it would take a year to plan adequately and make arrangements to finance the project.

At this point the developer might employ a real estate market analyst to make a study of the market for luxury apartments at the specific location. The market analyst would check out all competing projects, forecast the development of the area, and then recommend the size, character, and price range for the apartments to be built at the site. Some developers make their own analyses, using their own experience and whatever information can be readily gathered. In any case the developer will proceed with the project on the basis of market demand.

If our developer is satisfied that there is a market for a 200-unit luxury apartment building the next step is to find a mortgage lender who will put up most of the capital. Our developer may want to obtain a permanent commitment from a major insurance company for about 75% of the total value of the land and building to be constructed. Finding such a lender is so important that the developer may try to do this before "settling" on the purchase of the land. To cover the risk of being committed to a purchase of land on which one cannot build, our developer has a lawyer draw a contract with provisions that would protect against such a risk. One way to do this is to put up a small down payment and have provisions in the contract that would keep the developer from being personally liable for the balance due to the seller. The balance of the debt owed the seller is represented by a promissory note.

In addition the purchaser or borrower pledges the property as security for payment of the debt. As protection the borrower stipulates that the sole security for the payment of the balance of the purchase price of land is the land *itself*. Thus if unable or unwilling to pay the mortgage, our developer could default on the contract by losing the modest down payment without further liability to the seller. The seller would not have the buyer's personal guarantee for the land. The seller could take the land back and be in the same position as before selling the land, except that the seller would get to keep the original modest down payment the developer made on the land. Of course our developer would be obligated for other fees that were incurred in the original acquisition of the land, in addition to having spent a good deal of time and money unprofitably.

Our developer might have used another approach and got the seller to give an option for a year with even a smaller amount of risk capital. If the search for a permanent loan commitment was unsuccessful, the developer would have all of the other expenses, but would have lost only the option money instead of the larger down payment. Assume that our developer did not get caught in a period of tight money—as has happened to many—and assume that market research revealed that the building made good economic sense (which our developer believed all the time). Hence it is expected that money can be borrowed for the project and it is now time to prepare a "package" to submit to a lender.

The first step is to develop preliminary plans and layouts with the help of an architect. Some ground borings are also made on the land to determine soil conditions. An engineer is hired to make a topographic plan and survey of the property. A professional market research organization is also hired to confirm the original subjective guess as to the market and to discover what kinds of apartments would rent best in the current market. In addition information from zoning officials indicates that land-use regulations allow a 227-unit apartment building having the kinds of apartments decided upon.

The preliminary plans are revised and checked out with the zoning and building restrictions to make certain that a 227-apartment building is feasible on land of the particular size and shape. The design of the apartments appears to work itself out in such a fashion that the building will not be unduly expensive to construct. Since our developer is not a contractor (someone engaged as a general contractor), there are several conferences with a contract builder who has given some preliminary estimates of the probable building costs.

There are also conferences with a management firm whose chief property manager has supplied some valuable suggestions, both dos and dont's, based on experience gained in managing similar buildings. Neither the builder nor the manager charged our developer for their services. The builder hopes to be awarded the building contract and the manager hopes to manage the finished property.

When everything that could have been done by a responsible developer has been done, our developer is ready to present the lender with a loan application—a package that tells what is going to be done and what financing is needed.

Let us assume that the project will cost $4 million. Most of the money will come from the institutional lender whose buisness it is to make *long-term* amortizing loans on income-producing properties. Major insurance companies, large savings banks, and savings and loan associations are the prime sources for such mortgage money. The developer can go either to a mortgage loan correspondent of one of these major lenders (a mortgage banker) or to a mortgage broker who will canvass the major lenders. The developer may know the market well enough to go directly to an insurance company or other major lender, but in any case there now exists what is known as a *mortgage package*.

The developer will have assigned tentative rentals to each apartment and will have estimated operating expenses, taxes, and insurance costs. There is an estimate of the building costs, land costs are already known, and the developer has a good idea of the architectural expenses. Thus an estimate for the entire cost of the project is possible. As already indicated, the developer will seek financing of about 75% of the total value of the entire project when completed. All the larger permanent lenders (institutional lenders making amortization loans in excess of 17 years) as well as the mortgage brokers and bankers have staffs that independently estimate the costs. They have extensive files and are very experienced, hence are likely to know costs and expenses as well as the developer. If a permanent lender likes the location, appreciates the tentative design, agrees with the tentative rents and expenses, and has the money at that particular time, it may formally agree to commit its funds on a *long-term* basis, subject to certain conditions including the inspection and approval of the final working drawings prepared by the architect.

Although the conditions and terms are many, our developer knows that they can be met, and so the offer of the long-term loan for 75% of the total value of the project is accepted. Usually the commitment is for the *permanent* loan, the funds for which the lender will not advance until the project is completed. Our developer needs to find an *interim lender, such as a commercial bank that is in the short-term* lending business. Many banks will make loans to developers based on the permanent loan agreement, which calls for the institutional lender making the permanent loan to pay out the funds on completion of the building.

Even though the short-term lender has a guarantee, short-term money for construction costs more than long-term money. Our developer will also have to pay a fee for appraisal of the property and for interim inspections, as well as find a way to plug a *very large* hole—the holdback amount in the permanent commitment. The holdback means that the permanent lender is holding back of the funds committed, depending on how much of the apartment building is actually rented when the funds are disbursed by the institutional lender after completion of construction, thus paying off the short-term or interim lender. The holdbacks vary with different companies, but are generally present in commitments involving the development of a new building.

The holdbacks are usually based on the developer's generating enough *occupancy* to at least have enough cash flow to pay all operating expenses and the monthly or quarterly instalments on the mortgage. In garden apartments this occupancy requirement may be as high as 90%. Occupancy requirements vary among different types of properties, but are most important on unleased office buildings and shopping centers.

The reasoning behind holdbacks is simple. The lender says to our developer: "Look, when you rent 190 units or more out of the 227 units to people with acceptable credit and in accordance with the rent schedule you have submitted to us, we shall disburse on completion our entire loan of $3.3 million. Until you reach that point (190 units rented) we don't see how you'll be able to stand the payments on the full loan. So we'll only commit to disbursing $3 million until the rental requirements are met. Then we'll gladly give you the balance, another $300,000."

The developer knows that the spread between the minimum amount (the guaranteed amount of the loan) and the maximum amount, of the rental requirements are met, is $300,000. The bank is basing its short-term construction loan (generally called an interim loan) on the institutional lender's guaranteed minimum of $3 million. Therefore during construction the developer may not get the maximum loan $3.3 million because the rental requirements to obtain it may not have been met. Perhaps they never will be met thus the developer is short the $300,000 that had been expected on the assumption that the rental requirements would be met. Before construction began, the developer considered the various alternatives and arranged (but did not receive the money) for a separate loan to cover this possibility.

This separate commitment for a loan by a secondary lending corporation is called a standby commitment or sometimes a gap commitment. Its purpose is to plug the $300,000 hole, the holdback. The loan commitment says, "When this building is completed we will advance $300,000 regardless of how the rentals are going."

The permanent commitment of a minimum guaranteed amount of $3 million together with the standby loan commitment of $300,000 is sufficient guarantee for the interim lender, usually a commercial bank, to advance as the construction progresses the entire $3.3 million our developer is seeking.

The costs are not negligible for standby loan commitments. If the standby company actually disburses its funds, it knows it is doing so on a building where rentals are moving slowly. If the rentals were going great, the institutional lender that gave our developer the $3.3 million commitment would have disbursed the last $300,000, making the use of the proceeds of the standby loan unnecessary. Interest rates on standby loan commitments therefore are high—several percentage points higher in interest than on conventional loans.

Since standby loan companies are rarely called upon to disburse, most of their income is derived from the initial fees received when issuing their commitment. In other words they make money by issuing commitments for loans they hardly ever make.

Of course our developer could have planned to invest $300,000 more if the rental requirements were not met and the maximum permanent loan not received, rather than arrange for a standby loan. If the developer is responsible and not in a heavy cash position, finding investors to share in the project is not a very difficult task. Soundly planned real estate investments in good locations backed by responsible developers are very attractive to investors. The developer could form a group of close friends or relatives to help with the heavy cash requirements. Perhaps an investment trust with surplus cash might consider committing to an equity ownership of say 50% of the project. Or an investment club might consider this a fetching investment. Some lender might even consider a loan with an option on the lender's part to convert the loan to a portion of the equity when the project is completed. The mechanics of funding a project are almost limitless and the variations endless. Let us suppose however that the developer has enough cash or arranges the standby loan commitment to develop the project to completion with the minimum loan amount. Where does our developer go from here?

Construction Commences

A builder is needed. Although builders cannot be responsible for conditions they cannot see, such as a meandering stream under a tract of land, strikes, acts of God, and other similar contingencies, they can give the developer an "upset" price subject to some conditions. But the developer can never know for certain the final cost because of such uncontrollable conditions as strikes, the length of time needed to lease, and other uncertainties that are a part of the development process. The developer makes contractual arrangements with the builder; records the "loan package" (short-term; permanent—or standby, if any)—all of this through a title company or title lawyer; has an inspection by the bank (the interim lender); and is now ready to commence construction.

The construction proceeds with periodic inspections by the bank, the developer, the architect, and the local authorities (building inspectors). In addition to the contract builder's own employees, some work will be subcontracted among various specialists: plumbers, electricians, plasterers, concrete contractors, bricklayers, tilemen, and as many other trades as are necessary to build the project. Each subcontractor will have a contract with the builder, just as the builder has a contract with the developer.

It should be noted that in common usage the word "builder" has acquired a very broad meaning—everybody seems to be a builder. Here we use "builder" to denote a general contractor, as distinguished from a builder-developer who usually builds only on his or her own account.

Leasing Begins

The advertising of the project starts with the preparation of a sign to identify to the passing public what is being built. The developer may have hired an advertising agency to design the sign, to order it built to conform with local regulations, and to develop a brochure about the building as well as a plan for the proper advertising of the project on completion.

By now the developer will probably have made a commitment to a property management organization, which will be responsible for the leasing and day-to-day management of the property. This assumes that the developer does not intend to manage the building. Management of major properties frequently is controlled by either the organization that obtains the original permanent loan, frequently the mortgage banker, or the person or group that controls the equity cash, if loans are not too scarce. The management as well as the property insurance and other business generated can be profitable to someone—and usually everyone is looking for the business.

Management companies employ property managers, who each have a group of buildings under their direct supervision. The person directly responsible for leasing the apartments and maintaining the building is the resident manager. In unusually large projects the person in charge is sometimes called the executive manager. The day-to-day management rests in this person, who usually employs a resident engineer in the larger projects or a resident maintenance engineer or janitor in the smaller projects.

The developer, or subsequent owner, could bypass the management company and the property manager and hire the resident manager or resident engineer directly. But it may not be decided to do this for a variety of reasons, one of the most valid is that objectivity in administration can be applied by an excellent management company that manages similar projects. The developer can frequently benefit from such management. Benefits can range widely. They may include purchase of maintenance items such as light bulbs (the more you buy, the cheaper they become). In addition large management companies can shift personnel from one project to another, often benefiting both owners. Sharing such infrequently used pieces of equipment as power vacuum sweepers for cleaning parking areas, snow-removal equipment, and large power mowers can be advantageous, since one project alone often cannot afford to have expensive specialized equipment.

Whoever is responsible for the management will staff the rental office and prepare to show space, obtain leases, check credit, and arrange for the tenants to move in. If the project rents quickly and at the estimated rates, the permanent loan will be disbursed in full, without the holdback, and any standby commitment that exists will not be needed,

RESULTS OF GOOD PLANNING

A successful developer is an imaginative risk-taker who must plan a project as much as several years prior to the occupancy of a building. Developers are supposed to predict markets accurately several years in the future, plan perfect projects, obtain exquisite financing, and develop cash flow statements. These will all be compared at some later date with the financial facts and of course never will be precisely as predicted. The discipline of real estate development is subject to the limitations of the social sciences. Commitments today to a series of actions that may not be completed until some time well into the future are based on guesses and estimates, no matter how mathematically precise and statistically developed they appear to be.

Curiously there are many persons in the development business who treat the various phases of the process as if they were dealing with a physical science. Many investors as well, private and institutional, pretend or presume that their predictions are based on scientific data. The facts are that the necessary data are simply not available and forecasting is as much art as it is science. Thus the better the economic and financial research a developer brings to the development of a real estate project, the more consistent are the results. Only thorough developers seem to be consistently "lucky."

The only thing more hazardous than too much reliance on data and analysis is too little. Many projects seem to be built on faith and hope. Although fortuitous timing and location may enable the market to accept some mistakes, over the life of the property the quality of the original planning shows up.

The decisions are mainly those of the developer. However so many other people influence the final product that it is amazing that things turn out as well as they do. To an onlooker one building may appear architecturally appealing, while another building may look like a glob of bricks. The control over a project's appearance however is only partly in the hands of the architect. This is because the capital (equity cash) going into the project ordinarily want as much building on the land as is possible in order to lower the land cost per apartment. Meanwhile zoning limits the number of units and where they may be put, frequently giving the developer a box-like space in which to build.The lender who is committing the long term capital, sometimes three times as much as the developer, also exercises a subtle control over the design of the building. By the time the architect gets the project, many of the decisions have been made. The best buildings may well be built by developers who employ architects who understand the economics of development and management, who build in jurisdictions where the regulatory authorities judge on functional performance, and whose projects are financed by lenders who are willing to take on something different from what has worked for them in the past.

THE OCCUPIED PROJECT

The cast of characters who enter the stage after the project is completed includes practitioners in the field who are not necessarily known to the investing public. The tenants of an apartment building know the resident manager and resident engineer. "Resident engineer" has come to replace the old-fashioned term of a few decades ago, "super" (short for superintendent). He was someone who could fix anything. Alas those were the days before dishwashers, garbage disposers, automatic elevators, and highly sophisticated air-conditioning and heating systems. Once the only sure way to obtain more heat from the super (which meant shoveling more coal) was to bang loudly on the radiators. Today's youth know the term "radiator" only as something used in an automobile.

Today the licensing authorities in most jurisdictions require that a resident engineer have a stationary engineering background and can demonstrate expertise in the handling of equipment. So a call for a minor repair does not produce the resident engineer; the call is responded to by the "maintenance engineer," a modern euphemism for "janitor." Both the maintenance engineer and the resident engineer usually report to the residential manager.

The resident manager reports either directly to an owner or to a property manager who works for a realty management company. If the company is large, it employs several property managers, each of whom supervises several buildings, inspects them physically, and oversees the work of the resident managers.

These employees report to an executive who may be a certified property manager (CPM), so designated by the Institute of Real Estate Management, an affiliate of the National Association of Realtors. CPM's have passed specific tests and have demonstrated their expertise by serving a minimum number of years in the supervision of large income-producing properties.

Earlier in the investment development process, before the building was built, you will recall that the developer conferred with such a person about the layout of the space, the probability of collecting certain rents, and generally relied on this executive's practical knowledge in order to erect a building that would not require excessive maintenance. The same company will probably be handling the leasing and management of the occupied project. This is done by contract. The managing company is known to the public as the "agent," although sometimes by some less flattering names. Management companies make money by charging a fee that amounts to a percentage of the gross rental income they collect. Once the property is in the hands of professional property management, the investor will make the policy decisions and enjoy the benefits of investing.

TO REFINANCE OR SELL

Ten or fifteen years pass. The new project has gone through the first phase of its life and is now maturing. During this time few major decisions have been made by the owners because the most expensive items of equipment, although having needed minor repair, probably have not had to be replaced. The area is absorbing other people as new projects are built near the occupied project, and the owner hopefully has had a more or less assured income. Under current tax laws a sale or trade of the building would not have to carry an undue burden. But accelerated depreciation is getting low. Also the amortization is getting to be a big portion of the total payment. Tax shelter may be gone. The pressure is on to sell or perhaps refinance.

You will remember the formula for taxable income: cash flow plus amortization minus depreciation equals taxable income. To the extent that depreciation equals amortization, some, all, or more than all of the taxable income is not subject to federal income taxes. The emphasis at this point of ownership (after from 10 to 15 years) will be on decreasing the amortization in order that the cash flow may be tax-sheltered. Since it is impossible to increase the depreciation, the amortization must be decreased. As a practical matter the use of accelerated depreciation caused the depreciation amount to decrease each year while the normal amortizing mortgage causes the amortization to increase. Under normal conditions, the tax shelter thus becomes less each year, and no investor wants to be in a position where more than his cash flow is subject to federal income taxes. "What, pay income taxes on more than I'm receiving! Are you out of your mind?" This question is often voiced by owners of buildings 10 years or older. What can be done? Since the depreciation is declining, refinancing of the property is in order. Refinancing causes the amortization to decline sharply. This result is apparent when you remember that every payment of a mortgage consists of two parts— interest and amortization. Payments on a new mortgage consist largely of interest and very little amortization.

Let us assume two things: the building can be refinanced and the same amount of money as was required for the original mortgage can be borrowed. If the assumptions are correct, then all monies obtained through the refinancing may be pocketed by the owner and no federal income tax need be paid on this delicious chunk of cash. Why? You do not pay income taxes on borrowed monies, only on earnings. It also solves the horrendous prospect of paying federal income taxes on more than you are receiving because of the sharp decrease in the amortization. A quick look at the formula for taxable income will reassure you of this fact.

Who arranged the refinancing or the obtaining of a new loan? The same person, that is, the mortgage banker, the mortgage broker, the loan correspondent, or whoever obtained your original mortgage—or some other person in the same business.

If your choice is to sell, real estate brokers specializing in that type of property are your best bet. They know the market, both for buyers and general values. They are in the marketplace.

It may be that someone else who owned the property for 10 years or so is now putting it up for sale and you are interested in buying. For you the cost basis will be based on the price you pay. You start the depreciation based on your costs and the remaining useful life of the building.

THE AGING PHASE

After about 20 years of somebody's ownership of the property, some decisions must be made. These decisions may require substantial additional cash, which the owner may not be willing or able to advance. The replacement expenditures are up, the maintenance presents problems, and the quality of the tenancy may have declined. The decision on major replacements (new air-conditioning systems, maybe new elevators) are now in order. What to do?

Someone may be willing to upgrade it. Real estate investors and speculators often buy-20-year-old buildings, either because they are skillful at renovating, remodeling, and rehabilitation or they know what it costs to have this done by others. Sooner or later, depending on the management of the property and its location, the time comes when an additional investment is made in order to get the cash flow.

THE DEMISE OF THE BUILDING

When it no longer pays to maintain or upgrade the property, the end of the cash flow is near. The decision on rehabilitation or abandonment through the wrecking crane (or letting it become a slum) marks the last stage in the life of the building. Ordinarily in 40 to 50 years, all buildings not rehabilitated are candidates for the wrecker.

Some people are saddened by the demolition of an old building. Most real estate practitioners are delighted. It means they are back to the land from which it all began. Parking lot people often enter the process here or at the aging stage of the development process.

Many new downtown office buildings are often partially owned by the parking lot operator who either had a long-term lease on the land or an ownership interest in it. So the cycle begins anew.

Urban renewal is a classic ending of the aging and demise phases of the development process, yet it also is the beginning of a new development process.

CONCLUSIONS

The familiarity with the development process provides a basis for examining the risks and rewards inherent in investing at different stages in the process. This examination is a fascinating one because it clearly portrays how money can be made, consistent with certain risks, at all stages in the development process. To our knowledge, the different stages of the process have never been clearly identified in existing literature. The precise moment of risk change has not heretofore been identified at each *step* in the process. The clearly perceptible risk changes at each step could be the basis for helping you to further develop and refine your investment strategy.

The next chapter explains how the risks of investing during the development process decrease as the project moves from being vacant land to becoming a rented building.

5 INVESTING DURING THE DEVELOPMENT STAGES

Regardless of the kind of real estate you may eventually own and the legal form in which you may own it and regardless of where your investment strategy has its emphasis—cash flow, tax shelter, or capital gains—your risks and rewards are dramatically affected by *when* you enter the investment process. Precise information as to how you get in (and out) of any real estate investment is being deliberately postponed until the last two chapters. You will then have enough information to make a reasoned judgment in accord with your investment strategy.

The birth, youth, maturity, aging, and ultimate demise of a real estate investment may be viewed as a pyramid. It is continuum starting at the base, which represents the unimproved land; ascending to the apex, which is the occupied new project; and descending as it matures and ages until it is demolished and is once again unimproved land. *Where* you enter the pyramid determines what kind of risks you are taking and how much money you can make. The birth, life, and ultimate death of an income-producing property occur within a time cycle. The determination of the best possible place in the time cycle for you to invest is what the pyramid approach to investing is all about.

As described in the preceding chapter, entrepreneurs

(either developers or builders) purchase land on which they intend to build an apartment or other improvement. They put up option money, or a cash deposit, and agree to consummate the land purchase within a specified period of time. What do they know about the project when they make the commitment to buy the land? They may have very few facts. They may not know whether they can even build apartments (and may have contracted to buy the land "subject to rezoning"). They may not know how many apartments they can build; how much it will cost them to build; how much they can borrow, at what rate of interest or at what speed of repayment. Nor do they know how much it will cost to operate the building and how much rent they can receive. They do not know how many nor what kinds of units they can best rent, nor at what price to rent, or if the units will rent well. In fact they do not appear to know very much.

You can invest at this stage of development or at subsequent stages when the developer knows more about costs (and cash requirements) and about the benefits, such as cash flow. The longer you wait, the more time the developer will have had to go through the various stages on the upside of the pyramid. During that time the risks will become reduced—and so will the rewards. We now turn to the various stages at which you can "get in."

THE GROUND FLOOR

We call the first point in the project the ground floor. If you as an investor put up money along with the entrepreneur's immediately after a commitment for the land is made, you had better be rewarded mightily, for everything about the project factually known at this stage is what entrepreneurs call "guesstimates." Let us assume that our developer has prior experience and is a successful business person. The zoning attorney is consulted and thinks that there is a good chance of obtaining the rezoning that will permit the entrepreneur to build a 16-story high-rise building containing x number of units. We shall also suppose that they are right in this assumption and that the authorities eventually agree with the developer that the land should be rezoned from single-family-dwelling use to apartment-house use. What, then does the developer know? Nothing factually, except as a general comparison with similar projects (if they exist). However soon the developer will begin to put together a "mortgage package," which is an array of facts, analysis, and conjecture designed to aid a mortgage lender in arriving at a favorable decision to lend.

The "mortgage package" starts when the developer goes to the architect. The architect, with the help of a topographic map and other indicators of site usability, tentatively lays out a structure that will conform to the permitted zoning rules and will make effective use of the site. The architect however will be instructed as to which types of apartments are desired after the developer determines the neighborhood characteristics and reaches certain conclusions. The developer will instruct the architect on an appropriate mix among various kinds and sizes of apartment units and discuss physical features (room size, apartment layouts, and so on) as well as the desirability of other features, such as balconies. While the plans are being drawn, the developer will prepare rent schedules based on a projection of what the apartments that the developer decided on can ultimately command in rent.

The developer could have had a land-use study made by expert land planners prior to or during discussions with the architect. Socioeconomic studies could have been made of the typical profile of the prospective tenants by an examination of income characteristics and life styles of tenants in buildings, located in similar areas. A market analysis could have been made to decide on size, type and rental rates for the apartments, or the developer could have made these rental decisions relying on personal experience or experiences of fellow developers. One way or another, the developer would at this point in the process have started to prepare a gross income schedule based on a design of a building that would produce it.

The developer could speculate on how much of a loan a lender would give, the rate of interest of such a loan, and the speed with which it would have to be paid off. Some preliminary inquiries may have been made of a mortgage banker to find out what is happening in the mortgage markets.

The developer could estimate the building's operating expenses, based on either previous personal experiences or by relying on operating expense data furnished by professional and trade associations.

A chat with a builder friend or two could provide some estimate of building costs.

When all of this preliminary data is put in writing and the plans are drawn by the architect, the developer has what is known as a mortgage package. The estimates, all beautifully written and statistical, have an aura of precision. These are for presentation to a lender from whom a long-term mortgage commitment is being sought.

From an investor's point of view, the developer has not significantly affected the *investors* risk. Everything the developer has reduced to writing relating to the mix (the lender might not like it), the general design (the lender might not like it either), the estimated rents (the lender might think they are too high and so may the ultimate renting public), the costs to operate the building (the lender might think they are too low), the amount of the loan (the lender always thinks it is too much), and the cost to build it (may be too low)— all these are conjecture. The whole project may be a "bomb". Yet the developer has moved the project along the way toward a significant point in the pyramid.

Would you invest at this point, now that there is a mortgage package? You do not know that the risk has been reduced; all that has happened is that the papers show what the developer believed all along. Nothing has happened to change the risk—only the estimates of the risk. A milestone has not occured for you to consider that you have moved up the pyramid. You and the developer are still at the ground floor. If you invest your money at this point, you can *make or lose* the maximum, compared with any other place on the upside of the pyramid. Nothing has happened to change your ground-floor risk. However *your estimate of the risk* may have changed. The risk looks different because the developer has a lot of numbers on paper. From your point of view the only thing that has happened is that some information has been gathered that is valuable to the developer since it tends to confirm the original decision and influence others. As for you, unless you are a professional and can come up with an appropriate evaluation of the risk and rewards, you have to proceed on faith that the developer knows the score.

As an investor, are you prepared to take the risks inherent in entering the pyramid on the ground floor? Probably not; only a small number of investors have the need to make the most profit or the compulsion to take such a heavy risk. After all neither you nor the developer knows for sure whether the project is going to be worthwhile or even whether it will go forward. The uncertainties at this point are the greatest they will be for the project. Here is where professional judgment counts the most—where you can make or lose the most. It is a stage for those who are in the business of development, not for investors who want to conserve their investment capital.

LOAN COMMITMENT STAGE

The mortgage package has been submitted to a lender by the developer through either a mortgage banker or a mortgage broker, and usually, after several weeks of oral and written negotiations, the lender makes a written offer to commit funds to the project in the form of a permanent loan commitment. Let us assume that the commitment amounts to 75% of the project's value and will be honored upon completion of the building, subject to many practical and legal considerations. The loan commitment is the significant milestone on the upward continuum of the pyramid. The first milestone was the ground. The second is the loan commitment.

There are four steps on the upside of the pyramid. In addition to the first two steps, there are interim processes (short-term financing and the building contract) and tenancies. An acronym called GLIT describes the upside of the pyramid. It means ground, loan, interim (financing and building contract), and tenants. Where you commit your money on the upside of the pyramid determines how much money you can make.

At the stage after the permanent loan has been committed, you know that some lender likes the project. The project is feasible and should be profitable. The lender is committed to put up more money than anyone else and is experienced (but not error free). Despite the loan commitment, you still cannot be sure the project will be profitable or will be well constructed. The lender may have been under pressure to lend with relatively few other attractive choices available. This happens at times and the lender may not have properly evaluated the project in terms of quality considerations.

Once a permanent loan commitment is made by a lender. the likelihood of the building construction moving forward has been enhanced. This is because the lender charges a *standby fee* for the loan commitment. The standby fee is forfeitable if the project does not move forward prior to an agreed-on time. Most standby fees are sufficient to commit the developer to move forward. It is common practice to post a standby fee between 1 and 1.5% of the permanent loan commitment. On a $3 million loan, the standby fee could be any amount between $30,000 and $45,000, depending on the policies of the lenders.

You as an investor, although uncertain of the reliability of the projected gross rents, can be reasonably confident of the expense projections. You know how much you are borrowing and the speed with which the loan is to be repaid. Other expense items are not too difficult to estimate; each is relatively small when compared to the mortgage payments.

You still do not know two major things: the cost to build the project and whether the projected rents will hold up. The project seems feasible, but it is not as yet a proved and profitable building.

Since repayment of the loan is almost always the largest single item among the payouts, it is critical to have this fact before you in order to make a reasonable investment decision. You still may not be sure of the costs of construction, nor of the validity of your rent projections, but you are now reasonably certain of the estimate of your cash payouts. There is a psychological point that should also not be missed. Since everybody in the development process is guessing as to probable rents and probable expenses, it is reassuring to know that your developer's estimates are being confirmed by an experienced lender who is commiting more cash to the project than anyone else. The lender expects to be repaid out of income, and this commitment influences you. Thus when the permanent loan has been committed, the L milestone of the GLIT has been reached. The risks have been dramatically reduced because there is a loan commitment, which solves a major problem— getting most of the necessary money for permanent financing. The rewards are less uncertain than they were before because you know the amount of the long-term mortgage and mortgage payments. But the cost and the cash flow are still estimates.

THE INTERIM STAGE

The land has been bought, a loan has been obtained, and a standby fee has been put up by the developer. Where does the project go from here? It has to be built. Hence we need the builder who cannot build without money. Hence we need an interim lender, frequently a commercial bank.

The next act that commits the project to going forward is a combination of two things: a signed contract with a builder and, more importantly, the recording (placing on the public record) of the interim loan. The recordation establishes a lien in favor of the lender. A lien is a claim on the property and represents the security for the payment of a debt. The major lenders may go so far as to cancel their commitment if one blade of grass is disturbed prior to the recording of the loan. They want to make absoultely certain that no actual work has commenced before their lien is recorded in order to be sure that no one had a prior claim to the land as security for a debt. Since theirs is the first mortgage, any work performed by anyone, even dumping of dirt, could result in a prior lien. Many states allow mechanics to file liens for work done, but for which the owner has not paid. These are known as mechanic's liens. On-site inspections are made by either disbursing officer's or by representatives of the lenders, prior to recording of the loan, to make sure no work has been started and thus assuring the lender or lenders that they have first claim.

The recording of the interim loan is a powerful force in assuring the investor that the project will proceed. The builder has posted some kind of assurance that it will go forward or else the loan would not have been recorded. Builders may be required to furnish performance or completion bonds as an assurance to the lender that the construction will be completed. Bonds are usually purchased from a bonding company at rates that are rarely under 1% of the estimated cost of the building. If the builder has sizable assets, the lender may accept his personal signature in lieu of a completion or performance bond; thus a saving of 1% (the usual charge for a bond by a bonding company) may be effected. On a $4 million apartment project it amounts to $40,000. This expense or commitment to the lender assures the investor that the project will be completed. Uncompleted projects not only fail to produce rents, but are expensive to hold. Anything that delays completion increases costs.

The contract with the builder will call for a payment schedule as the work progresses,and the interim loan will state how the bank will disburse the funds. Simultaneously with the recording of the interim loan some funds may include reimbursement to the developer for expenses that have been incurred in carrying the project to its current stage. Lenders vary in the schedule of disbursements as the work progresses. The individual disbursement policies of each interim lender are labeled by developers and builders as draw schedules. They indicate, by percentage of the total loan, how much the developer may "draw" or take "down" at various stages of construction. These draws are disbursements from the lender, which earn interest on the day the money is drawn (disbursed). Developers and builders seek to do business with those lenders whom they know and trust and have come to consider tractable and understanding.

Construction loans are profitable for banks; banks like them because of their short-term nature and because they are guaranteed to be paid off by the permanent lender on completion of the project. It is a rare situation where the monetary system is so unbalanced that there is a shortage of short-term money and plentiful long-term money, but it has happened. Fortunately these imbalances are not of a permanent nature. Yet the obtaining of a long-term commitment by a major lender and the signing of the contract with the builder do not guarantee that the project will move forward. The interim loan must be obtained and recorded; then everyone can be confident of a completed project.

Let us assume that the developer with whom you plan to invest has a firm contract with the builder with an "upset price". The upset price is the maximum construction cost. Wouldn't it be nice if all the costs of the project were firmly established? Unfortunately they cannot be established. All building contracts provide for exceptional occurences, such as conditions under the ground, acts of God, and strikes over which the builder has no control. For example a strike, of elevator installers in a proposed 16-story apartment building could run costs well above your estimates. Since elevators are rarely completed until near the end of the building project, most of the interim funds would have been withdrawn from the bank at this stage. If the amount withdrawn from the bank is $3 million, and the interim loan bears interest at 9% per annum, each month you wait for the strike to end costs you $22,500 with no way ever to recapture that expenditure. As another example running into a soil problem could raise your costs. Thus what the "upset" price really does for you is to shift *some* of the risk to the builder and reduce *some* of your risk on total costs.

The cost of money is a very important factor in any building project, and any delay increases this cost. Unfortunately the risk of unknown cost is still with you at this stage of the pyramid and will remain unknown until the project is completed *and* occupied. Why do costs depend on occupancy? Suppose the estimated rents are higher than the market will pay? To return to our example, $3 million at 9% annum still costs $22,500 each month that the building is unoccupied and you are hoping to fill the project at the rents you had originally projected. If you take 12 months instead of 3 months to fill the project, the projected costs will be increased by $202,500. If the developer had planned a project calling for an investment of $1 million and a loan of $3 million, the cash investment costs would be 20% higher than originally planned, attributable solely to the slowness in renting up.

At the I point of the GLIT you know two things more than you did before. First you are fairly sure of your construction costs. Second you have a good forecast of a completion date and the beginning of some income. For the first time you have a solid idea of how much money has to be invested.

The I, or interim state, is a popular point for investors to get in on real estate investments when they are involved in new construction. From the investor's point of view, it is the first time that you can get a reasonable picture of the cash flow and tax shelter that you will get for your investment. In the developer's view, it is the point at which there is enough information to be able to get an attractive price from those who will participate with him in the investment (or from a sale, assuming completion). It is also the point at which the developer will need the balance of the equity funds for completion.

Investing at the G, L, or I stage provides some tax benefits beyond those obtained by investors who buy completed projects. During construction interest is paid, and some of that interest is tax deductible during the year of construction. The rest is capitalized and written off over an additional nine-year period. In addition other expenses, such as property taxes, are incurred. These expenses are written off during construction and an additional nine years. This is a reduction of benefits brought about by the Tax Reform Act of 1976.

Under the *Tax Reform Act of 1976*, construction-period interest and real estate taxes must be capitalized in the year in which they are paid or accrued, they are then amortized (written off) equally after a 10-year transition period. Thus 10% of the total amount capitalized may be deducted in the year it has been paid or accrued. The balance is written off over a nine-year period, beginning with the year in which the property is placed in service. Therefore *new* property investors who come in at the I stage (or earlier) obtain a deduction not available for investors who buy at the end of the deduction period. The deduction period ends nine years from the date the property is placed in service.

The phase-in of the new rule for nonresidential property began in 1977, but the full 10-year amortization period does not apply to construction-period interest and taxes paid or accrued before 1982. For projects commencing in 1977, 20% may be deducted in each year; in 1978, 16⅔% may be deducted; in 1979, 14²/₇% may be deducted; while in 1980 the figure is 12½. In 1981, 11¹/₉% may be deducted and commencing after 1981, all nonresidential projects will be treated as indicated earlier, that is at 10 per annum.

Residential real property, other than low-income housing, also has the construction-period interest and taxes phased in, but the phase-in time is slower. Commencing in 1978 the residential development receives a speedier amortization schedule. The phase-in time is even slower for low-income housing, with phase-in starting in 1982. Residential real property must start using the 10-year amortizing rule commencing in 1984, while the low-income rental housing rule doesn't start the 10-year amortization rule until 1988.

There is still another aspect to investing at this point. It should be obvious by now that developing is a separate business from investing. The two frequently go together, especially since at times the best way to get a good project is to participate in building it. The investor in the development process earns a profit—or should for taking development risks. But since our income taxes are paid on profits that are realized (not on increase in value), investors who get in during the development stage are able to acquire real estate investments at favorable prices (representing their taking the risks of getting in early). By investing at even as late a stage of development as the I stage, you can get very high returns for your investment because you provide capital to develop the project as well as to buy it.

If the risks of getting these higher benefits are not for you, the next stage may well be—because it is there that the risks are the lowest.

THE TENANCY

The milestone of completion and occupancy brings forth the facts, which you may compare with projections. The costs are in and so the total amount invested for development is known. The project is tenanted and the rentals are now verified or adjusted. The still unknown fact is the accuracy of the estimated expenses necessary to operate the project, hence the accuracy of the cash flow projection. The expenses will be all known or capable of solid estimates within one year of occupancy. The T in GLIT is the last point on the upside of the pyramid—the apex of the pyramid. It has been reached when the property has been occupied for 12 months, revealing not only the costs but the cash flow.

At this stage of the pyramid the risk is ordinarilly the smallest it will ever be. The project has started to produce income, and is usually at its best capability. If you paid a fair price and did not borrow too much, and if the project makes sense to begin with, the risks of loss are minimal.

SUMMARY AND CONCLUSIONS

Where on the upside of the pyramid would you invest your money? It depends on your strategy. Are you ready to take the risks of the development business? What rewards do you need or want? If you want the least risk, you will find it at the top of the pyramid, the T stage. It is the place in the pyramid where you will make the least on your investment, but even the least can be more than enough to make the investment attractive. The ground floor, where the risks are the greatest, may reward you the most.

There are opportunities to buy new buildings and get first-owner depreciation. You can get in during the early stages and own the property by yourself taking possession upon completion. Many investors, however, get into projects in some form of group ownership with a developer. It is axiomatic to developers that the longer they can wait before introducing capital other than their own throughout the upside of the pyramid, the larger the portion of the ultimate cash flow that they may retain for themselves. Put another way, the final cash flowing to developers for all the risks involved in the upside of the pyramid could be all retained by them if they did not need additional capital. They know that if they can wait until full tenancy, they can get a higher price for the portion of ownership that they sell; the longer they wait the more they get to keep. This makes sense because all the risks of development have been eliminated.

To the investors getting in early, this means that they will get a higher cash flow in relation to the amount of their investment. Your rewards are increased of you share some of the earlier risks with the developers. You are getting some of the cash flow they could have had if they waited for your capital until the project was tenanted. At the G stage of GLIT, the risks are enormous, and so are the rewards. As you ascend the pyramid through L and I, risks decrease and so do the rewards. When you reach T, both the risks and the rewards are the least.

The majority of investors, especially first-time investors, are not emotionally comfortable in the early stages of the development process. It makes sense to acquire the experience in the less risky ventures and then work one's way up to one's own upper limit of risk. You can increase your risk and reward not only by getting in before the peak of the pyramid has been reached, but also after. The next chapter describes the risk and reward on the downside of the pyramid.

6 INVESTING DURING THE DECLINING STAGE

After the property has been developed, occupied, and undergone a year of minor adjustments, it should begin to produce the anticipated cash flow. Normally the property is at its peak of performance at this point: all the space is rented and the building is in excellent condition. Things might improve further because of increase in the demand for the property, but you can be sure that the income-producing ability is being used up with the passage of time. Eventually the building will be torn down or abandoned.

En route to the end of the building's life, the rents will drop (at least in relative prices, so that even if the dollar amounts remain the same, the newer apartments will get more rent relative to the old). Also, as the building ages, the expense will rise. There are four recognizable stages through which the property will progress. Although ordinarily slow, each change taking a decade or longer, the changes do occur with the passage of time. Each of the four stages in the life of the property, on the downside of the pyramid, have different levels of risk. The investor may choose the kind of risk he can accept and will seek to be compensated for the risks he takes.

The downside of the pyramid is explained by the acronym, AMAD: absorption, maturing, aging, and demise. Incidentally, the entire pyramid sounds zany if you say it all at once; GLITAMAD.

92

ABSORPTION

The absorption stage of the downside of the pyramid refers to the time during which the real estate market is absorbing the new construction of competitive buildings in the area where your building is located.

On the day of completion the building starts to wear out and the value starts to decline. Some of the loss occurs simply because the newer structures are more desirable. Whatever the combination of causes, it is a fact that the structure will lose value. Many persons seem to be confused by the combination of facts: the building is losing value, yet sales prices are rising, thus making it seem that the building is gaining value. Except for extreme circumstances over a short period of time, it is only an appearance. Knowing that the building will eventually be useless helps to understand the fact that the moment the physical structure is built, it begins to deteriorate and lose value.

This confusion stems from what people hear, read, or know concerning someone who has owned real estate and has sold it for considerably more than the original purchase price. They believe that it has "gone up in value."

What has gone up in value? Certainly not the bricks and mortar; certainly not the elevators, nor the refrigerators, dishwashers, disposal units, carpets, venetian blinds, nor such mechanical equipment as the air-conditioning and heating systems, nor any other component parts of the structure. It may cost more to replace these parts because of higher labor costs and some inflation. But unless the construction costs rise faster than the general inflation level, it is not possible for the building to go up in value. It is the *land* that increases in value.

The increase in land value comes about because the location gets better (more desirable) as the city grows. Add to that the general increase in prices and you can readily see that it is the rise in the price of land that really makes the difference when you go to sell. The best that can happen with a building is that inflation will provide some compensation for the building's loss in value, but it can only postpone the decline. It can never stop it.

You can see that property developed five years ago and resold for considerably more money today has been profitable because of the increase in value of the land. You can make very profitable investments by selecting the locations that will get better—you do not need the "best" location, only the one that will get better.

The investor who comes into the pyramid during the A stage, that is the absorption stage, will receive the benefits of cash flow, tax shelter, and the proceeds of sale. The fact that the building starts to wear out immediately is not necessarily a liability. Part of the cash flow is payment for the loss in value of the structure. The depreciation allowances permitted by the tax laws may more than offset the amortization, so that some, all, or more than all of the cash flow is not subject to federal income taxes. The investor dare not be lulled into a sense of security with respect to the physical structure of the building, The building is deteriorating and losing value. The amount of loss in value may never be accurately determined, but the fact of depreciation is an important investment consideration.

For tax purposes the speed at which the building is being depreciated is more or less geared to the fact that the building is wearing out. In practice it may be correctly assumed that the faster the building will physically deteriorate, the faster the depreciation may be taken.

Depreciation may be taken more quickly by the original owners or developers. The more accelerated forms of depreciation are available to the original investor, not because the structure wears out more quickly at the beginning, but because Congress deemed it beneficial to the economy of the country to encourage investment in capital improvements. This fostered the development of income-producing properties. Congress therefore allowed more accelerated forms of depreciation to be used by the initial owners.

You know that the building must eventually wear out. The ability of the building to produce income will decrease. As it ages, it is going to become less desirable. Competitive new buildings will be built nearby, with better room arrangements, more thoughtful design, and better equipment. As a result the building itself will suffer financially, and at some point in time it will definitely wear out. While this wearing-out process is going on, the land tends to increase in value. It is incorrect to assume that the land will go down in value—ghost towns are a rare real estate phenomenon—although some cities do go downhill and some land values do decline in those parts of a city that become undesirable. At some point in time the building will be demolished and the land will once again be reused.

We see examples of this reuse of land in virtually every metropolitan center in the form of either public urban renewal or private development. There is a constant rebuilding of our cities through the tearing down of inefficient structures and replacing them with new buildings.

When you invest you should make some kind of forecast as to how long the building will last. You need to know how long it will be an income-producing investment.

Fortunately, if you identify the significant milestones of the downside of the pyramid, your forecast need not be accurate. If you recognize that you are in the absorption stage, the first A in the downside of the pyramid, you need only concern yourself with the fact that it is highly unlikely that major relacements of the component parts of the building will be necessary. Generally you will not have to make substantial replacements for 10 years, more or less, depending on the quality of the components that were originally installed in the building. During this time you should not have to replace refrigerators, mechanical or heating systems, swimming-pool filtering systems, roofs, or any of the other major and relatively expensive components of the building. Ordinarily you will need only to maintain the building and replace a few minor items.

If you commit your funds during the earlier part of the

10-year period of the absorption stage of the pyramid, you will have relatively little risk. If your purchase is conservatively financed, you will not lose, unless you bought a substandard structure in the world's worst location. If your building is adequate, your location is excellent, and your timing appropriate, you will have it made.

You should realize that the longer you wait to enter the pyramid on the downside, the greater will have to be the cash flow and potential benefits because of the shorter life of the structure. At the end of the first full decade of ownership, you will find yourself under pressure to make some decisions, since at some time during the second decade you will have to replace some fairly expensive component parts of the buildings.

You will also realize that during this first decade other building owners will be absorbing tenants in the same general area. Because their buildings are newer, these frequently will be more desirable. Your rents will be lower than those of the newer and better buildings.

The absorption stage is a good place to enter the pyramid. Under some conditions the risk can be less here than at the tenancy stage. In any event it is easier to assess the benefits during absorption because an operating history has been developed and the investor can see the development that has followed. The absorption stage is one of the two best times for a real estate investor to get started.

THE MATURING PROCESS

If you enter the pyramid after the first decade, you must get your cash out faster than if you had entered during the first decade. This means that you must seek a higher cash flow if you enter after the absorption stage.

The second stage on the downside of the pyramid is the maturing stage. The quality of the improvements and location will govern your investment during the maturing process.

Amazingly enough certain parts of the country seem to have more skilled and quality-conscious building crafts-men than are available in other parts of the country. It is of course quite possible to take excellent materials for a building and put them together so ineptly that glaring errors are apparent even to the casual observer. Yet modest materials that seem to fit together more perfectly, give a better visual effect. The good reputation of a building developer can be based on an insistence for quality materials and workmanship. An investor need only buy one "package of garbage," as a builder has euphemistically called an apartment house, to realize that an exceptionally high maintenance cost can completely negate the possibility of any cash flow. The poorer the quality of construction, the sooner the pressure on investors to replace several highly expensive components of the building in which they have invested.

By the same token, the emphasis the builder places on quality design, such as well-thought-out room layouts, ample closets, decent size kitchens, and bathroom facilities dramatically affects the desirability of the building from a tenant's standpoint. The better-designed buildings do not become obsolete so quickly as the ill-designed buildings. One need not be an expert in architecture to appreciate easily apparent differences in quality in different buildings.

As you recall, although land does not depreciate, it does change in value. The location with a building on it may be so desirable that it tends to offset the forces for obsolescence in building design. Certain older areas that are highly desirable because of their location and nearness to community facilities, along with the general atmosphere of the area, may tend to slow down the rate of building obsolescence, even for those projects, built with something less than quality materials. Yet the maintenance costs will be higher on lower-quality buildings. Because of its highly desirable location, the value of the land supporting such buildings may be increasing at so rapid a rate as to offset the advantages of a better-built building in a less desirable location. Despite such exceptions as a result of improving locations, the normal pattern nevertheless is for buildings to wear out at various rates of speed and to become obsolete for many reasons. Still the land tends to go up in value except in very poor locations.

An astute investor recognizes that when the first decade (more or less) of ownership is over and the area around the project has been established as a result of more buildings being placed on the land, it may be a propitious time to sell because the maturing process is about to begin. *Do not invest near the end of the absorption stage at beginning absorption prices.* The project will have a proven history—but you are investing in the future hence should assess the future.

During the maturing process, certainly some of the major components of the building have worn out and major replacements are necessary. It is reasonable to assume that refrigerators; dishwashers; disposals; and cooking ranges, electric or gas, would all have to be replaced some time during this 10-to-20-year period, probably at some time between the fourteenth and twentieth year of the maturing process.

Also during this period the air-conditioning and heating systems (practitioners call air-conditioning and heating systems the mechanical systems) may be in need of major replacement. At least the air-conditioning compressors; water towers; the boiler used for heating hot water; and other items of considerable expense, such as the elevator motors (if not the cabs themselves) may need replacement. The filtration systems of the pool may need replacement. Hence near the end of the maturing process, say in the twentieth year after the buildings first full year of occupancy, you will have to make some decisions that you certainly would not have had to be concerned with had you entered the pyramid prior to, or at the beginning of, the M stage and had subsequently sold before the end of the M stage. It is inevitable that the amount of income that goes to expenses will have increased, and unless inflation and location have moved up rents substantially, the cash flow will decline.

One of the frequent benefits cited to prospective investors in purchasing a building during the maturing process is that depreciation quite frequently exceeds the amortization by a large enough margin so that most of the cash flow is not subject to federal income tax. This is as it should be. The investors must reserve a substantial portion of the cash flow for the items that he will have to replace eventually. They should consider the possibility that the proceeds of sale will be less than the amount of cash they invested.

Investing during the maturing stage is suitable for investors who require a high cash flow.

THE AGING PROCESS

The aging process has arrived when expenses are up and expectations are down. Investing at this stage requires the determination of what kind of replacements to make with what kind of materials and how to finance old properties. This kind of specialized knowledge is normally acquired only by the full-time practitioner because the risk is too great for the prudent amateur to learn by experience. The inexperienced investor will not have the knowledge of financial markets and will not have the knowhow to remodel and replace. There are specialists who renovate, remodel, and repair older buildings in areas where the land values have not only held up but also have increased so rapidly that the location can command good tenants if the building were restored. The professional remodelers restore older buildings that, if kept in the hands of less sophisticated investors, would soon become prime targets for the demolition experts.

In some areas the aging process may appear to come on rather slowly. The neighborhood may be highly desirable and replacements are being postponed because of an exceptionally high level of maintenance. On the average, when the aging process does set in, for example somewhere near the beginning of the third decade, it comes on with a rush. When the aging process is upon the property and the property is owned by a full-time practioner, there are three possible plans: remodel, renovate, or rehabilitate it. It will only prove to be a profitable and solid venture if the location is such that for all practical purposes when the remodeling, renovation, and rehabilitation process is completed the building will be at the top of a pyramid once again.

The decision to rehabilitate involves much of the same kind of analysis as the decision to build. The problems, in many respects, are even more difficult and so the risks can be high. Viewpoints about the rewards vary. Some time ago at an investment property seminar a major developer of new structures sat on the dais together with the largest principal in the area specializing in "the three R's" (remodeling, renovation, rehabilitation). The developer of the new projects had an estimated net worth of $200 million, while the practioner engaged in the three R's had a net worth of about $2 million. A question was addressed to the three-R man by one of the audience of Realtors: "Which produces the best economic result, what you do for a living or what the new building developer does for a living?" The gentleman who specialized in the three R's turned the question around to the Realtor and asked:"Whose net worth would you rather have?" The audience reaction reflected their opinion that there are greater economic benefits in coming into real estate on the upside of the pyramid than in coming in on the downside of the pyramid. Since then however it has become much more difficult to build new apartments profitably and there have been many more profitable opportunities in rehabilitation, including conversions to condominiums.

The professionals who make money in the aging process fall into two basic categories: those engaged in the three R's or those who are sometimes accused of being slumlords. If you want to go into remodeling, renovation, and rehabilitation, it is a business and not a real estate investment—although it is one way of acquiring real estate investments at costs lower than usual. Owning properties that are in the aging stage, even with a proper maintenance program, is a difficult proposition. In the earlier stages of the maintenance program it is necessary to protect properly the investment and earn the cash flow. In the aging stage it is difficult to strike the delicate balance between proper maintenance on investment criteria and proper service on social criteria. Part of the difficulty is that the tenants have low income and are thereby severely limited in their ability to pay. Part of the difficulty is that many investors take a shortsighted view and use all the shortcuts available because the risk of continued operation is high. As is well known, conflicts between landlord and tenant then develop, and these do not help the maintenance of the property.

Owning and managing older properties is a specialty. The novice investor would be well advised to appraise such investments with exceptional care. The experienced investor may find some good opportunities in upgraded older properties.

THE DEMISE

All things come to an end. So it is with the pyramid and the structure. The pyramid is completed when the structure can no longer produce sufficient income to warrant continuation of operations. The buildings are frequently in ramshackle condition with broken windows and have all the trappings of slum property. Yet many professionals who have come in just prior to the demise of the property and have bought during the aging process did so knowing the end was in sight, Many have been well rewarded for the level of risk by studying the possibilities of urban renewal. Land and ramshackle buildings have been taken over by metropolitan authorities, and many such areas throughout our major cities are in the process of being redeveloped by local authorities, or by private industry with local-authority approval, along with federal aid. Investing at this stage is virtually the same as investing at the G stage of GLITAMAD. You are buying land that is to be reused. Such investments may be made by land speculators who are waiting for a change in zoning.

Another approach is to assemble small parcels of land which, when combined, will permit a more economic use of the property. Such assembly may take 5 or even 10 years, and investors carry this land while trying to assemble a more usable plot. A big difference between buying this land for its reuse possibilities and buying land not previously in use is that the land for reuse may have buildings on it that generate some cash flow. The cash flow might be miniscule or even negative, but the interim use of the structure reduces the costs of holding the land.

Investors may depreciate the structure while holding the land. Under certain circumstances they may even write down their cost basis when demolishing the building to clear the land to make way for the new use. There can be attractive tax shelters in such investments, but note that the risks are high and the problems more difficult than anywhere else on the downside of the pyramid.

SUMMARY AND CONCLUSIONS

It is impossible to answer the question, "Where is it best to enter the investment cycle of the pyramid so as to make the most amount of money with the least amount of risk?" There is a tradeoff between risk and reward, and so it is impossible to get the most profit with the least risk. However, it is possible to get the most profit within some set limits of risk. The investor may determine his or her strategy by first setting the limit of risk. Those who want the least risk will buy only after the first tenant (or tenancy) is committed, preferably on long-term leases. Selection of in-between areas is based on the amount of risk with which you can be comfortable, both in terms of chance of loss and of confidence in the decision.

The benefits you seek will also influence your strategy. The most money is made in getting in on the ground floor—the land. There is no cash flow on the upside of the pyramid, but there are tax write-offs, tax shelter, and the provision for some future proceeds of sale. At the top of the pyramid the cash flow starts and is generally the most stable (least risk), tax shelter is great for first owners, and proceeds of sale will depend on location and timing. On the downside of the pyramid the cash flow should be larger. The later you get in on the downside, the shorter the remaining useful life and the greater the depreciation. Generally the longer you wait to get in, the less you can expect in proceeds of sale, unless the trend in desirability of location shifts. Near the end, the cash flow is all used up, and the proceeds of sale will be negligible, unless there is some use for the land. Another way of looking at it: the bigger risks get the bigger rewards. If you do not need high risk and rewards, but want a stable cash flow for a long time without taking a big chance on losing your capital, you need the safety and stability of investing at A (absorption) stage, If you need more income, then invest at the M (maturing) stage. The last stages of A (aging) and D (demise) are really for the pros.

The stage in the pyramid is only one determinant of risks and rewards. Financing influences tax shelter as well as cash flow and proceeds of sale. The type of property—apartments, office buildings, or shopping centers—will also influence the mix of benefits, as can the different methods of owning real estate. Pick your place for entering the pyramid based primarily on risk rather than the mix of rewards. There are ways of increasing tax shelter and other benefits by financing. These are discussed in the next two chapters.

PART THREE

FINANCING REAL ESTATE INVESTMENTS

7 THE RISKS OF USING BORROWED MONEY

Many real estate investors believe that the best way to make money is to buy real estate with little or no cash down payment. They reason that you cannot lose money that you have not put into a venture, and if you borrow large amounts of money at a fixed rate of interest and repay the debt with cheaper dollars, you have enhanced your profit. Inflation works to the advantage of those who have borrowed large amounts of money. These beliefs have much merit.

There are however some hazards. You may not be able to pay back the money you have borrowed. You can lose money even though you borrowed all of the purchase price. You are committed to the agreed interest rate even though interests rates in the market may have declined. Having to pay the higher rate of interest when the property no longer produces the necessary cash may force an unfavorable sale. If cheaper dollars are not forthcoming because the expected inflation failed to materialize, the cash flow may become negative and lead to an unfavorable sale. Even if the property is held, the investor may be paying a higher rate of interest than the real earnings of the property.

Other real estate investors do not consider it wise to use little or no cash down payment. They believe that investment success requires a substantial equity. An amazing number of large-income-producing properties are held entirely debt-free or have an extremely low debt in relation to their value. One of the largest and best known real estate investment trusts in the United States has a history of operating with total mortgage debt equal to approximately 35% of the value of its properties. Many "old" money investors own their properties free of any debt.

Which of these opposing views is for you? It depends on the risks you are prepared to take to obtain the rewards you seek. You can make a greater return on your investment if you have borrowed to the "hilt" and the property is a winner.

If the property is a loser, you can be clobbered. If the inflation fails to materialize, you will have to pay back very "dear" dollars. On top of that the failure of prices to rise may unfavorably affect your rents, so that you wind up with a negative cash flow. The mortgage terms may turn out to be oppressive because the interest rate is greater than that obtainable in the market and because the high mortgage payments have you putting more cash into the property in order to prevent foreclosure. The investor with a debt-free property does not face this problem because without debt there is no foreclosure. The property that is clear of debt, or can carry itself until it is, will generally produce enough cash flow to enable even investors who have invested in poor-quality property to get their money out eventually.

This chapter explains the risks that are inherent in buying with a low down payment. The first section points out that too low a down payment may force you to sell the property because you cannot make the payments on the mortgage. The next section then introduces the concepts of leverage (examined at greater length in chapter 8), which serves to set the stage for discussing the effects of heavy borrowing on the cash return from a down payment.

After considering the basic features of the ability to repay debt, this chapter proceeds to discuss foreclosure, which comes about when the debt is not paid. The income tax consequences of foreclosures are then examined, as is the personal liability of the borrower. The final section of the chapter tells the investor how he may protect himself from the possibility of a deficiency judgment.

FORCED TO SELL

You cannot have lost your money until your property is sold and you have less money left than you started with. One danger in using borrowed money is that you may be forced to sell the property at a time when a sale is not advantageous to you. Your inability to repay the debt may force such a sale. One positive method of protecting yourself is to be sure that the gross income is high enough to cover all operating expenses and to make payments on the debt with something left over. Since the property may generate a fluctuating gross income during the years of . ownership, the debt can be serviced (repaid with interest in installments) only if a prudent amount was borrowed when the property was acquired.

Knowing that the gross income and expenses will vary from year to year, you will want to control from the outset the amount of debt that is to be repaid each year, The cash that is left after servicing the mortgage should be planned so that it is sufficient to cover either decline in gross income or increase in expenses, unless you are willing and able to add to the initial capital to carry the property through troubled times.

If you are forced to sell because you cannot or are not willing to make the payment on the mortgage, chances are that the timing of sale is poor. Frequently the condition that caused the decline in income is the same one that will adversely affect the price you will be able to receive on a sale. A major hazard of overfinanced property is that the borrower loses control over his timing of sale.

USING LEVERAGE

Leverage is the use of borrowed money to magnify gains and losses. Naturally, buying with a low down payment means using a great deal of leverage. To use leverage you have to use borrowed money, usually by pledging the property as security for the debt.

If you borrow money at 7% and earn 8%, leverage is working for you. The more you borrow, the more you make. If you borrow an amount equal to your equity (a one-to-one ratio), then if the investment earns 8% and you pay 7% for borrowed money, you make 9%, for example:

Borrow	$100,000	Earn on	$200,000
at 7%	0.07	at 8%	0.08
	$ 7,000		$ 16,000

Effect of leverage then is:

Earnings on	$200,000	$ 16,000
Interest on	$100,000	7,000
Earnings on	$100,000 equity	$9,000

Ratio of earnings to equity $\dfrac{\$9,000}{\$100,000} = 0.09$ or   9%

If you borrow at a two-to-one ratio, you make 10%, for example:

Borrow	$200,000	Earn on	$300,000
at 7%	0.07	at 8%	0.08
	$ 14,000		$ 24,000

The effect of leverage is:

Earnings on	$300,000	$ 24,000
Interest on	$200,000	14,000
Earnings on $100,000 equity		$ 10,000

Ratio of earnings to equity $\dfrac{\$10,000}{\$100,000} = 0.10$ Or 10%

A three-to-one ratio beings you 11%—you make $8 per hundred on the amount you put up plus $1 per hundred on each of the $300,000 you borrowed.

It works in reverse too. If you borrow at 7% and earn only 6%, then at a one-to-one ratio of borrowing to equity you will earn 5%, for example:

Borrow	$100,000	Earn on	$200,000
at 7%	0.07	at 6%	0.06
	$ 7,000		$ 12,000

The effect of leverage is:

Earnings on	$200.000	$ 12,000
Interest on	$100,000	7,000
Earnings on	$100,000 equity	$ 5,000

Ratio of earnings to equity $\dfrac{\$ 5,000}{\$100,000} = 0.05$ or 5%

At the two-to-one ratio you make 4% and at the three-to-one ratio you make 3%. The investment of say $400,000 might earn 6%, or $24,000. You have to pay 7% on $300,000, or $21,000 interest. you are left with $3000 for your $100,000 equity, or 3%.

It should be obvious that buying with a low down payment, such as 10% (which is a ratio of 9 borrowed dollars to 1 equity dollar), will work wonders in leverage. If you pay 7% and earn 8%, the leverage brings you up to 17%. If you earn 6%, it brings you to a minus 3%—that is a loss of 3% per year. In a few years you could thus lose your asset. If costs of borrowed money are two, three, or more percentage points above earnings, it takes less time to lose your equity.

The situation is complicated in real estate because you really do not know how much you are earning until you have all the benefits, including proceeds of sale. You hear

THE TERMS "yield," "rate of return," "earnings," and "profit." These terms as applied to real estate are ambiguous. You cannot really know what has been made on the investment until the property is sold and all the monies are in the hands of the seller. Estimates of course can be made, but frequently the investor will simply look at the cash flow relative to the down payment.

Cash flow relative to the down payment is a reasonable measure of benefits when the proceeds of sale are equal to the down payment. That is if all you get when you sell is a return of your down payment, then the cash flow is your major benefit. Frequently the concept of leverage is applied to the cash flow as though it were earnings. Investors when speaking of leverage may mean that they are modifying their cash flow (relative to down payment) by using borrowed money.

BORROWING EFFECTS ON CASH FLOW

The cash flow, as you will recall, is computed by deducting from the gross income all cash outlays, including servicing of the debt. The relationship of the cash flow to the down payment is a ratio, or a percentage. We call this ratio the *cash on the down payment,* which can be abbreviated to COD. The COD is the ratio between the annual cash flow and the down payment, expressed as a percentage.

The COD differs from yield or earnings because during the ownership of property many things are going on for which an accurate accounting cannot be made. Although it is easy to calculate the amount of debt that is being repaid, the actual depreciation of the building is going on at a rate that is not accurately determinable. The land may be appreciating in value. But at what rate? You could make estimates on all of these items, but you will not know what you have made until your property is sold and all the monies from the sale are in your hands.

The COD is usually stated as a positive figure. A $10,000 cash down payment on an investment that produces an annual cash flow of $1000 is a 10% COD. If the property produces a negative cash flow, that is you paid out more in cash than you took in, the COD would be a negative percentage.

You no doubt recall that one of the benefits of owning income-producing property is the cash flow. The relative importance of the cash flow compared to the other benefits, tax shelter and proceeds of sale, is highly dependent on how the property is financed and on all the other factors that affect the income- producing ability of the property as well as your own tax picture. Almost any property can be transformed into a winner, on paper, by using gimmickry on the financing. Therefore astute investors use the COD only as one indication of how well they are doing.

Just as the cash flow and its relationship to your down payment is an indication of how you are doing, so is the tax flow (taxable income or loss). The cash flow is the bottom line of an operating statement; the tax flow is the bottom line of the same operating statement for federal income tax purposes. Sophisticated real estate investors appreciate being able to see on the same page the annual results of their investments. Their accountants therefore may be asked to prepare operating statements showing the cash flow and the tax flow side-by-side. (See Table 6.)

Operating statements on which the bottom line is the cash flow do not show an allowance for depreciation. The tax-flow operating statement does however show the depreciation allowance.

The cash-flow operating statements reflect the total mortgage payments including amortization. The tax-flow statements do not show a deduction for amortization. The difference between the two is apparent when the formula for taxable income is recalled: cash flow + amortization minus depreciation = taxable income.

Just as the cash flow and the COD are highly depen-

Table 6   Cash Flow and Tax Flow

		Cash Flow	Tax Flow
Rental Income		$10,000	$10,000
Expense of operation			
Property taxes	$1,300		
Insurance	200		
Utilities	1,200		
Maintenance	1,200		
Other Expenses	700		
		4,600	4,600
Income before deprecia-tion and amortization		5,400	5,400
Depreciation			3,400
Mortgage payments		3,600	
Interest	3,000		3,000
Amortization	600		
Cash flow		$ 1,800	
Taxable income			($1,000)

Cash flow + amortization minus depreciation = taxable income
$1800 + $600 minus $3400 = ($1000) or a tax loss of $1000.

dent on the financing, so is the tax flow. The tax-flow statement concludes by showing the amount of taxable income or loss. The taxable income decreases when mortgage borrowing increases because of the larger deduction for interest. Investors need to see both the cash flow and the tax flow to obtain an indication of the benefits they are receiving while they own the property. On the basis of these two statements, investors can easily compute the tax shelter. All of the items in the formula (CF + A − D = TI) appear in the combined statements of cash flow and tax flow.

Within certain limits the COD can be increased by borrowing more money. The lower the down payment, the more attractive the COD appears. One cannot argue against the mathematics involved. Generally the less the down payment, the higher the COD. Imagine an annual cash flow of $1000 on property purchased with absolutely no cash down. It has happened. The COD is not calculable. It is infinite. The splendor of such a magnificent COD could cause an investor to lose sight of the fact that it is merely a ratio, a percentage. Will there always be enough gross income to repay the debt? If your down payment is under 20% of the purchase price, the COD is very sensitive to minor changes in cash flow. Since the COD is computed by using the cash flow as the numerator and the down payment as the denominator, it is generally not a significant factor if the down payment is relatively small in relation to the cost of the property. (See Table 7.)

OVERFINANCED PROPERTY

A property is considered overfinanced if it does not produce enough income to cover the payments on the mortgage and still have a positive cash flow. A property may also be overfinanced if the total debt against the real estate exceeds the value of the real estate. If the property is overfinanced on both criteria, there are very serious problems.

Most real estate mortgage money is loaned by four kinds of financial institutions—savings and loan associations, savings banks, commercial banks, and life insurance companies. These institutions are regulated by state or federal authorities and in some cases both. The regulatory authorities regulate the lenders to deter them from lending too much on the property.

Lending more than the value of the property is obviously "too much." Since the value can only be estimated and since it changes in time, the lenders by regulation and policy limit their loans to some percentage of their

Table 7   Cash Flow with a Low Down Payment

Assume: Price of $60,000
          Down payment of $20,000
          Loan of $40,000
          Interest 7.5%

Annual constant 9%, so annual mortgage payment is $3,600

Cash Flow

Income	$10,000
Expenses of operation	4,600
Income before depreciation and amortization	5,400
Less mortgage payment	3,600
Cash flow	$ 1,800

Cash on the down payment $\dfrac{\$1,800}{\$20,000} = 9\%$
    If gross income drops 10% or $1,000
    then cash flow becomes $800

Cash on the down payment would be $\dfrac{\$800}{\$20,000} = 4\%$

Assume purchase with 15% or $9,000 down and balance in two mortgages
    1st, $40,000
    2nd $11,000, payable $900 a year at 8% interest
New cash flow $900

New cash on down payment $\dfrac{\$900}{\$9,000} = 10\%$

But the 10 % is very sensitive to changes in income and expense. For example a 10% decline in gross income would wipe out the cash flow. The COD would be negative.

116

estimate of the property value. This can be as little as 50% for property that has a very limited market or as much as 80% for real estate enjoying a strong market. It can be more in certain cases when the repayment of the loan is guaranteed by something other than the security of the real estate. Most of the time loan-to-value ratios of two-thirds (66 $^2/_3$% of the value) or three-quarters (75% of the value) can be expected.

When you own or are acquiring property, you may use the property as security for the debt. That means that you promise to repay the debt and add to your promise the pledge of the property. If you fail to pay, the lender may use your property to get his money. This is done by foreclosing on the property. Foreclosure is discussed later in the chapter.

When the property is very valuable and you have only a modest mortgage on it, you may borrow additional money and pledge the property to secure the debt. Naturally lenders who first loaned you the money have first claim in the event of foreclosure. They have a "first mortgage." Second lenders have a "second mortgage," and so on. The number refers to the priority of claim among the mortgage lenders.

The institutional lenders will lend only if they get a first mortgage or a first trust deed. The difference between the mortgage and the trust deed is mostly in the foreclosure process. As already mentioned, the institutional lenders may lend two-thirds or even three-fourths of the purchase price, There are some private lenders who lend on the security of a second mortgage or trust, but at high interest rates. Sometimes the seller of a property will "take back" a second or even third mortgage to facilitate the sale. Taking back a mortgage means that the seller holds the mortgage personally. The seller may hold a first mortgage if, for example, you buy a $100,000 property for $15,000 down and the seller takes back a mortgage for $85,000. Or the seller may take back a second mortgage if there is a first on the property. For example you buy a property for $100,000 with an existing $60,000 loan and put $15,000 down. The seller would take back or carry a $25,000 second mortgage.

If the amount of the loan is high relative to the value of the property and the terms are good, the price might be more than the value of the real estate to reflect the value of the financing. Sometimes the price paid is so high that the loans against the property add up to more than the value of the property. If the property cannot generate the income necessary to make the payments, the property is overfinanced and the risk of a forced sale is very high.

DEBT MUST BE REPAID

A high COD is a reward for using borrowed money. The risk is that the cash flow may become low or even negative.The property just may not generate enough gross income to cover the expenses and repay the debt.

When money is borrowed, someone promises to repay it. Pledging the property to secure the debt does not by itself relieve the borrower of the obligation to repay. The real estate investor who uses large amounts of borrowed money may face foreclosure as a result of unwillingness or inability to repay borrowed money.

In real estate circles many people do not like to talk about the thought of foreclosure. Nevertheless it is important.

Precisely what happens under foreclosure varies from state to state, but the largest single misunderstanding is that "the lender takes over the property." Many people are under the impression that if a mortgage or deed of trust note is in default, that is the payments have not been met on schedule, the lender forecloses and thus takes over the property. To clear up this misunderstanding it is important to realize that most states require an auction process (with the property to be publicly advertised). Under a deed of trust the auction is conducted by trustees who have been named by the lender. After a period of public advertising, in which the date and place of the auction of the property are specified, the auction sale of the property begins.

The lender's representatives frequently bid the principal amount of the debt remaining on the property plus costs. If no one bids a higher amount for the property, the property has been deemed to be purchased by the lender.

The foreclosure procedure may vary depending on whether the mortgagee (the lender) is secured (protected) under deed of trust or has a mortgage, but on the whole the procedure is similar. One exception is that under a mortgage the mortgagee's representatives must have the permission of the court in the jurisdiction in which the property is located in order to proceed with the auction. It is rare that a strict foreclosure takes place, that is a foreclosure without a sale. The form and method vary by state laws, but in most cases a mortgage foreclosure is actually an auction sale of the property ordered by a court.

LIABILITY OF THE BORROWER

The note that the borrower signs, whether secured by a mortgage or a deed of trust, usually stipulates that the borrower is *personally* responsible for repayment of the debt. Thus the borrower is liable for any deficiency if an auction sale under foreclosure proceedings does not bring enough proceeds to pay the debt in full. In considering the amount of the bid, many lenders will sometimes bid less than the amount owed to them if they feel the property has depreciated severely and in fact is not worth the unpaid balance of their loan. They may do this because the person who signed the original loan is personally responsible and they feel that there is a better chance of getting the rest of their money by going after that person, than only the property. Another reason for bidding a price lower than the debt is the possibility that a real estate speculator will bid more than they are bidding. Having admitted to a loss, they may be delighted to have whatever cash they can get, rather than the ownership of the property that does not produce enough to pay the mortgage. Most lenders have no serious interest in owning properties obtained through auctions caused by the borrower's inability to pay the loans they have made. But if the lender does not bid the amount still owed, someone else may purchase the property at the foreclosure sale for less than the amount of the debt, leaving the borrower still liable to the lender.

Many lenders prefer not to bid below their loan balance. Institutional lenders do not want to admit a loser to the regulatory authority that watches over their investments. The life insurance companies are under scrutiny of the state insurance commissioners, who frown on any policies or procedures that would get a lender any large amount of foreclosed properties. Should the lender be a federal savings and loan association, its policies and procedures are under the scrutiny of the Federal Home Loan Bank Board and it too does not want to be subjected to criticism. State-chartered institutions may have their deposits insured by a federal agency and thereby become subject to federal as well as state regulating authorities.

If neither the lender nor anybody else is willing to bid the remaining balance on a mortgage plus the advertising and other costs incident to foreclosure, a deficiency exists. The deficiency is the difference between the balance due plus accrued interest and costs and the amount paid to the lender out of the foreclosure sale. In the event the lender uses a judicial process, a judgment may be obtained against the initial borrower. Such a judgment is known as a "deficiency judgment." It means that a lender can attach the borrower's other assets, not being necessarily confined to real estate, in order to be repaid the difference between the debt and the amount received by the lender at the public auction.

One consequence of borrowing money in large

amounts for real estate investments is that the investor may be exposed himself to the risk of a deficiency judgment if the property does not bring in enough and should it be auctioned under a foreclosure sale.

INCOME TAX LIABILITY

The auctioning of property under foreclosure establishes a sales price for internal revenue purposes. You will recall that the formula for determining profit for federal income tax purposes is sales price minus book value = taxable income. It is therefore possible to have a substantial profit for federal income tax purposes by defaulting under the deed of trust or mortgage, and thus have a sale at a price that is substantially higher than the book value. This is why many tax-conscious investors cannot walk away from a property, so to speak. They will have a tremendous tax liability, especially if they were using one of the more accelerated forms of depreciation. Table 8 shows how the tax liability could develop out of a foreclosure.

There has been an emphasis on being sure that the depreciation exceeds the amortization so that some, all, or more than all of the cash flow is not subject to federal income taxes. Thus foreclosures by auction on income-producing property can frequently result in a heavy tax burden for the defaulting investor. Investors who deal in large amounts of borrowed money must consider that there may come a time when the property is producing a negative cash flow and they may be unable, or unwilling, to continue adding fresh capital to the project. If they have held the property for several years and used the accelerated form of depreciation, they may have to continue, despite their unwillingness to feed the property, because of the large spread between the sales price and book value. An auction sale under these conditions, with a "bid" at a price considerably higher than book value, is

Table 8   Calculation of Income Tax Liability

Assume previous purchase price of $100,000	
Down payment	$ 15,000
Assumption of existing mortgages	85,000
	$100,000
Assume original tax basis	
Land $10,000	
Building $90,000	
After elapse of time	
Depreciation reduces building cost basis to	$ 60,000
Land basis remains	10,000
Cost basis for income tax purpose	$ 70,000

Loans reduced from $85,000 to $75,000
If foreclosure occurs and the sale satisfies expenses and mortgage debt remaining, a sale price of $75,000 gives a taxable gain of $5000 to the investor, even though he receives no cash. Part or all of this amount might be taxable as ordinary income under the recapture rules discussed in chapter 3.

really a sale. Even if no money flows to the owners they may have to pay a substantial tax and have no money for doing so.

Paying incomes taxes after a foreclosure in addition to paying on a deficiency judgment are the two ways in which an investor can lose money aside from putting up a down payment or adding cash to cover a negative cash flow.

AVOIDING DEFICIENCY JUDGMENTS

Investors may protect themselves from the potential liability of a deficiency judgment by arranging that the mortgage or deed of trust have a clause that specifically relieves them from being personally responsible for the payment of the debt. This type of clause is generally known as a "sole security clause." It is rarely used for loans on owner-occupied residences, small apartment buildings, or other small-income properties, but it is often employed on loans for large-income producing properties. This is true for many reasons, the most important being that many large real estate investors have a vast portion of their wealth in the form of real estate investments and the total mortgage debt may be large relative to real estate equity and non-real estate assets. Thus the personal liability may be relatively little protection to a mortgage lender, but a great hazard to a borrower.

Real estate investors would do well to protect themselves against personal liability by using either the sole security clause or, if this is not available, by taking title to the property in the name of a corporate entity organized exclusively for the purpose of taking title and financing the property. The corporation may retain title to the property, or after all the necessary documents have been signed, the property may be immediately transferred back to them individually; thus the corporation that initially signed the loan is held responsible and not the individuals. However a lender who has a firm policy of requiring personal guarantees from large real estate investors would ask that the corporation's duly appointed officer not only sign the deed of trust note in the name of the corporation but also have it *personally* endorsed by the individuals. The advent of transfer taxes at the local level has complicated the technique of corporate borrowing and transfer because of the fairly substantial costs of transferring property out from under a corporation into the names of the individuals.

It is possible to have the real estate owned by the corporation, with the corporation earning the investment income. There is a complicating factor, relating to federal income taxes, in the corporate ownership of real estate. Investors using this method for holding property may find that they are paying federal income taxes twice, once for the corporation and once on personal income.

To avoid the liability of a deficiency judgment and for other reasons, some real estate investors are prepared to pay taxes twice (once when the corporation earns the income and the second time when the investor receives it). The cost of the taxes is reduced when the amount of tax-sheltered income is high. A real estate investment corporation with a portfolio of properties may be liable on the individual loans as a corporation, with the owners of the stock not being personally liable. Thus, certain circumstances the corporation may be used to protect the individual against personal liability. But it is not the best device if protection from liability is the only purpose.

Investing in real estate as a limited partner is another way of avoiding liability for deficiency judgment. Investing through a limited partnership has a number of advantages and disadvantages, as pointed out in the last section of this book. Since protection from liability is only one consideration, it should not necessarily be the determining reason.

Some borrowers have attempted to avoid the responsibility of personal repayment by transferring their assets to their spouses. One hazard is that some court may disregard the scheme and proceed against the spouse, especially if it is determined that this was done specifically to avoid repayment or liability under the note and the person who transferred the asset remained the real owner. Also someday the investor may not be able to locate his rich spouse, who having discovered that all the worthwhile assets are in her name, might decide that the spouse no longer seems attractive.

There are other methods of protection against liability of a deficiency judgment. One frequently used method is to find a property already mortgaged by the seller and buy it, taking title "subject to the mortgage." This means that in the purchase of the property you are actually buying the equity of the seller, and although you know about the mortgage and understand it, you personally are not obliged to pay it. You do not assume the mortgage nor do you agree to pay it. Of course if you do not pay, the lender can foreclose through the auction procedure, but *you* would not be liable for a deficiency judgment.

Persons unaware of the option of taking title subject to the mortgage sometimes assume the mortgage. The phrase used is "assumes and agrees to pay." This means that the investor assumes personal liability. The seller is not released from the liability and can be held responsible by the lender, along with you the purchaser, in the event of a deficiency. In some states when the seller personally takes back the mortgage and serves as the lender, the law is that in the absence of a promise to pay, the mortgagor (the borrower) would not be liable for a deficiency judgment. Thus the two main methods of avoiding personal liability for real estate debt are: either buy property that is financed and take title "subject to " the existing financing, or be sure that there is a sole security clause in the mortgage or trust deed.

Of course the best way to invest in real estate is to avoid personal liability for the mortgage, but it is even more important that the amount borrowed and the terms of repayment be such that the risk of foreclosure and of a deficiency judgment against you are minimal or nonexistent. It sometimes happens that the error in judgment was so bad that all one wants to do is get out from under the mortgage. Like the mouse caught in the trap, one does not want the cheese any more—one just wants out. As previously noted, getting in is easy—it is getting out that is sometimes difficult.

SUMMARY AND RECOMMENDATIONS

When you buy with a low down payment, you increase the risk of being forced to sell the property because of a negative cash flow. In deciding how much to borrow, you should balance the risk of a forced sale with the potential increase in profit by the use of borrowed money.

Your strategy on borrowed money should be tailored to your needs. If you are confident that the property will earn more than the cost of borrowed money, and have evidence to justify that confidence, then it makes sense to borrow as much as you can be sure you will be able to repay. It is unusual for an investor to buy without the use of any borrowed money. Most investors who desire a conservative approach will borrow using one mortgage that is repaid in monthly installments until the loan is fully repaid. Those investors who wish to magnify gains, and are presumably prepared to magnify losses, use two and three mortgages. It is thus possible that a fully rented property will generate a negative cash flow.

Buying property with loans for 75 or 70% of the value provides substantial leverage. Repayment of such borrowing ordinarily would not take an inordinate proportion of the rental income. The result is that a positive cash flow remains. Thus you can expect that the property will "carry itself" (provide a positive cash flow), even if vacancies are unusually large or rents are substantially reduced. Many investors like properties that will carry themselves in the face of a 10 to 15% decline in gross income.

If you get an 80 or 85% loan-to-value ratio, chances are that cash flow will be very sensitive to changes in income and expenses. At 90 or 95% financing, it is unusual to expect and get much, if any, cash flow.

The catalyst to a forced sale or foreclosure frequently is a negative cash flow. The owner may put the property up for sale in order to avoid foreclosure, but the timing is likely to be poor. The same conditions that weaken the cash flow weaken the market for the property.

The results of a foreclosure sale go beyond the sale of the property to satisfy the debt. If the property does not bring enough money to satisfy the debt, the borrower may still owe the money and pay the debt out of other assets.

Borrowers may also find themselves with an income tax liability, even though they do not receive any proceeds of sale.

While the 75 and 70% borrowing will ordinarily provide a substantial cushion in the cash flow, some high-risk properties are financed with loans of only 60 or 65% of value. Some conservative investors will use these low loan-to-value ratios to get the very lowest of interest rates. Buying well-selected properties with such low amount of leverage magnifies gains with very little risk of having debt service so burdensome as to force a sale.

When borrowing, you may protect yourself from the liability of a deficiency judgment by use of a sole security clause in the mortgage. There are other methods that may be used, but they are less desirable. When buying and taking over an existing loan you may protect yourself from the potential liability of a deficiency judgment by taking title "subject to" the existing mortgage rather than by "assuming" the mortgage.

It is wise to use borrowed money to invest in real estate, but you should not borrow too much, pay too much for it, or have to repay it too quickly. Then, even when you fully expect to repay according to the terms, it is prudent to protect yourself from the liability for a deficiency judgment whenever feasible.

This chapter has explained the risks of using borrowed money, while pointing out some of the rewards. The next chapter examines the rewards of using borrowed money.

8 THE REWARDS OF USING BORROWED MONEY

You may have just concluded that using borrowed money can increase your rewards, although it increases your risks. Yet many of the risks can be controlled. For one thing you will want to use protective techniques in your borrowing to eliminate personal liability wherever possible. You will also want to borrow on terms of repayment that will keep the risk within the bounds you can accept. Understanding how you may use borrowed money to obtain the rewards you seek, without taking undue risk, will help you decide how much to borrow and the kind of loan terms you will seek.

This chapter explains how to use borrowed money profitably. As you may recall the profitability of the investment will not be known until after the sale. Thus many investors will look to the cash flow and the COD (cash on the down payment) as indicators of the profitability. Under such circumstances it is important to understand the relationship between the income-producing ability of the property and the repayment of money borrowed to buy the property. This chapter begins by considering how the use of borrowed money may appear to magnify the benefits.

Since the benefits of the original financing may diminish as the original loan is repaid, it may be desirable to refinance the property to obtain more benefits from the use of borrowed money. The second section of this chapter identifies the several benefits obtainable from refinancing.

Most of the discussion about leverage (use of borrowed money to magnify gains and losses) assumes that the investor will make more on the money borrowed than the cost of borrowing. There are times however when the mortgage lender really earns more than the borrower. This chapter points out how leverage working against the real estate investor can be disastrous.

The chapter goes on to explain that the cost of money is more than the interest cost. Not only are there extra charges that increase the costs of borrowed money, but there are provisions in loan agreements that may make it expensive or impossible to pay the entire balance of a mortgage loan in one payment.

FINANCING CAN INCREASE REWARDS

Unlike loans on personal property (automobile, furniture, and the like), loans against income-producing real estate are long-term, mostly from 20 to 30 years. The loans are normally repayable out of the cash generated by renting the property. Usually the principal is repaid in small monthly amounts, together with interest computed on the unpaid balance. As you may recall from an earlier chapter, the total *annual* payment, which includes the principal and interest divided by the *original* amount of the loan, is called the *annual constant.*

Annual Constant

The annual constant as the ratio of annual payment to the original mortgage amount is expressed as a percentage. For example an annual payment of $9000 ($750 monthly) on a mortgage of $100,000 means that the annual constant is 9%. The interest rate could be 6 or 7%, but the annual constant is 9%. The annual constant of 9% is equal to a monthly payment of $7.50 for each $1000 borrowed.

Here are some truisms about the terms of repayment:

1. With a given annual constant: the lower the interest rate, the higher the amortization, and the shorter the term of the loan. For example with an annual constant of 8.5% and a 6% rate of interest on the loan, the loan would amortize in 20 years 9 months. With the same annual constant of 8.5%, a reduction in the interest rate to 5% would increase the amortization, and the loan would be paid off in 18 years (instead of 20 years 9 months).

2. With a given rate of interest: the lower the annual constant, the lower the amortization, and the longer the term of the loan. For example with an annual constant of 8.5% and a 6% rate of interest, the loan will amortize in 20 years 9 months. With an annual constant of 8% and with an interest rate of 6% it would take 23 years 6 months to amortize the loan (instead of 20 years 9 months).

3. It is possible to increase the interest rate slightly and lengthen the term of the loan substantially, with the result of a lower annual constant. For example a 5.5% loan with a 9.5% constant amortizes in 16 years. One could with a 5.75% loan amortized over 18 years reduce the constant to 9%. If the loan were amortized in 20 years, the constant would be down to 8.5% (instead of 9%).

You may be willing to pay higher interest if you get lower amortization with the result of a lower annual constant. This is so because one of the benefits you seek is a higher cash flow. Those investors who are interested in a higher cash flow, even at a higher cost of borrowing, reason that they can do better by getting the cash in hand.

What has happened to the old-fashioned philosophy of remaining debt-free? It still makes sense if you cannot make more on the borrowed money than it cost or if the risk is too great. Debt-free investment was popular at the beginning of the depression in the early 1930s, when most debt proved to be burdensome. It is an inapplicable financial strategy under conditions of relatively low interest rates and an increasing rate of inflation.

Balloon Payments

Some lenders will not allow their loans to extend beyond the fixed limits by their own lending policies. To remain competitive with those of other lending institutions, their interest rates must be comparable and so must their annual constants. To bring the loan into their length of term policy, they will frequently call for loans to be all due and payable prior to the time when they would ordinarily expire if allowed to run until paid through constant amortization.

It is possible to borrow money from a lender such as a bank that ordinarily would not make a loan in excess of 10 years for example. Commercial banks, when they have unusual or excessive monies to loan sometimes make loans that are competitive with those of insurance companies, mutual savings banks, and other long term lenders, but with a "balloon" on the principal balance, frequently at the end of 10 years.

It is important to recognize that, when arranging financing, it might not be possible to arrange for the refinancing of your loan in order to pay off a large principal balance as a result of a ballooned mortgage loan. Unless the balloon represents a relatively small amount of the principal amount you are borrowing at the outset, it is not wise to enter into a loan agreement making the loan all due prior to maturity through normal amortization. It is our opinion that an "all due and payable" clause in a loan prior to the amotization of at least 60% of the original amount of the loan is risky. Life insurance companies and mutual savings banks sometimes write payments on a loan to amortize over 20 or 25 years, but with a balloon at the end of 15 or 20 years. Such a provision might be used if a major tenant in a shopping center has a long-term lease, but the lender does not want the term of the loan to last longer than the lease, although they will accept a lower annual constant than that necessary to amortize fully the loan over the life of the lease.

Frequently the seller of a property will carry back a second mortgage (a trust deed) for part of the original price. The annual constant is generally 12% (1% per month of the original unpaid balance). Most of the time there is a balloon payment at the end of five to seven years, sometimes longer, sometimes shorter.

Debt-free Comparisons

It is wise when contemplating the acquisition of income producing property to look at the property as if you were not going to use any financing whatsoever. This will give you a clear idea of what the property would produce in terms of cash flow for an all-cash purchase. For simplicity assume that you could buy a property for $100,000 on an all-cash basis. If the property will produce $10,000 per annum cash flow, the ratio of cash flow to down payment is 10%. As you remember we call this ratio COD (cash on the down payment). We use it also when the property is mortgage-free. In such an instance of all cash, the use of the cash flow as the numerator (that is $10,000) and the down payment as the denominator (that is $100,000) results in a COD of 10%.

Once this percentage has been established, it is possible to make an objective analysis of the benefits of borrowing money. First you should find out what the competitive interest rate is for this type of property at the time you expect to buy. Let us suppose that the current interest rate is 7%. Assume that you can borrow through normal channels about 75% of the value of the property. In other words you can borrow $75,000 on a $100,000 property with an interest rate of 7%. The lender insists on an annual constant of 9%. Is it worthwhile for you to finance the property or should you pay all cash?

Assume that the property will, when debt-free, produce a cash flow of $10,000 per annum. If you borrow
$75,000 with repayment based on a 9% annual constant,
you will be paying $6750 per year, which would include
interest and principle on your loan until the loan was fully
amortized. Your cash flow would no longer be $10,000,
but would be $3250 ($10,000 less $6750).

The borrowing of $75,000 has changed the COD from
10% to 13%, because only $25,000 was paid in as cash
down payment and $75,000 was borrowed, with the
result that the $3250 cash flow was generated with
$25,000 down ($3250 divided by $25,000 is 13%). The
calculations are as follows:

	Before	After
Income before mortgage	$ 10,000	$ 10,000
Less mortgage payments	0	6,750
Cash flow	$ 10,000	$ 3,250

$75,000 loan at 9% annual constant = $6,750 payment per year

	Before	After
Purchase price	$100,000	$100,000
Less Loan	0	75,000
Down payment	$100,000	$ 25,000

Determination of the COD ratio:

$$\text{Cash flow to down payment}\quad \frac{\$10,000}{\$100,000} = 10\% \quad \frac{\$3,250}{\$25,000} = 13\%$$

Although many real estate investors analyze a property as if it were owned free and clear, they do so only to
determine the extent to which they can improve the COD
by using available financing techniques. In the example,
if an annual constant of 10% were the lowest that could
be obtained in the loan market, the investor would be
receiving the same cash on the down payment because
the annual constant and his COD before he borrowed are
the same. Some investors would still borrow, reasoning

that they could deduct the interest for federal income tax purposes and that by borrowing they could invest in more property. Under some conditions it will make sense to borrow money with an annual constant equal to the amount of the COD, but most investors try to obtain an annual constant that is lower than the COD, so that the loan can increase the COD. A difference of even 1% between the annual constant and the COD on a free-and-clear property can make a significant difference in the resultant COD. A difference of 2% is quite substantial; a difference of 3 or 4 points dramatically increases the COD.

It is axiomatic that the greater the loan, the greater the cash that will be required to service the loan, so that the results will be of course a lower cash flow. It is important to emphasize the point continually however because many investors have gotten into deep financial trouble by seeking to obtain maximum loans only to find that a slight change in the cash flow of the property has caused them serious financial difficulties.

COD and Constant

The relationship between the COD and the annual constant determines the effect of financing on cash flow. If you compute the COD as though the property was free of mortgage debt and compare that with the annual constant, you can see how the financing will affect the cash flow. For example if a property produces 9% cash on the down payment without any mortgage, then any borrowing with an annual constant lower than 9% will increase the COD. The converse is also true. That is, if the COD without a mortgage is lower than the annual constant, then borrowing will reduce the COD.

Comparison of COD and constants can help in selecting a loan. Generally speaking you will prefer as high a loan as a first-mortgage lending instituion will provide, so long as the annual constant is no higher than the COD.

Property cost at $200,000
9% COD   0.09
Cash flow $ 18,000

Use a $100,000 loan with an 8% constant
   Cash flow without mortgage $18,000
   Less mortgage payments
     8% of $100,000   8,000
New cash flow $10,000

$$\text{New COD } \frac{\$10,000}{\$100,000} = 10\%$$

Furthermore the more you borrow the greater the effect.

Cash flow before
   any mortgage $18,000
Borrow $150,000
   at 8% constant   12,000
Cash flow after
$150,000 mortgage $ 6,000

$$\text{Ratio of cash flow to down payment } \frac{\$6000}{\$50,000} = 12\% \text{ COD}$$

($200,000 minus $150,000)

There are however times when, because of high real
estate prices (meaning low COD's) and high interest
rates, you may be willing to borrow with an annual constant slightly above the COD. You may even pay a higher
interest rate to get more leverage if you believe that the
property will make enough to pay for the risk that you
take in reducing your cash flow. The profitable use of
such leverage is of course predicted on the proceeds of
sale.

FINANCING AFFECTS TAXATION

Aside from the problem of variation in rental income and expenses, causing negative cash flow on overly financed property, there is the problem of income taxes.

The amortization of the loan is typically increasing every year of the loan, while the interest payment on the loan is decreasing. The result is that the excess of depreciation over amortization narrows because amortization is increasing. At the same time depreciation is decreasing if accelerated methods are used, which was frequently the case before the change in IRS recapture rules. In conservatively financed property this presents no problem for quite a while, because even when depreciation no longer exceeds amortization, there is a cash flow out of which to pay income taxes. Very heavily financed properties have little or no cash flow, so that when tax shelter runs out, the investor has taxable income from the property without cash from the property sufficient to pay the taxes. This exerts a pressure on the investor to sell the property. As you may recall, it is important for the investor to choose the time of sale.

You may have heard stories about people who have borrowed 100% of the cost of their property (called "mortgaging out") and sometimes have even obtained "windfalls" in the financing of income-producing properties. Mortgaging out and the obtaining of so-called windfalls was considered the intelligent and sophisticated thing to do in the old "608" FHA heydays, which lasted from approximately 1946 to 1952. The government, through the FHA, decided to insure mortgages for 90% of the value of the real estate. The emphasis was put on the immediate construction of garden-type apartments, which became known in the industry as "608's" (referring to the section number of the Nation Housing Act administered by the FHA). The insuring office of the FHA was in effect guaranteeing the loans made by savings and loans associations, mutual savings banks, and life insurance companies. Many so-called smart operators took advantage of the program by obtaining extremely low-cost land, which could be valued at a price considerably higher than they paid for it. The tremendous shortage of housing during this period was a result of a five-year moratorium on housing between 1941 and 1946. The land prices were rising so rapidly that many of these projects were appraised and mortgages insured for more for 100% of their cost, but not necessarily of their value. The results of the "608" program was to produce thousands of new housing units in virtually every major metropolitan area of the country. The loans were very long-term with exceptionally low interest rates because they were guaranteed by the FHA. The program sometimes put cash in the hands of the developers over and above the actual cost of building the projects. This cash is called a "windfall."

The FHA was strongly criticized as were some developers at Congressional hearings on the subject in the early 1950s. The most profound remark was made by one multimillionaire who had received a windfall through a large FHA-insured loan. The Congressman questioning him asked, "Mr.—, is it not true that you borrowed 114% of your actual cost on the job, which loan was insured by the Federal Housing Administration branch of the Federal Government?" The witness testified, "That is true, Congressman, but don't forget it was a loan. I have to pay it back. If I don't pay it back, then you would have the right to criticize me." A windfall does not seem like a windfall when it must be repaid.

Following these experiences Congress included a provision in the Internal Revenue Code of 1954 taxing as dividends distributions by corporations having government insured mortgages in excess of cost. The effect of this is to tax windfalls as ordinary income.

While some developers became millionaires through the FHA "608" program , others eventually lost their properties through foreclosure that cost them heavily in federal income taxes. Their book value was far less than the amount of the loan. The profit income formula, sales price minus book value = taxable income, put them in an intolerable tax position. The sales price was the foreclosure price, usually the amount of the loan balance; hence their tax liabilities were heavy because of their low book value, which is cost less depreciation.

The lesson learned from the overfinancing of the "608's" was an important one. It is also a simple one: don't borrow more than you can pay back. On the happy side some "608's" were well planned, fairly well constructed, and in good locations. These withstood the large degree of overfinancing, while those constructed sloppily and in poor locations had no chance of success. Some owners who felt they could get rich on 110% loans from the government are now back at their former occupations. Without quality construction and without a winning location, an overfinanced property has no place to take its owner except to the land of the troubled.

The latest version of highly leveraged real estate investments is in subsidized housing. It has been possible to develop such property and retain ownership with as little as 5% equity. The cash flow is limited, but the big benefit is tax shelter.

Some developers have syndicated the equity and provided the tax shelter to the investors, while retaining cash flow. With or without these variations the investor gets a potential tax liability. Thus, as discussed in the previous chapter, the investor cannot simply let the property go to foreclosure and be done with it. IRS will construe a foreclosure as a sale, so that to the extent the mortgage exceeds the tax basis there will be a taxable gain.

Prior to the *1976 Tax Reform Act*, death was a way out. The inheritors of the property would get a stepped-up tax basis with no one ever having to pay a capital gains tax on the appreciation during the life of the decedent. The rules have changed, so that passing property by will does not fully step up the tax basis of property acquired before 1977, and there is no step up of basis for property acquired after 1976.

Financing may be well used to increase tax benefits, but borrowed money is expected to be repaid. Negotiating away that liability to the lender does not take care of the liability to IRS. It is therefores better to plan on paying loans back, even if the intent is to increase tax shelter.

REFINANCING

The benefits of original financing disappear over a period of time. They diminish because the annual constant remains the same, having been calculated on the original amount borrowed. In time the mortgage payments are very high in relation to the loan balance, prompting many investors to look again to the benefits of borrowing. Borrowing again is called refinancing. There are three major benefits you can obtain by refinancing:

1. You can obtain a very large amount of cash that is not subject to federal income taxes. You will recall that borrowed money is not subject to federal income taxes. Refinancing of income-producing property is just that—you are borrowing money. What you are doing is enjoying the benefits of your prior amortization. This has been made possible by a combination of amortization and an increase in value of the property (or at least no decrease in value of that property).

2. You can increase the cash flow. If you do not increase the debt, but arrange for a new annual constant based on your current loan balance, the payments should be considerably less. (This process is called recasting.)

3. You can financially prepare for a sale of the property in the immediate future. Because a new purchaser may not be able to obtain the financing that you can obtain, you should consider refinancing the property yourself. You are in a better position to obtain the refinancing because you know the history of the project and can present facts that generally are not available to the new purchaser.

When refinancing property in order to prepare for a sale, it is especially important to make sure that the new loan may be assumed. Most lenders now provide an acceleration clause which provides that the mortgage becomes due and payable if the borrower-owner sells or otherwise alienates title. You may be able to negotiate away such a clause.

Some time during the owning process, pressure builds up for you to refinance or sell. When you first bought the property, you were weighing the choices available to you in terms of the speed of depreciation. If you are like most investors, you want to obtain a reasonable cash flow and the maximum amount of tax shelter; hence you may have used accelerated depreciation. If you bought after 1976, you may have used straight-line depreciation because of the change in the tax law requiring recapture of all post 1975 depreciation in excess of straight-line depreciation regardless of how long the property is held. At any rate, when amortization exceeds depreciation by more than the cash flow, you will pay federal income taxes on cash you do not receive. No one enjoys paying federal income taxes on more cash than they are receiving, so that consequently the pressure builds up to refinance.

Keep in mind benefits. Which of the three benefits are important to you in your refinancing? Do you want a maximum amount of extra cash? Do you want to increase the cash flow? Do you want to pave the way for a sale? These benefits are sometimes in conflict with one another. It may make more sense to take less cash out in the refinancing if you could keep your annual constant low enough to make the financing appear very attractive in the event that you are seeking a sale. If you do not contemplate a sale within the next few years, you may want to emphasize the cash flow by not borrowing more money, but merely reducing the mortgage payments through the acquisition of a new and lower annual constant recasting. Whichever benefits you are seeking, you may be sure that sooner or later the original financing will have to be changed, and the decision to do so will be yours.

LEVERAGE AGAIN

Using borrowed money to magnify your gains or losses is, as you recall, termed leverage. You magnify your gains when you can make more by using borrowed money than the cost of that money. The losses are intensified by the use of leverage when the costs of the money exceed the gain that can be derived from it. The use of leverage in real estate has produced some magnificent results. The more money you can borrow, the better off you are, provided that the cost of the borrowed money is less than you can make through its use. Unhappily the demise of nationally known real estate developers can be traced largely to the negative side of leverage. What happened to these gentlemen is that—among other things) the cost of the money was higher than the amount they were making and the speed with which it had to be repaid called for more cash than they could get their hands on.

Some mortgage bankers predict the demise of a real estate developer by analyzing the cost of his borrowed money. One reason for this is that the real estate investor does not know how much money he is really making. Earnings from real estate are not known until the property is ultimately sold and all of the monies from the proceeds of sale are in the hands of the seller. Since real estate is a long-term investment, it may take as much as 20 years to accurately determine the profitability of the investment. Yet when one is highly leveraged, one is paying money back on a certain predetermined schedule. When interest on such money ranges from 12 to 20% and the property cannot stand that kind of cost, it is only a question of time until the property is lost. One fact that all real estate investors should accept is that they will not know how profitable an investment they have made until the proceeds of sale have been received. They can make precise calculations, but not all of their data will be accurate. The sure road to success is to borrow money at rates that are assuredly lower than the property will earn and to borrow such monies with a repayment schedule that is less than the monies forthcoming through the ordinary operations of the property, without regard to future sales and indeterminate profits.

OTHER COSTS OF MONEY

It has been traditional when refinancing real property for the lender to charge, in addition to the interest rate, a "point" in connection with the placing of a loan. The "point" in real estate practice is 1% of the total loan. In other words paying a point for a $100,000 loan on a property will cost the borrower $1000 in cash. The early justification for charging of points is fairly well understood. The intent is to return to lenders some of the overhead costs involved in the setting up of a loan. It was intended to cover costs of their own appraisers and the costs of staffing offices devoted exclusively to the originating of income-producing loans or to paying mortgage brokers to obtain loans. In the 1960's, points were being charged to cover more than initial expenses of setting up loans. They were used as a device to increase the interest income, and they were especially prevalent in the states where the usury statutes prohibited loans exceeding 6% in interest, but were silent on add-ons, such as points. They are used for FHA-insured and VA-guaranteed loans as well, which have traditionally operated with maximum interest rates.

It has also become usual to charge a penalty for paying off a loan prior to its normal expiration through steady amortization. The original intent appeared to be to help the lenders recover some of the expenses incurred when they receive the large lump sum payment and must close out the loan on the books of the company and endeavor to get an unexpected sum of money back into use. The typical income-producing loan may contain a clause stating that if the loan is paid back any time during the first 10 years, 1% of the remaining principal balance will have to be paid off as a penalty for prepayment. In recent times however the prepayment penalties have become stricter and more onerous. Some will argue that the charges appear to be just another device for accumulating more interest and thus increasing the yield for the lender. The cost can be three or six months' interest, which could amount to several percentage points on the loan.

Points paid by the borrower are an additional cost of money and should be spread over the expected life of the loan along with and prepayment penalties to determine the true cost of interest, especially if one is a large borrower.

The prepayment penalties have been used more and more by lenders who suspect that high interest rates can best be protected by forbidding the payoff of loans during the early years and even by severly penalizing borrowers when they attempt to prepay them in the later years. Prepayment penalties as high as 5% are not rare, although they usually decline to as low as 1% as the loan ages.

The absence of a prepayment privilege in the early years of a loan is called a "lock-in." The lock-in forbids borrowers to pay off the loan with a single payment; thus even if interest rates should drop, together with lower annual constants, investors finds themselves in the position of not being able to take advantage of changing market conditions. In cases of rising current interest rates, some lenders aggressively canvass their more well-secured loans, which carry low interest rates offering the owners lower annual constants, but with a higher interest rate. As a result of such canvassing and negotiations with the owners, lenders frequently are successful in removing some low interest rate loans from their books.

Every investor should be aware that owning real estate is a long-term proposition. Profitable investments demand that owners control their options, while holding income-producing property for a very long time. That is they should try to depend on their own judgment in picking and choosing the correct time to refinance and the correct time to sell, which can make real estate investing a rewarding experience. Some loans become due and payable if the borrower sells the property. The clause that so provides is called an acceleration clause.

Surrender of the right to refinance through lock-ins or excessive prepayment penalties is a severe limitation in managing an investment. The acceleration clause also provides a limitation in the management of the investment. Thus sales may take place at a time that is not advantageous for the owner. Your investment rewards can be severely limited by giving up some of your rights in timing both financing and sale.

During times of tight money, the developer or investor may have no choice but to accept a lock-in situation. In these cases, you would do well to examine the policies of the lender compared to those of other lenders during previous times of tight money. Such an examination will help you select those lenders who may be willing to renegotiate when the time comes for refinancing or sale.

Should you find yourself in a difficult situation because of an unwillingness of your first-mortgage lender to refinance your loan, even though the loan to value ratio (based on the current worth of the property) is very low, you may wish to consider a "wrap-around mortgage."

As its name implies, a new loan is wrapped around a first mortgage without disturbing the first mortgage already in place. A new lender, who will recognize the low loan amount already in place, may wish to make a new loan at 75% of the current value. This new value, let us say on an eight-year-old office building, may be very high as a combined result of inflation and an improving location with excellent tenants. A new loan is negotiated with a new lender who leaves the old first mortgage (usually with an interest rate much lower than in the current market) and advances the *difference* to the owner. The new lender is secured by a new debt instrument, the wrap-around loan, which includes both the unpaid balance of the first mortgage and the new amount advanced by the lender. Thus two debts are combined into one, which distinguishes the wrap-around mortgage from a second mortgage. Each new payment, usually monthly, goes to the wrap-around lender who remits to the original lender the amount necessary (principal and interest) as called for on the original first mortgage, keeping the balance. Inasmuch as the single interest rate on the wrap-around mortgage is higher than the original first mortgage rate, it is cheaper than new second mortgage money would be. Wrap-around lenders realize a healthy return on the "new" money lent out because their new money is earning not only a decent rate, but—since the older first mortgage is still on the property—they also collect the interest differential on what their wrap-around mortgage requires plus the interest rate on the existing first mortgage. These borrowers are getting new money at less than prevailing rates had they borrowed or negotiated a brand new first mortgage from a lender for the full amount.

The wrap-around technique works best when the following conditions exist:

1. When the first-mortgage lender refuses to refinance or "recast" the existing loan.
2. When high rates are being charged for second mortgages (12% to 20%), along with short terms resulting in onerous annual constants.
3. When the interest rate on the first mortgage is low compared with current rates.
4. When the property is producing large amounts of cash flow and can thereby service additional mortgage debts.

SUMMARY AND CONCLUSIONS

The annual constant is the ratio of the annual payments to the amount of the mortgage. Most investors want low annual constants because they prefer to get cash flow now rather than proceeds of sale later. Some investors want this tradeoff badly enough to pay a higher interest rate to get it.

The cash on the down payment (COD) is the ratio of the cash flow to the down payment. The COD also works as a measure of the current income-producing ability of the real estate when there is no mortgage on the property.

Borrowing money affects the COD. The higher the annual constant, the lower the COD; and conversely, the lower the annual constant, the higher the COD. With a given relationship between COD and constant, the more you borrow the greater the effect of using leverage.

While there are many ways to increase borrowing, they all require repayment of debt. If debt is not repaid, the consequences go beyond loss of property through foreclosure and the possibility of deficiency judgments. The consequences may include a substantial income tax liability. Thus the total amount of financing should be within the bounds that will enable investors to stay with the property until they are ready to sell.

The use of borrowed money should contribute to the profitability of the investment. The benefits of financing fade as the mortgage is reduced. Thus sometimes it is desirable to get anew some benefits of borrowed money by the process of refinancing. The benefits include getting more cash out of the property now rather than later, increasing the cash flow, or preparing the property for sale by attractive financing.

The refinancing, though valuable, is also costly. Costs include interest, points, and prepayment penalties. It is wise to have the flexibility to adjust the financing to changed conditions.

In recent times we have experienced some dramatically changed conditions in the environment that affect the cost and availability of mortgage money. These changed conditions can significantly influence the profitability of real estate investments. The next chapter discusses the process by which these conditions change and provides some guidance to the investor in meeting these risks.

9 THE COST AND AVAILABILITY OF BORROWED MONEY

SAVERS AND BORROWERS

Investing in any type of real estate is a long-term proposition. Therefore institutional real estate financing is also long-term, running for periods of up to 30 years and sometimes longer.

Most investment real estate is financed by borrowed money, and the cost of the borrowed money is one of the most important costs. It is determined by its availabilty and the number of people who want to borrow it. Usually there is brisk competition among institutions to attract savers and an equally fervent competition among those who wish to borrow money.

As an investor in real estate you are vitally affected by the cost and availability of money both when you buy and when you sell. You ought to understand where this money comes from and the factors that affect its cost. Financial knowledge about the money markets can help you time your purchase and will have a significant effect not only on when you should sell, but also on the selling price itself.

The presidents of institutional lenders, for example

148

savings and loan associations, want two types of customers. They need a source of money, that requires attracting savers to their institutions. They need interest income, that means they need some borrowers. They will have to pay their savers a rate of interest as favorable as those of other savings institutions or they will have difficulty in attracting the savers. In short they must be competitive with other savings institutions.

They will need borrowers, and it will be difficult to find them if they charge more for the money than the borrowers can obtain in the marketplace, namely from competitors.

Savings and loan associations make profits by paying savers less for the money than the associations can get by lending it out to the borrowers. The "spread" between the amount they pay for the money and the amount they can charge for lending it varies from time to time, but it is usually a couple of percentage points, more or less. The savings and loan association is in competition not only with other savings and loan associations (both for savers and borrowers), but also with other institutions, namely mutual savings banks, commercial banks, and in a less direct way insurance companies and credit unions.

In a sense the savers are loaning their savings to the savings and loan institutions because they have no immediate use for the money and want the liquidity. As incomes rise in an expanding and booming economy, not only people, but also profit-making institutions accumulate excess cash. The market works in such a way as to allow the financial intermediaries to make the spread on the savers' money because of *one* all-important fact. The savers are quite *liquid.* They can withdraw their money from savings and loan associations almost on demand. On the other hand the borrowers from these institutions are obtaining long-term loans, usually for 20 years or more. If it were not for the *liquidity* demanded by most savers, the savings and loan associations would serve a very limited function. They, the savers, could lend the money themselves at higher interest rates than the association can pay, assuming they could evaluate the mortgage loans and they had the money in reasonably large sums. But very few savers would be willing to accept a rate of interest paid by savings and loan associations if they could not withdraw their funds on very short notice. They appreciate the fact that their deposits (up to $40,000) in some associations are insured by the Federal Savings and Loan Insurance Corporation.

As lenders the institutions are forced into competing with other long-term lenders. The rates you may be charged are related to the demand and supply of money in the marketplace. If more people and institutions are saving money, more money is available for lending. If income taxes are low, more money is available because of a greater "after-tax" income.

There have been times when it was government policy to urge all citizens to "spend, spend, spend," for example during the depression in the early thirties or as a means of getting out of some recessions. At other times our government has endeavored to cool off over-heated periods (leaping inflation) by urging people to save, rather than spend. While these urgings either to spend or save may have a salutary psychological effect on us, the largest single force influencing the money markets are the policies of the national government. If it spends more money than it takes in from taxes, it becomes a borrower and competes in the open markets for loans (certificates, notes, and bonds). When it runs up staggering deficits, it increases borrowing to pay for goods and services. After all it gets its primary income from taxes, and if taxes are too low, it must borrow like any of us who spend more than we take in. This heavy borrowing drives up interest rates since the money market is under pressure to come up with more savings than it has available to lend. Aside from savings, where does the money come from?

THE FEDERAL RESERVE SYSTEM: ITS SIX GAUGES AND THREE VALVES

The "manufacture" of money is seemingly a highly complex process, but may be understood by considering the six gauges under constant view of the Federal Reserve Board. These gauges show the condition of the economy. In addition there are three valves that the Board can open or close as they deem necessary.

Creating Money

First let us examine the money system at work. Assume for a moment that you "panned" some gold while on a vacation in California and you received $1000 for it from our government. You deposit the money in your checking account. Your bank "sends" approximately $160 to the Federal Reserve District in which the bank is operating. The bank usually retains about $40 in cash, therefore approximately $200 of the $1000 that you put in your checking account cannot be used by the bank for lending purposes. The other $800 however may be loaned out. Because the bank cannot make money unless it earns interest, you may be sure they want to loan out your $800. Of all sources of bank income, the major one is interest on loans and investments.

Who borrows the other $800? It is loaned out, frequently to a customer who already has an account with the bank. The person obtaining the loan places the $800 in his checking account, normally the same day. The bank again takes approximately 16% of this $800, allocates it to the Federal Reserve Bank, retains about 4% of the $800 for its immediate cash requirements, and loans the balance out again, and again, and again. The process may involve many banks, but the result is the same. The expansion of "original" money placed in checking accounts would, under the assumption just noted, increase the

money supply by an amount five times the amount
originally deposited. In other words for every $1000 you
placed in your checking account, for all practical purposes, the banking system can loan approximately $5000.
Not *all* banks are required to "send" 16% of demand
deposits to the Federal Reserve Bank. The ratios vary
among banks and from time to time.

The bank is interested in making the most money on its
loans consistent with safety, and the bank policy dictates
that the loans be of a relatively short-term nature. Banks
are severely limited in the amount of long-term loans
because the banking authorities are concerned that the
money (mostly checking-account money), can be
withdrawn on short notice. This is why on examining the
bank's statements you will find a very small percentage of
their total assets in long-term mortgages. They make the
most money on consumer credit loans. These are loans on
automobiles, appliances, television sets, and furniture
bought by the consumer. The loans are also made to individuals, partnerships, and corporations for relatively
short periods of time. The rate charged bears a direct
relationship to the financial strength of the borrower.

Let us make some assumptions. Let us assume that the
total money supply—what we lay persons understand as
money, that is printed money and coins—amounts to approximately $50 billion. If we were to look at the total
deposits on hand in all the banks of the country, let us
assume we would discover deposits, of approximately
$350 billion, while we only had approximately $50 billion
in currency and coins. We also know that some of this
currency is being carried around in our pockets in coins
and bills. This seemingly incongrous situation exists
because our economy actually evolves around
"checkbook" money. The Federal Reserve Boards policy
of reserves, that is the portion of each deposit that must
be sent to the Federal Reserve Bank in the area where the
commercial bank is located, has different requirements
on what is known as time deposits. These time deposits in
the commercial banks are known to lay persons as sav-

ings accounts. The expansion of the money occurs through the process of lending depositors money. Both time deposits and demand deposits are involved, but demand deposits are of greater significance.

Tight money comes about when there is an excess of demand for loans over the available money supply defined to include deposits in commercial banks. To illustrate, consider what happened in the tight-money crunch of 1966. In order to do that let us go back a few years to 1962 when the total demand and time deposits on hand in commercial banks averaged approximatley $245 billion. In 1966 the total demand and time deposits in banks showed $326 billion. So during this four-year period, there was an increase in the money supply of approximately 33%. Plant expansion increased 65% during the same four-year period. Mortgage borrowing increased 50% during the four-year period; consumer borrowing increased 47%. With an increase of 33⅓% in the money supply and with the government borrowing huge amounts to finance a war, a tight- money situation had to develop. Or did it? The Federal Reserve Board controls the *monetary* policy of our economy while the Administration and the Congress establish the fiscal policies. This double-headed administration of our money system usually works fairly well—much better than in most countries. But like in any business, or in any family, that spends more than it takes in, the end result could be financial trouble. This situation requires action: lower the overhead or make more money. Quite simply we needed to do both in 1966.

The term "fiscal restraint" used by some economic writers simply means tax more and spend less, or at least do one or the other. The Congress did not think that our economy could stand both guns and butter and therefore, before increasing taxes, extracted a commitment from the administration to quit spending so much money (it took two years before the President agreed). Tied to the cut in federal spending was the surcharge, which increased our federal income taxes. Fiscal restraint, at last.

Fiscal restraint was a cry in the wilderness in 1966, so the Federal Reserve Board turned off the supply of money by tightening the screws on all three money valves. More of the valve tightening in a moment, but the result of the shutting off the money supply toppled several nationally known real estate and construction men from positions as multimillionaires to near bankruptcy in some cases and others to actual bankruptcy. The entire spectrum of the real estate industry immediately went into the doldrums. Money that was ordinarily available to the real estate industry simply dried up overnight.

Since the combined real estate and construction industry is one of the nation's largest, you can be sure that many influential people became greatly concerned. Construction was choked off, and investors holding land for future development discovered how terribly frenetic it is to own mortgaged land with no one to buy it.

Controlling the Money Supply

Did the Federal Reserve Board make a correct decision? In retrospect it could not have done anything else other than to turn the screws on the valves to shut off the money. It did not have much choice since it looks constantly at six important gauges:

1. The gross national product (total value of all goods and services produced).
2. Bureau of Labor Statistics Consumer Price Index (inflationary trends).
3. Employment rate (unemployment among persons wishing work).
4. Balance of payments (money should be flowing into the country at the same rate at which it is flowing out).
5. Trends in industrial production (steel, automobiles, and other industrial-type production).
6. Trends in housing (ups and downs of our total housing construction).

Mickey Mouse, upon seeing all six gauges in 1966, could have seen the word"tilt," and thus would have had to start a new game. And that is precisely what the Federal Reserve Board did. All six indices registered tremendous increases, especially the inflationary pace as well as the loss of our money to foreign countries (when we buy more from foreign countries than we sell to them, or at least send more dollars abroad).

We believe that there should have been higher taxes or some other fiscal restraint. However, under the circumstances, the Federal Reserve Board had to decrease the relative supply of money, which made it more expensive to borrow and dropped some would-be borrowers out of the market.

The three valves controlling the money supply may be simply labeled as follows:

1. The open market transactions (buying or selling of federal bonds or other debt instruments).
2. Change in reserve requirements (raising or lowering the proportion of each deposit to be sent to the Federal Reserve Bank).
3. Change in the discount rate (the amount that member banks pay for loans from the Federal Reserve Bank).

As for the first valve, what the "Fed" (Federal Reserve Board) does is sell a government bond from its own inventory. Assume that the Chase Manhattan Bank buys the bond for $1000 out of monies that it has available to loan out. It does not loan the money out because the bond rate is so attractive that it takes $1000 of money available for loans and instead buys the bond. When the Federal Reserve gets this cash, it does not deposit it anywhere, hence this $1000 has been removed from the money supply. The result is that the Chase Manhattan Bank's deposit at the Fed is reduced by $1000. The expansive effect operates in reverse, reducing the money supply by approximately $5000 under our assumptions. Actually something close to $6000 that would be available ordinarily for loans is no longer available. This pushing of the sell button is what can make money dry up virtually overnight. If the Federal Reserve Board wanted to close off the supply of money, it could technically do it in virtually one week under existing law, by merely selling some $15 billion worth of bonds at prices so attractive that no bank in the country could resist; if the Board did this our money supply would of course be reduced virtually overnight by about $90 billion. Out of a total money supply of $350 billion, a $90 billion reduction would be a trauma, which would cause a dramatic shortage and virtually panic the money markets. Of course, the Board has no intention of doing such a thing, but the pressing of the sell button of the Federal Reserve is the easiest and quickest method of shutting off the supply of funds available to the banks. It did some bond selling in 1966, and the result was almost, but not quite, a financial crisis.

Coupled with selling bonds at a fast clip, the Fed changed the reserve requirements on time deposits. This turning the screws on the second valve—changing the requirements by making the bank send a larger portion of their funds to the Fed—reduced the amount the money available for their banks to lend. Remember that the loss of $1000 to lend shuts off some $6000 or more in the money supply; it depends on reserve ratios.

The third valve was also screwed down a little by increases in the discount rate. This makes the banks pay more for money than they can afford to pay, considering what they can get for the money from borrowers. Sometimes the banks are told specifically the conditions under which their requests for such borrowing will be honored. Have you ever had a tellers window slammed down on your fingers? The bankers have.

Screwing down all three valves surely had its effect,

but until recently our dollar looked stable to investors and business persons in other countries. Lately however, the outrageous exploitation of oil-importing countries by the Organization of Oil Exporting Countries' cartel (OPEC) has disturbed the stability of the dollar and other currencies. But back in 1966 we made a few attempts by way of Congress to slacken the demand. Then certain tax incentives, mainly relating to depreciation of new buildings and a tax credit for purchases of new plant equipment, were temporarily suspended by the Congress and approved by the President. In 1969 real estate depreciation allowances were reduced and the tax credit for equipment was eliminated.

As talented as the Federal Reserve Board is, we think it seemed to overcorrect our economy in 1966. This manipulating of our money supply is an art and not yet a precise science. So, as one might expect, we either undercorrect or overcorrect.

Some Other Forces

Let us go back to 1966 again for a look at some other federal actions. The Federal Home Loan Bank Board, which acts as a regulatory agency overseeing the operations of the savings and loan associations, increased the interest rate at which members could borrow from them. The rate was increased from 4.5% in early January 1966 to 6% in November 1966. In all there were six rate increases in the calendar year of 1966 by the Federal Home Loan Bank Board. That meant that savings and loan associations could not make any money by borrowing from the Federal Home Loan Bank Board. To make the situation even more difficult, these institutions owed some $6 billion to the Federal Home Loan Bank Board, which said, "No new loans until you pay us back." The operations of the Federal Home Loan Bank Board are "tuned in" to the operations of the Federal Reserve

Board, both working in concert with each other. The gentleman sitting in the White House was politically receptive to complaints from a large number of citizens who were under some distress. As a matter of fact it appeared as though the President of the United States ordered a full investigation of the Federal Reserve Board through the Chairman of House Banking and Currency Committee. Possibly, the end result of this complaining and investigating was that the Chairman of the Federal Reserve Board made several trips to the White House. One can only speculate on what was said during this period of time, especially when the agency was being so thoroughly investigated by a Congressional Committee. We do know however that in 1967 the Chairman of the Federal Reserve Board was reappointed by the President and that one of the vacancies on the Board was filled by a man whose financial policies were thought to be similar to those of the Chairman. We also know that the same valves that were used to decrease the money supply were gently unscrewed to increase the money supply. In the latter part of 1967, approximately the third quarter of 1967, money became more available once again.

In fact it expanded with such rapidity that the highest recorded period of inflation since World War II was recorded in the fiscal year from July 1967 to June 1968. It has gone higher in some subsequent periods.

The Federal Reserve Board once again had to tighten the valves, while the hoped-for tax surcharge was in limbo in the House Ways and Means Committee. This is another reason why real estate investors should realize that they can benefit by owning leveraged real estate investment. We are living in an economy where the money supply can be expanded or contracted by the use of the techniques of the Federal Reserve Board and to the extent that we have inflation, such as occurred in the calendar year of 1967, investors can benefit by owning leveraged real estate.

ENCORE

In 1968-1969 the resurgence of inflation increased the demand for borrowed funds. The cost of borrowed money hit record levels, and some would-be mortgage borrowers could not get a loan commitment. Those who obtained loans did so at higher interest rates and higher annual constants.

The result of the resurgence of tight money was a drop in the volume of construction and subsequently an increase in the general level of rents. Investors who financed their property prior to the sharp rise in interest rates paid and may still be paying low rates for borrowed money, but they are able to charge competitive rents. The result is an increase in cash flow.

Those who owned land for sale to a developer found less of a market because projects that are profitable at lower interest rates may not be profitable at the higher rates. Those who had property for sale and needed a loan to help with the sale found money scarce and expensive.

The problem of tight money was back again in 1969, 1973-1974, and in 1978-79. Tight money will also be with us again. If this seems like a four-year pattern of scarce and expensive money, don't count on it. The factors influencing the availability and cost of money have been discussed earlier in this chapter. Although the gauges and valves are monitored intensively by the Federal Reserve Board, changes are not accurately predictable. No one person in authority has yet learned how to 'fine tune' our monetary system.

SUMMARY AND CONCLUSIONS

It is important that real estate investors time their investments as best they can by buying in a period of relatively easy money when financing is relatively inexpensive and the annual constant can be relatively low.

They should hold the property through an inflationary period and then sell when expectations of inflation and prosperity are exceptionally high. The end result of course is a higher price to the sellers and a dramatic increase in the value of what they had purchased earlier. During the very brief period of easy money in the third quarter of 1967, a few sagacious (or lucky) investors obtained financing for new projects or refinanced their existing ones, and since these commitments and mortgages were of a long-term nature, their problems were solved during this period. The opportunities recurred following other periods of tight money and will continue to recur.

Understanding the forces that influence the costs of money and inflation should be a great aid in reducing risks for the real estate investor. It makes no sense to build or buy during a tight-money market when one is forced to pay much higher interest coupled with a much higher annual constant, considering that these loans may be on record for as long as 20 years. Provided of course that one can predict with some degree of accuracy that the same real estate can be acquired with less costly money, if you but only wait. Some investors will buy during a period of tight money and commit to high interest rates with the intent of refinancing when rates are lower. Such a strategy is workable if there are good terms in the loan for prepayment privileges and if in fact interest rates come down. Otherwise the investor may get a very long period of low cash flow because of the high annual constant.

Nevertheless if the increasing costs of land and increasing costs of construction seem to be moving up faster than interest rates, it makes sense to acquire or build even in a tight-money market.

Some financially able people have been waiting since 1941 for prices to drop because "real estate is too high." Whether real estate is "too high" or not depends on the future. The next part of the book discusses making investments in the future of various kinds of real estate.

PART FOUR

SELECTING THE
TYPE OF REAL ESTATE

10 RISKS AND REWARDS IN LAND INVESTMENT

Everyone knows of land that was used for farming a few years ago, but today is part of suburbia. In the cities, older downtown buildings have been replaced by new skyscrapers. These changes in land use have caused changes in land values.

The value of land is dependent on its income-producing ability (or potential ability) or its use, such as for a homesite. When its income-producing ability (actual or potential) changes, its value changes.

An investment in land is made with one major hope: a substantial increase in the land's value. This increase could come about because of an anticipated or actual *change* in the use of the land. If the change in land use takes too long, or indeed if it never comes about, investors can lose their investment and more.

Holding land and supporting it by paying property taxes and meeting mortgage payments are typical of an investment with a negative cash flow. Purchasing land with the hope that in the near future a change in use will occur involves risk that the change may not come about soon enough, if at all. It follows therefore that an investment in land must be timed to an intended use.

More money has been lost in land investment than in

163

any other area of real estate investing; yet it also probable that more money has been made through land appreciation than in any other area of real estate. The rapid growth of urban America has transformed many farmland owners into real estate investors of considerable wealth.

LAND SPECULATION

If you invest in vacant land, you are one of three kinds of investors:

1. A farmer or other user who works the land for income.
2. A developer who will eventually develop the land.
3. An investor who hopes for a profit as a result of a potential change in land use.

One who buys land to build a home for personal use is not an investor in land, but is serving as a developer. Investors who hope for a profit because of potential change in land use are in reality *speculators*. They make money because they are prepared to take the risk that the land-use change may not occur. Speculators will pay only the amount necessary to produce a substantial profit based on their estimate of how long they will have to hold the land. Astute speculators invest only in what in horserace parlance is called an "overlay". All racetracks have tote boards that show the odds on each horse in the forth coming race. If a horse is in fact a two-to-one shot, but the public betting at the track ignores the horse's possibilities and on the tote board the horse is shown as a six-to-one-shot, professional gamblers call this lack of confidence and the resultant high odds an "overlay." Professional gamblers bet only on the overlay.

An overlay in land occurs when the land can be profitably developed sooner than is generally expected. For example the investing public may expect a parcel of land on the urban fringe to be ready for development in 10 years. If in fact profitable development on it can begin in 5 years, it is an overlay. Professional speculators in land invest only in overlays. They leave the other land investments to the uninformed.

Amateur speculators may buy land, and while the chance of its turning out to be an overlay is small, they may in fact have a winner. By the same token, some poker players may draw to an inside straight and take the pot.

There have been times in the history of land speculation when it would have been difficult to make an investment that would not turn out to be a winner. It is like the person who said to his stockbroker in 1928: "Buy." When asked what, the reply was: "Anything, they are all going up aren't they?"

Opportunities for successful land investment arise in communities that exhibit substantial sharp increases in the rate of growth. The typical cause of such increases in growth rates is an increase in employment opportunities.

Growth in employment opportunities is influenced by industrial location and expansion, government spending, and a variety of socioeconomic factors, including a higher standard of living and greater mobility of the population. The land speculators who find themselve buying in a community where the timing just happens to be "right" would find it difficult to pick a loser. Of course identifying the right time for a community is another matter.

In the ordinary course of growth of a community a pattern of land use will emerge. Frequently the pattern will be constrained by master planning for community growth and the associated zoning and programming of public improvements.

Zoning is the regulation of land use by a local government body. It limits the kind of use to which the land may be put. Thus land zoned for single-family dwellings may not be used for a shopping center. Frequently a change in zoning will permit a more profitable land use, and the speculator may realize a substantial profit. In some communities, speculators constantly look for land that may be rezoned and make their profit from land investments by successfully getting the change in permitted land use.

Sometimes zoning authorities allocate more land for a particular use than is necessary for the operation of real estate markets. Obviously if there is to be any competition, more land must be zoned for a use than is currently required. Otherwise the owner of the only zoned land may have a monopolistic position. On the other hand there may be excessively large amounts of land available for a particular use with the zoning already obtained. Just because the land is zoned for apartments, a shopping center, or an office building does not mean that it can be profitably developed into that use.

Public improvements, such as roads, sewers, and water supply, are necessary in order to develop land. The local planning authorities consider these improvements along with zoning when they draw up the master plan. Some communities have ample facilities, at least considering the amount of land available for development. In other communities the shortage of some public improvements, such as a sewer system with mains and treatment facilities, provides a severe limit on growth. Under such conditions one could predict the pattern of growth by predicting where the sewer main will go or in some cases the water main.

When one considers the advent of freeways and beltways and other major forces that make the pattern of urban growth different from that of an earlier generation, one readily sees that forecasting the pattern is difficult even for a professional urban land economist. An amateur may make an analysis and predictions and for various reasons may find himself at the right place at the right time. But without professional advice, or sufficient knowledge, the amateur speculator in land will find the risks out of line with the rewards. You may play the land game if you so desire, but you should realize that unless you have specialized knowledge, you are trying to fill an inside straight.

ACQUIRING LAND FOR RESALE

Unless you are willing to pay all cash and hold the land for perhaps decades, you will probably seek a highly leveraged investment. The highest leveraged investment in land is accomplished through the use of the option technique. You put up money for the right (but not the obligation) to buy the land. If you think you have a winner, you exercise the option; if not, all you can lose is your option money.

Why would anyone in their right mind sell you an option? Perhaps because the seller thought you were paying too much for the land and had no objections to being overpaid. You can use the option when you need time to examine some uncertainties. For example you might need time to look into the possibility of rezoning the land, to check on the location of proposed roads, or just to gain time to arrange for the down payment. To use options as a financing device to gain control of overlays requires a superb handicapper. That is you must get some big winners to compensate you for the unexercised options. An expired option is valueless except for the experience it brings.

The most frequently used technique for buying land with little money is to simply use a small down payment. A mortgage is usually given back to the seller for the remaining balance. The seller expects, and gets, a higher price for the land when it is sold for a low down payment. Small-down-payment purchases on large tracts of land and resale on equally easy terms is the realty "action" market, not too dissimilar to the "sardine" market.

The "sardine" market is the classic tale of the sardine dealer who buys and sells sardines. A case of sardines sold for $35. It was resold at prices of $65, then $85, and finally $110. The ultimate purchaser (the $110 buyer) opened one can and tasted the sardines. They were horrible. This purchaser went back to the seller, and bitterly complained, and was told, "You ate the sardines? They aren't for eating, they're for selling."

Buying and selling land is similar to buying and selling sardines. It can be profitable even at prices higher than those at which the sardines are worth eating or the land worth developing. But unless you want to take inordinate risks, the price should be related to what a user can afford to pay.

One approach to investing in land is to select land on the fringe of urban development. There is a large amount of such land surrounding the metropolitan areas of our nation, much of it used for farming. Each year more of it becomes part of suburbia. Somebody makes money and is going to make money buying farmland that is eventually sold to developers as subdivision land. Consider the example of farmland purchases for $1,000 an acre, while land ready for subdivision sells for $10,000 an acre or more.

Making the most money in this market usually requires that the land be bought with very little money down. If you buy for $2,000 an acre—all cash—and sell for $4,000 an acre, you have not made a spectacular gain on your money, assuming that it took five years for the land value to double. You would have less than doubled your money after paying property taxes.

If you bought the same land with $200 down and put in another $800 for interest and taxes while holding it for the same five year period, the average amount invested would be over $400, You would net a profit of $1200 (gross profit of $2000 difference in sales price over cost, less $800 for interest and taxes), which about triples the average amount of your investment. In addition the interest and property taxes you paid were deducted from ordinary income, which provided you with tax benefits. Furthermore when you sell and recover your investment, you pay a capital gains tax rate, assuming you sell the entire tract to a single purchaser. Tax benefits would then enhance your after-tax profit. You may make your investment in land a safe one if you pay all cash, but you cannot make the most money by paying all cash.

TIMING THE SALE

The timing of the sale is especially important in a leveraged investment. To return to our previous example, if you resold after 1 year at the $4000 price, having put up only a $200 down payment, the return would be fantastic. If you have to wait 10 years, the profit is negligible. And waiting 20 years means losses even if the price doubles.

If you decide to invest in the land market for large profits, do it with highly leveraged purchases and get out as quickly as possible after the price rise. The ultimate subdivider and user of land is the last purchaser and, as the last purchaser, must eat the sardines. If you bought the land at a low price, the ultimate purchaser will be able to use the land at a price that is favorable.

Ideally land investments should be made prior to the change in land-use expectations. A sale of such investments should be made when the change in expectations has pushed the price up. You may sell land or sardines, but you need a sale to make a profit. Waiting too long is expensive.

Most of the information that you get relating to city growth and structure will refer to forecasts of *demand*. This is the key to profitable land buying and selling. Your land purchases must be geared to trends in employment opportunities, population increases, and other related factors that cause the city to grow and as a consequence pull your land into the subdivision pattern.

Since forecasters of demand are educated guesses about the course of events, you need to be properly concerned that the prediction of growth will happen within a reasonable period of *time*. The timing of when your land will be pulled into the city structure is one of the most important factors influencing your purchase. It should be keyed to the ability of developers to use your land, and they cannot use it if the usual land improvements are not available to them. The ultimate users of the land need to be assured of fire and police protection, adequate schools, and the ability to get to hospitals, churches, and shopping facilities. Developers cannot use your land unless they can manufacture it into a lot.

WHAT IS A LOT?

Some people have purchased lots, often through the mail which consisted of four lines drawn on a piece of paper representing a portion of the earth's surface. A lot is not a usable lot merely because a promoter owns some raw acreage and has a draftsman draw four lines on a map which is then recorded. Many Americans have bought "lots" on which they thought they could build their primary, vacation, or retirement homes, only to discover that without the utilities and other improvements just mentioned they own a small plot of raw land. They have nothing else, except the company of other disillusioned owners who have also purchased a similar "lot" in the same fashion. It is incredible that not only have thousands of persons purchased one such "lot," but also often two or three, the extra "lots" being an "investment". An investment in what? Probably sardines. As a result, some state governments have enacted legislation to protect the buying public by requiring that land promotions be registered with the authorities and that promoters ensure the availability of all the utilities and improvements that the public has a right to expect when they purchase a "lot." The Federal Government also has some regulations of land sales. A good policy is not to buy a lot that you have not seen. When you see it, check out all the necessary items to assure yourself that you can build on it.

In areas of very rapid city growth legitimate developers have bought land for subdivision purposes, only to discover that they have been burdened with land on which they cannnot build. Public authorities have not been able to keep pace with the growth. Sewer and water facilities which generally come before major improvements roads, are lagging as much as several years or more behind the demand for such facilities.

If you are buying land for resale, you must be able to predict *when* and where the sewer and water will be available. After you have determined the availability of public facilities, such as city sewers and water, you must make sure that roads are also available.

Land is frequently acquired without the investor concerning himself with the fact that road construction may be several years away, even if the sewer and water are available. Since road maintenance requires tremendous expense, you must be certain that local authorities are willing to accept this responsibility. It may surprise many that a fairly large number of roads are in fact private, even though they were intended to be public. If the local authorities do not accept such roads for maintenance in their regular system, they are private roads. They lower the value of the land that they serve because landowners must pay for maintenance of the roads in addition to paying their real property taxes.

Road standards are set by the local authorities. If the road you see running through an attractive tract of land is not accepted and maintained by some political subdivision, it may be best to forget it. If the road has not been accepted by the taxing authorities for maintenance, chances are that it has been built in a way unacceptable to them, no matter how elegant, clean, and seemingly adequate it looks to you. It may not be high or wide enough or may not meet certain construction standards required by the local authorities.

Zoning also plays an important part in evaluating land you may wish to purchase. Some farmland, unzoned for any other use, may necessarily have to remain as farmland or be converted into large-lot subdivisions of perhaps two acres per dwelling unit. The authorities may refuse to rezone the land for residential or other uses because they plan a public use, such as for a park or school. They may also limit the kind of use because of a general plan or because other landowners, usually homeowners, want nothing except low-density high- priced developments. The result is that land investments that depend on rezoning can be risky investments. The land you select should become *usable,* and that requires utilities, roads, community facilities, and zoning. The chances you take depend on the availability of facilities as well as on the demand.

DEVELOPABILITY

No growth, slow growth, and other local limitations on development significantly limit the supply of buildable sites. These limitations include sewer moratoria and time-phased ordinances that regulate which land may be developed and when.

Such limitations can severely hurt the land investor by delaying the time for development. They can however mean big profits if they apply to someone else in a way which restricts competition.

The increased difficulty in developing land has made for a sharply restricted supply. Yet some land someplace needs to be developed to accommodate increasing population. If you own the land that becomes developable, while others own the potentially developable land that governmental authorities are keeping from being developed, that regulation can make you rich beyond your wildest dreams.

Putting yourself in such a position involves a much

more detailed discussion than is appropriate for this book. The information is, however, available elsewhere.[1]

FINANCING LAND FOR RESALE

Many investors have lost a great deal of money by trying to hold on to highly leveraged land purchases. Professional land speculators know that land eats three meals a day, often requiring sirloin steaks for more than one meal. For breakfast land eats taxes; for lunch, interest payments; for dinner principal payments. Taxes on acreage are usually very low. Some states give a tax break, by law or custom, to farmers. Land in a developed areas may be taxed heavily. The annual taxes may be equal to 2 or 3% of the value of the land. On a highly leveraged investment this could be a substantial cost. The interest payments on highly leveraged investments are always a high-cost item. Usually 6% is low and in some circumstances even 8% or more is low. The principal payments are sometimes deferred, by paying interest only on the loan for up to five years. But sooner or later the principal payments must start. If the principal is amortized, it could be at a rate starting somewhere between 2 and 4% per annum. Thus an annual constant for a long-term land loan could easily be 10 or 12%. Whether the loan is interest only or amortized, you can be sure that the principal payments ultimately add up to the total amount borrowed.

Since to make the most profit you need highly leveraged land, the question is "Who will lend on land?" To obtain financing on very favorable terms requires the cooperation of the seller, because few lenders are in a position to make such loans except at seemingly

[1]See Maury Seldin, *Land Investment.* Dow Jones-Irwin, 1975; and Michael Sumichrast and Maury Seldin, *Housing Markets, The Complete Guide to Analysis and Strategy for Builders, Lenders, and Other Investors.* Dow Jones-Irwin, 1977.

outrageous interest rates or discounts. Having the seller carry back the financing under an arrangement where the land is the sole security for the debt provides you with a measure of protection. If you must hold the land for twice as long as you anticipated, you might just walk away from the investment and take your loss of the cash you put up and not be liable for the unpaid balance of the mortagage. It is possible that the land may not go up in value fast enough to compensate you for the taxes and interest you are paying. It happens.

You might consider that the land in which you are investing can be made into a more profitable investment if you also arrange for clauses in your purchase money mortgage that provide added flexibility. For example you could arrange for releases of certain portions of the land on the payment of a portion of the principal of the mortgage. This allows an investor or the developer to sell off certain portions of their investment over a period of time. A well planned land sales program might call for sales over a period of years at succeedingly higher prices. Under such a planned sales program, proceeds of sales are frequently used to cover the costs of carrying the land. If the land has been selling profitably and quickly, the carrying costs go down and the profits go up. And that is what all investors want.

You could also consider that certain portions of the mortgage you give back would not necessarily have to be paid off in their entirety, if you (or your ultimate purchaser) decide to subdivide the land into homesites. The portions of money then due on the subdivided lots could be made subordinate to (give way to) bonafide institutional mortgage loans on the lots on which houses are constructed. Mortgages have priority on the basis of date of recordation. The "subordination" clause subordinates the priority of claim to a later recorded mortgage, usually a construction loan. Sometimes the subordinated mortgage becomes a long-term second mortgage. This provides additional leverage to the investor, who purchases land improved with a building. Your ability as a purchaser to convince sellers that the release and subordination clauses are in the long run beneficial to them depends on your ability to convince then that you are paying a higher price for the land because you expect them to cooperate with you in the financing.

Many high-income investors used to prepay interest for as much as five years on their land purchases in order to deduct all of this known carrying charge in the first year of purchase. It provided some assurance that they would be able to carry the land for five years without being burdened with interest payments in years in which their own income was uncertain. The seller had to pay taxes on the interest received, but did not mind because the cash would be received earlier. Then in November, 1968 the Internal Revenue Service rules on deductibility of prepaid interest were tightened to limit the amount of time for which there is a deductibility of prepaid interest. Prepaying of up to one year's interest is still deductible. You may prepay more, but the tax advantage is gone.

Most investors try to arrange terms of the purchase money mortgage in such a way as to defer principal repayments on the mortgage for periods of up to 5 (or even 10) years, thus avoiding additional cash outflow during their ownership of the undeveloped land. Under this arrangement the total payments of a $100,000 mortgage at 7% would be $7000 per year. There would be no amortization. But at the end of the 5 or 10 years the entire $100,000 would become due and payable.

If an interest-only provision is not available, most investors try for as low an annual constant as possible. A frequently used annual constant is 12%. Thus the annual payments on a $100,000 loan would be $12,000. Sometimes the payments are quarterly, which in this case would be $3000 per quarter. The payments include interest.

Frequently seller-lenders may insist the contract stipulate that they will be paid in full at the end of 5 or 10 years, even though the amortizing mortgage might take 15 or 20 years to be paid off. These "balloon" payments frequently force a choice between expensive refinancing and a sale. Since it is important for you as an investor to choose the time of sale, you should be cautious about using balloon mortgages.

Some sellers are frequently advised to sell their land with down payments of less than 30% of the total price to avoid being taxed on the entire proceeds of sale in one year, namely the year of sale. As a result many parcels of land are offered with a payment of only "29% down." The tax reason for the "29% down" is to provide for a margin to safeguard against being taxed on the total capital gain in one year. The seller under these circumstances is usually willing to provide financing for a reasonable period of time.

INTERIM USE HELPS IN CARRYING COSTS

While holding the land for resale many investors put it into interim use to obtain income. Some investors work out partnerships for the farming of the land, cancellable on relatively short notice; others sell off timber; while still others develop acres of their land into turf. Most of the sod you have seen rolled up like carpets on trucks heading into cities comes from land that is being held primarily for investment since farmers are apprehensive about selling off their topsoil. Land is also often rented for use of carnivals, horse shows, rodeos, and the like, as well as for grazing by adjacent or nearby farms. In the more densely populated areas, kiddie lands, pitch and putt golf courses, parking lots, and various other temporary uses help carry the land.

Not all interim land uses appear temporary. Some of the garden apartments built to last 40 to 50 years have in less than 20 years been torn down to make way for more permanent land uses. This type of development has taken place along the Wilshire Boulevard section of Los Angeles. The more rapid replacement of structures than would seem to be justified by physical deterioration is reflected in a cartoon that shows a New York office building under construction with a sign saying, "Upon completition this eight story building will be torn down to make way for a 40-story skyscraper."

Many of these uses were not intended to be temporary. But when land values increased ten-, twenty-, thirty-, or even fortyfold within a decade or two, the intended long-term use of the land became obsolete. There are many land investments today containing buildings that are rapidly becoming obsolete. When rented, these buildings provide enough income to help "carry the land." There may be no cash flow, but there is some tax shelter and hopefully substantial proceeds of sale.

In the boom of the twenties the idea of an interim use of land was so attractive that many buildings were built with interim uses in mind, In such areas as New York, one-story buildings were built in the hope that their rent would cover the property taxes. Such buildings are called "tax-payers." Four decades later many of the "tax-payers" are still standing. So-called interim use turned out to be permanent. The quality of their tenancy has deteriorated. What would have been a marginal investment in a store building if the price were right, turned out to be poor investment as land speculation.

A strategy of interim use as a hedge against the possibility that the expected development will not materialize is an excellent one. You should however not pay too high a price for that hedge.

FINANCING LAND FOR DEVELOPMENT

Land that may shortly be developed because of the combination of demand and availability of utilities and other community facilities is not as difficult to finance as land that is many years away from such development. Commercial banks, savings and loan associations, and other conventional mortgage lenders make loans on well-located land to responsible investors or land developers as well as to home builders in the process of subdividing the land. These loans are generally tied to the fact that building lots for which all utilities are in, or will be in shortly, are "ready to go."

The construction loan on a house is generally for a lesser amount than the permanent loan obtained for the home buyer. A builder may reduce capital investment by obtaining individual lot loans as well as construction loans. The lot loans are then paid off when the permanent loan is placed, usually when the house is sold.

Sometimes land loans may be worked out as the first draw on the construction loan. For example if lenders are willing to make a construction loan of $38,000 on a house to be built, in many jurisdictions they may be willing to advance $3800 to the builder to help cover the cost of the lot purchase. Although not strictly a land loan, this loan is made in the form of a first mortgage and is frequently called a land loan because a portion of the loan is advanced to cover part of the land costs.

There are some institutional land loans that could aid the investor in financing this land. Frequently investors are also developers who simply wish to inventory the land while he develops plans or until they are ready to start the project. Land loans are generally not available to speculators except when there are private lenders who will supply high-risk loans for very high rates of return.

Major institutions, such as life insurance companies, large oil corporations, and other industrial organizations, have been joining major land developers who acquire gigantic tracts to build new towns near major metropolitan areas. So much capital is required that few private developers have the resources to feed the land its three meals a day while it is being developed over a 5 to 10-year period. Some large organizations have acquired development companies and use the credit of the parent company to gain adequate financing.

As an investor in land you cannot hope to bring the

land to the development stage until all the problems of roads, utilities, and zoning are solved. And here lie your greatest risks. You are in competition with others who are doing the same thing, that is holding the land for resale to developers. If you cannot solve all these problems and thus make the land attractive to a developer, you run the risk of not selling out at the right time. You may have to hold the line for such a long time that during your holding period the market demand is satisfied in your area by other landholders. Your land may be in demand, but if it is not ready for development until the demand has slackened off or if home-mortgage financing is not readily available because of a tight-money situation, you may not find a developer at any price. Developers want land that they can subdivide and build on in the immediate future. If there is little or no mortgage money available, you may not be able to find a buyer in the development business. Your only buyers then may be land speculators looking for an overlay. To make your land attractive to them in a tight-money situation most often means selling at sacrifice prices and that is the time to buy, not to sell.

THE BENEFITS

The benefits to the successful land investor can be fantastic. Of the major benefits discussed in Chapter 3, the one most relevant is proceeds of sale. Land held for long-term investment qualifies for long-term capital-gains tax. For individuals who are investors the maxium tax on long-term capital gains is based on inclusion of forty per cent of the gain in their ordinary income. For corporations, the maximum tax on long-term capital gains is 30%. The tax is computed using the same basic formula of sales price minus book value = taxable income. The book value of land probably does not change because land is not depreciable and there may have been little if any, depreciable improvements.

Making a profit assumes that you sell the land for more

than your costs. You have the costs of sale, which are deductible, and while you were owning the property you could deduct the interest and taxes from your taxable income. You cannot deduct the amortization on your mortgage. So the real benefit comes at the end, when the property is sold and you try to recover your investment and then some.

If, for example, you purchased your land for $1000 an acre and bought 100 acres, your book value is $100,000. If you bought it heavily leveraged with a small cash down payment of $100 an acre, your cash investment would be $10,000. If you held the land for two years, paying interest only on the $90,000 mortgage, your outgo (negative cash flow) would be the two-year interest on the mortgage and the taxes. Assuming that the interest on your give-back mortgage to the seller was 6% per annum and the taxes were $3000 annually, your negative cash flow for the two years you held the property was $16,800 ($5400 in interest annually plus $3000 annual taxes). This negative cash flow was deducted by you each year against your other income. Therefore you deducted as expenses $8400 each of the two years. (In the case of individuals this interest might constitute a tax preference item for purposes of the minimum tax or for purposes of the limitation on deduction for interest on investment indebtedness.) Your book value remained the same however since you had no depreciation. You carry the land on your books at the original $100,000 purchase price.

Assume that you sell the land for $2000 an acre after the two years. Your taxable income, subject to capital-gain rates, would be $100,000 less expenses of sale, which let us assume amount to $20,000. Thus you will be taxed on $80,000 capital gain let us say (at 25% on $50,000 and 35% on $30,000) for a maximum total of $23,000 in income tax (The tax liability under the minimum tax and the tax preference items are being ignored here to simplify the illustration.)

Out of a gross of $200,000 you would have to pay expenses of sale of say $20,000, the $90,000 mortgage, and the income tax at capital-gains rates amounting to say $23,000. Thus the $200,000 price less $20,000 expenses leaves $180,000 less the $90,000 mortgage and give you $90,000 pretax proceeds. After $23,000 taxes you have 67,000 for an original investment of $10,000 for two years, plus additional cash investment of $16,800. You would have an after-tax net profit of over $40,000, which is a very handsome return. To the extent your maximum tax rate is less than 70%, the tax on the gain in excess of $50,000 will be reduced and the after-tax profit increased. The numbers are shown in tabular form in table 9.

The profit opportunity in such investments is exciting to any investor prepared to take the risk. There have been many purchases of land with such attractive results. Any real estate broker located in rapidly expanding metropolitan areas during the past 30 years can recall numerous instances of rapid land appreciation. Such gains are legion, especially as reported by winners at cocktail parties. They cover such areas as Los, Angeles, California; Washington, D. C.; New York City; Atlanta, Georgia; Phoenix, Arizona; and Las Vegas, Nevada—all among the many cities where rapid expansion has occurred since the end of World War II. The land investor who made purchases, especially with very small down payments; paid carrying costs while holding the land; and was right about the utilities, other improvements, and zoning changes has indeed done very well.

Others who invested in land hoping for huge profits have lost their original investment in addition to the costs of feeding the land. Where did they go wrong? They failed to check out the zoning in the master plan; the road pattern existing or planned; and the locations and probable timing of sewers, water, and other necessary utilities. And chances are that they did not buy directly in the stream of expansion.

Frequently well-intentioned real estate brokers speak

Table 9   Example of Land Investment

Purchase		
Cost 100 acres @$1000 per acre		$100,000
Down payment 10% ($100 per acre)		10,000
Mortgage		$ 90,000
Carrying cost		
Interest 6% per year of $90,000	$ 5,400	
for two years	5,400	
Total interest		$ 10,800
Taxes @$2000		6,000
Total carrying cost		$ 16,800
Sale		
Sales price 100 acres@$2000		$200,000
Less expenses of sale		20,000
Sales price less expenses		$180,000
Less mortgage		90,000
Proceeds before income tax		$ 90,000
Income tax		
Sales price less expenses	$180,000	
Cost basis	100,000	
Taxable profit	$ 80,000	
Taxes		$ 23,000
After-tax proceeds		$ 67,000
Less original investment	$ 10,000	
Less carrying cost	$ 16,800	26,800
After-tax net profit		$ 40,200

in conclusion words, not in facts. Prospective land investors sometimes hear only what they want to hear—so raced are their speculative engines. The broker points out how the land is "bound to go up in value," And speculates on the effects on the value of the land if some large organization he or she has heard about builds in the immediate area. Any conclusions at this point are guesses at best, even if the broker has heard that some new factory is considering a site nearby. But has it already bought the land nearby? Is it going to build in the immediate future? Why is land "bound to go up in value?"

Land goes up in value if it is in the path of urban growth and if it is not already too heavily priced. The intelligent investor expects some evidence of urban growth. Favorable happenstance helps—but who can count on it?

GETTING OUT

Assuming that you have made an intelligent land purchase, is there anything you can do but sell and get the benefits of sale? First, unless you are getting all cash, do not accept more than 29% down payment since *all* the gain would be taxable in the year of sale (include any mortgage payments to you, or on your behalf, in the year of sale in your 29% down-payment calculation). If you sell the land for less than 29% down payment, the sale might qualify as an instalment sale. The law reads 30% but most investors use 29% in order to play it safe. Thus you could pay your capital-gains tax a little at a time, in proportion to the cash you receive. Since tax laws are complicated and are subject to change, see qualified tax counsel before you commit yourself.

Instead of selling the land, you may wish to trade it for a much larger piece of land, since you do not need the cash now and believe that the larger tract has a good future. This can usually be done without payment of federal income taxes. To handle this properly you should consult a tax attorney or an accountant who is familiar with real estate transactions.

Probably the most profitable procedure other than selling the land, is to join forces with a responsible and skillful developer to turn your land into a fine income- producing property. This not only postpones the payment of taxes on the increased value of your land, but also converts a non-income-producing asset into an income- producing asset.

Very often a fine developer with a solid reputation has difficulty in locating choice land on which to build. The developer would welcome a call from a reputable landowner to discuss the possibilities of a change in zoning which could make it not only possible but also profitable for both of you. Exchanging your land for a percentage of an owning entity that will ultimately convert your nonincome-producing asset to an income-producing asset, without first selling the land and paying taxes on the sale, is a legitimate way of postponing taxes and increasing your income possibilities by amounts of up to 33% more than if you sold the land first.

Here is an example of how this works. You own land that 10 years ago cost you $25,000 and is worth $225,000 today. If you sold it, you would have to pay capital-gains taxes of say $50,000 on your $200,000 profit. After taxes you would have $175,000 left to invest. If the developer would pay the market value of the land, that is $225,000, for development of the land into an apartment house, the same value in partnership interests would certainly be allowed. Moreover if the developer really needed a partner, even a bit more might be allowed. Contrast this with your after-tax investment capital of $175,000 if you had sold and subsequently would be willing to invest in an apartment house venture with another developer. You are $50,000 better off by exchanging your land for a $225,000 interest in the apartment-house venture. Stated another way, your land will get you a $225,000 interest if you trade, but only a $175,000 interest if you sell. In this example you would receive an interest of approximately 28% more by using the exchange technique rather than selling. As with most tax advantages, the IRS collects its share, but at a later date. You are postponing your capital-gains tax which will be eventually paid when the new income-producing apartment house is eventually sold. Thus the major benefit of owning land, that is the proceeds of sale, may be enhanced, while the tax liabilities are postponed.

If you can properly assess the risk and remain emotionally comfortable while you own it, land is unquestionably the most profitable of all real estate investments, provided that you have chosen a winner.

CONCLUSIONS

Land is where the big money can be made. But land is not the place for an investor new to real estate. The risks and rewards are great because it is land that changes value dramatically, not buildings. Leveraged investments in land magnify the gains, if any.

Investors in land should be prepared to carry the land because of the negative cash flow. The big benefits are at proceeds of sale and that depends on timing and location. Some of the benefits from selecting land at the right location and at the right time are available through investing in income-producing property. The next few chapters describe these risks and rewards.

11 HOUSES AND SMALL APARTMENT BUILDINGS

Of all real estate investments, rental houses are probably the easiest to get into, the easiest to get out of, and the least profitable. At least they used to be before the inflation of the seventies. In any event they are a good starting place for active investors in real estate.

Active investors manage their own investments. They may employ a property manager, but they must still spend time and effort to protect their investment. Passive investors on the other hand might put their real estate in a trust or invest in a syndicate where a managing partner does everything, including having the checks drawn in favor of the investor.

If you are interested in having a bank or trust officer manage your investments, forget rental houses because as investments they require active management and are at least a part-time business. You will find very few syndicates for houses because such investments are usually of smaller scale than investments in larger-sized housing projects.

Managing rental houses is an excellent training ground for the real estate investor. It also provides some business opportunities associated with real estate investment.

AN INVESTMENT IS A BUSINESS

An investment is an asset that has the potential or capability to produce a profit. You may invest in real estate much the same way as you might invest in stock traded on the New York Stock Exchange. But real estate investments require more attention than common stocks because an investor must make decisions about operating the property.

As a real estate investor you might retain an experienced professional property manager to supervise the operation of your investment properties. You might retain a Certified Property Manager (CPM), who is a member of the professional property management organization affiliated with the National Association of Realtors (NAR). You could then be confident of proper supervision of the operation of the property, but you still have the top management responsibility.

Having such responsibility requires you to set the rents and make the major decisions on expenditures. You could rely on counsel for help and leave the details to them. In large investments it would be wise to do just that. However in rental houses it rarely pays for you to employ a property manager. Nor is it profitable for management companies to manage single-tenant residences. If the property manager charged a fee based on his costs, you would have little income from your investment. Sometimes however real estate brokerage firms that have house resale departments will provide some property management service at a very modest price in the hope of getting the listing on the house when you decide to sell. Management of single-family dwellings also helps brokerage firms in prospecting for house buyers. Generally the brokers will collect the rents and provide some minor management services, such as ordering repairs and accounting. If the fee is modest, you would not expect them to spend time away from their offices and personally show the properties to prospective tenants.

Most investors who buy houses collect the rents themselves. They also order the repairs, do the accounting, and perform a multitude of other property-management services, thus saving the fee for professional management. In fact they are in the property-management business, at least on a part-time basis.

Some investors have found houses to be investments sufficiently attractive to employ staff personnel to aid in the management of the properties. Business owners occasionally borrow staff from their own businesses.

Maintenance and repairs on rental houses can be expensive items if one calls in skilled workmen for every job. Plumbing and electrical repairs are expensive. Painting and gardening contractors generally have lower rates. But calling in a contractor for every job would lead you to believe that you are in business for the benefit of the contractors which frequently seems to be the case.

Investors who can also double as mechanics (performing the work of the contractors) can save a great deal of money. They find being a do-it-yourselfer for their own investments to be a profitable part-time business.

Investors in rental houses will find that the cash they save by doing the work themselves adds up to a substantial portion of the cash flow. If you do all the property management, repair, and maintenance yourself, the results of the investment will appear quite attractive because they will include the "business" income that was saved by not paying for the property-management and contractor services.

THE REWARDS

The rewards of investing in rental houses include the opportunity to retain more of the gross income by performing yourself the property management, maintenance, and repair services.

In addition it is an excellent way to learn about real

estate investments because most houses have wide enough markets to enable investors to know the value of what they are buying. An investor can shop the market and see enough sales of comparable property to be able to get into an investment and out of it without the high hazard of having overpaid, or undersold, or having picked a loser. You may also be able to evaluate the physical characteristics of the house and lot by taking into account the same criteria you would use in selecting your own home.

The forms of benefit from investing in real estate are: cash flow, tax shelter, and proceeds of sale.

Cash Flow

The cash flow benefit is generally negligible in single-family rental properties and may even be negative. It is very small because the price of a home is usually high relative to the rent. An old rule of thumb was that a house would sell for 100 times its monthly rental. For example a house that rents for $240 a month might sell for $24,000. In recent years it seems that the price of the house is greater relative to the rent. For example a house that rents for $300 per month might sell for 120 times its monthly rental, or a sales price of $36,000. There are some houses that sell for 150 times the monthly rental. Usually this occurs where there is not much of a rental market and the house is expensive. You can estimate the prevailing gross-rent multiplier for the type of house and location in which you are interested by checking with various real estate brokers, owners, sellers, and tenants and by computing the ratios for a number of sales. You will conclude that the higher the monthly rent multiplier (ratio of sales price to monthly rent), the more difficult it is to get a substantial cash flow. And in recent years, the multipliers have become exceptionally high.

The amount of the mortgage and the monthly payment are significant determinants of the cash flow. Since the security for the mortgage usually includes the borrower's unequivocal promise to pay, as well as the pledge of the property, and since the borrower's earning ability in itself is generally sufficient to pay the mortgage, the loan-to-value ratio can be very high. Conventional loans (those not guaranteed by VA or insured by FHA) can be for 75, 80, or even 90% of the value. Under VA and FHA if the loan was originally acquired by an owner-occupant, the ratio could be up to 100% of the sales price; that is a lot of leverage.

The level of expense is also important in determining the cash flow. Much of the cash flow is frequently attributable to owner-investors performing their own property management and maintenance services.

Many investors in houses are satisfied to have little or no cash flow from the property because they have put up very little cash and need not pay out a lot for services to operate and maintain the property. If you buy a house with a $1000 down payment, rent it out, manage it, and make minor repairs yourself, do not bother to calculate the COD (cash on the down payment) because the percentage is a meaningless figure. If you are able to get a positive cash flow, you are doing well because the cash flow is only a significant benefit in rental houses when you have a high equity. Table 10 shows a sample cash flow for a rental house.

Tax Shelter

The tax shelter of a rental situation is appealing. The depreciation usually exceeds the amortization if you buy a house whose lot is not of high value and where you use a mortgage with a long term to repay. Under most conditions you could get relatively high tax shelter per dollar invested. You would however have to amass numerous houses in order to get a substantial dollar amount of tax shelter. If you need the benefit of shelter and have the capital for numerous houses, you should consider rental

Table 10   Sample Cash Flow for a Rental House

Rental income		
$150 per month × 12 months		$1800
Expenses		
Taxes	$ 250	
Insurance	30	
Utilities	100	
Maintenance and repair	100	
Other	20	
Total expenses before interest and depreciation	$ 500	
Mortgage payments		
$14,000 payable $100 per month including interest@ 7% per annum	$1200	
Total cash expenditure		$1700
Cash flow		$ 100

houses. But unless you are able to handle the management problems involved in the "business" of owning rental houses, consider investing in apartment buildings. Table 11 shows a sample of a tax shelter for a rental house.

Proceeds of Sale

The third benefit, proceeds of sale, is where the profit is in rental houses—that is when there is a profit.

You will recall that proceeds of sale are determined by the sales price, less expenses of sale, less debt. There are some investors in rental houses who hold them for 10 years or more and are able to get the benefits of proceeds of sale because of amortization of the mortgage. If the price of the house holds up, a steady reduction of the mortgage will ultimately bring substantial proceeds of sale. This investment strategy is sound if your objective is to buy a management and repair business and if you want to build up equity that will ultimately provide a cash flow. However this strategy is not the best if you are a high-income business or professional man with a tax problem, since you would not have enough benefits from amortization to warrant your time and effort. After approximately 8 years, depending on your depreciation and amortization schedules, taxable income from the property would be higher than the cash flow.

The strategy suitable to most investors is one that is based on a projected increase in the price of the house. As an investor in rental houses, you must get this rapid increase, if much benefit is to accrue to you. This worked well for many investors in many areas over the last decade.

A rapid increase means a sharp rise in price over a short period of time. You should look for a house that might appreciate substantially over a three year period. You could get lucky through spurts in prices over a

Table 11   Sample Tax Shelter for Rental House

Rental income (assume no vacancy)		$1800
Expenses		
Expenses other than interest and depreciation	$500	
Interest (0.07 × $14,000)	980	
Depreciation		
Improvement $15,000		
Remaining useful life, 25 years, depreciation rate 4%		
125% straight-line rate, 5%		
$15,000 × 0.05	750	
Total expenses		$2230
Net income (loss)		($ 430)

shorter period of time, but if you have to wait for more than five years, your average annual rate of return will be modest.

Most of the price rises occur because of inflation and because the value of the land changes. The change in the value of the building is modest. Of prime importance to the value of the house is its physical characteristics, which affect its marketability. If your intent is to invest as a hedge against inflation, then the house is a good vehicle for borrowing.

The greatest profit potential lies in selecting a house in a location that will improve. The extent of the land appreciation will govern whether your investment was mediocre or excellent.

SELECTING THE RENTAL HOUSE

The key considerations in selecting the rental house are location and timing. You need to get in at the very early stages of a boom in housing demand or inflation. If the market shows signs of weakening—postpone your investment in rental houses. You have a better bet at the end of a stagnant period than at the end of a boom. If you buy with a low "potential" at a low price, time should save your investment. If you buy at high prices and a high potential does not materialize, time hurts you. Your timing should place you in a position where time can help you.

As for location, start with the city. The city should have a growing employment rate and rising incomes. The rise in price will materialize because of the increasing demand for the housing by people coming into the city. Unless you live in a rapidly growing city, there is relatively little opportunity in rental housing for short-term investments.

A city does not grow evenly. The relative price rise of houses is greater where the affluent live than where the poor live. Thus you need to identify (relative to the price of housing that is being bought by new employees coming to town) the better sections of the city that are in the path of city growth. This should be locations that have not yet "arrived." They may be a little far out; the roads may need widening; the shopping centers may not yet have developed; the amenities that give the location value have not been provided yet—but they will be coming.

Within this location you look for neighborhoods that are attractive. The lot size and shape should be suitable to the kind of usage you require. In rental houses forget the unusual—you need marketability: easy to get in, easy to get out.

The house itself should also have a popular style, floor plan, and other features. You need not find something you would like to live in, but it must be something you believe other people would want to live in. If it has problems, or makes you feel uncomfortable, do not buy. Stay objective, but also trust your own feelings. Many investors have bought a "dog" because they were told "the house in not for you to live in, it is just for investment."

TOWNHOUSES

Townhouses refer to a physical type of structure. Essentially, townhouses are single-family dwellings that are built by using one or two walls in common with one or two contiguous single-family dwellings. In earlier years we had row houses in which there would be an entire block of houses in which each had two walls in common with the adjacent structure, except of course for the end units. Typically they were all set back from the street the same distance.

Townhouses, by way of contrast, run usually in clusters of 6 to 10 units (more or less) with variations in the setbacks (distance from the house to the front of the lot). This breaks up the monotony of the elevations (fronts). What we have to say about townhouses also applies to buying a single unit in a larger cluster, whether it be semidetached or a "plex" unit of some sort (usually one of three or four units).

Because of the rising costs of home ownership, especially land and interest costs, people have had to economize on housing. One way of economizing is to use less land. Townhouses and plex units do exactly that. A detached single-family dwelling may use a quarter, half, or full acre, or even more. But one can get 6, 8, or even 10 units to the acre (instead of 4 or less) by using semidetached units or townhouses.

The marketability of these units is generally not as good as the marketability of single-family detached dwellings because most people would prefer the detached dwelling. However it has been much easier to supply units at the price the mass market demands using townhouses and plex units. While some investors have done well with these units, you should make exceptionally careful evaluations of the competition and the potential competition.

Investment in these units does have an advantage over the investment in detached dwellings. Maintenance and management may be easier. Maintenance is less because physically there is less to maintain. Furthermore under some arrangements there may be common management of exterior space for all the units. One has to pay for this, but it does mean less time to spend in the day-to-day management of the investment.

The form of management may be through a property owners' association, which levies assessments against the owners. There are however other choices, One is cooperative ownership, which is currently not very popular. It serves the same purpose as condominiums, but the form of ownership is different and it usually applies to owner-occupied property. It is not a likely prospect for the investor.

The condominium is a form of ownership discussed in

the next section. Some townhouses and most plex units are owned as condominiums, rather than as structures on separate lots. In these cases the manager for the condominium association takes care of external maintenance and the common facilities, which really makes it easier on the investor.

CONDOMINIUMS

A condominium is a form of ownership not a physical type of property such as a detached single-family dwelling townhouse or garden apartment. Many condominiums however are of apartment-type construction. The basic physical difference between such units and traditional apartments is that such apartments are usually better equipped, or otherwise more desirable as housing, than the rental unit counterpart. Some apartment units have been converted from rental units to condominiums, for sale to owner occupants. During the conversion process most were upgraded substantially. Some of the new owners rent them out.

Other "condos" are office condos and even warehouses. Any place a builder or converter sees a market for ownership of individual units at prices higher than could be obtained on a pro rata share of owning the entire complex, there will be pressure for construction or conversion. It would follow that ownership for rental income is more profitable in the case of the larger scale project than in the case of the individual units. Investors in condominiums then should look for quick appreciation if they expect to get high rewards for investing.

Some condominiums are second-home condos. Investment in those is somewhat similar to investing in a second home, which is occasionally rented out. One difference is that the management of the seasonal rentals and the maintenance may be taken care of, for a fee, by a management company that handles many similar rentals.

The investor really has to get substantial appreciation or a substantial off-season use to make out on such investments. The big disadvantage, compared to other investment property, is that there are limitations in getting tax shelter for properties that are occupied by the owners from time to time.

USING LEVERAGE

The assumed objective of investing in rental houses or other individual rental units, is the potential of short-term appreciation. If this is the objective, you need to use mostly borrowed money.

The high-leveraged investment may be obtained by the use of several financing devices. One of the most popular is to take over a VA or FHA mortgage already on the unit. If the former owner has put in very little cash, you may be able to buy with a low down payment. If he has a substantial equity, you might buy with 10% down and give him a purchase money mortgage for the balance. This would be a second mortgage or a second deed of trust.

Under such circumstances you might take title subject to the existing first mortgage (or trust) and use a purchase money mortgage or (deferred trust) without (in some circumstances) personal liability for the balance. You could thus avoid personal liability for the mortgage if you have made a poor investment and decided to give it up.

If the property had a conventional mortgage at a low interest rate and was of reasonable loan-to-value ratio, you might just keep it on the property and give back the seller a second mortgage or trust. In many cases the loan may require lender approval of the buyers, which will not be given unless the interest rate is increased. If the existing mortgage balance is low, relative to the purchase price, or if the monthly payments are high, it may be desirable to get a new first mortgage.

The costs of a new first mortgage can be high in periods of tight money. You should be careful about the terms to which you agree when taking out a new mortgage or in taking over an existing mortgage. If the costs are very high, they may be too high to make the investment profitable.

As an alternative in buying with the use of a mortgage, you could use an agreement that is called a land contract or contract for deed. The use of this device varies from state to state. In essence you enter into an agreement to buy, put up part of the purchase price, agree to pay the balance, and take possession. However you do not get title until you pay all or a predetermined portion of the purchase price. The seller, still having title, can keep the old mortgage or get a new one. You could take title when you were ready to negotiate a new mortgage or take over the old mortgage. You could thus wait until you were ready to sell and have the new purchaser obtain his or her own mortgage.

The disadvantage of using the land contract is that you do not have the same protection as if you took title. However if you use the land contract, you may find many sellers who will sell with very little down payment, 5 to 10%. You may also want to use this method when you want to sell.

You may find that down payment of anywhere between 10 and 25% will be required for rental houses. If you are ready to buy at foreclosure sales, or from the VA or FHA, and do some rehabilitation, you could find yourself in another business. The rehabilitation business may be coupled with owning rental houses, but it usually requires quite different financing.

SPECIAL RISKS

If you own one rental house and have one vacancy, your vacancy rate is 100%—and that hurts the cash flow. You must expect with one house that from time to time you will have a 100% vacancy, so plan for it by keeping reserve cash. You should have the willingness, as well as the ability to keep up the payments when a vacancy occurs or you will be disappointed with your investment experience. You could of course buy two, three, or four houses to reduce the relative loss from a single vacancy. But the more houses you have, the more running around town you will be doing. You can take on a couple or a few houses in your spare time as a hobby, but for more than a few, the time requirement can be overwhelming.

With one or two houses the costs of mismanagement are relatively small. If you have many houses and you or your manager make mistakes, it may be very expensive. Poor selection of tenants can be costly. You can bear some excessive costs as part of developing experience, but a heavy commitment to a new business should be made only with some professional help.

Personal involvement with the tenants may develop because of the business relationship. Inability of tenants to pay or unwillingness to increase rents can of course influence investment results.

You may protect yourself from the personal liabilities of personal injury associated with ownership by using liability insurance. These hazards are risks ordinarily encountered in business and should be treated as such.

GETTING OUT

Getting out can be easy if you have a marketable house and pick the right time. In your investment program you should have some time horizon for getting out.

One way out is all cash. Pay your income taxes and start on the next venture. (See Table 12.)

Another way out is to sell with the low down payment, defer some of your income taxes, and get a high price by selling with good terms. (See Table 13.) You will then have

**Table 12   Sample Proceeds of Sale on a
Rented House (Sale for All Cash)**

Sale price		$22,000
Costs of sale		
Commission	$ 1,320	
Other costs	430	1,750
Net price		$20,250
Cost		
Improvements	$15,000	
Less depreciation	1,750	
	13,250	
Plus land	3,000	16,250
Taxable gain		$ 4,000
Taxes (assume)	$ 1,000	
Proceeds of sale		
Net price	$20,250	
Less mortgage	$13,550	
Pretax proceeds	$ 6,700	
Less income taxes	$ 1,000	
After-tax proceeds	$ 5,700	
Less seller's initial		
down payment		3,000
Net profit, after taxes, aside from		
cash flow		$ 2,700
After-tax proceeds, net proceeds		
in cash		$ 5,700

a second mortgage or trust. You could sell the second mortgage or trust, but at a discount; or you can keep it for income or perhaps even use it as part of a down payment on another purchase.

Table 13   Sale for Low Down Payment

Sale price		
Down payment	$ 2,500	
New first mortgage	18,000	
Carry-back second mortgage	2,500	
		$23,000
Sales price		$23,000
Cost of sale		
Commission	$ 1,380	
Other costs	470	
		1,850
Net price		$21,150
Cost		
Improvements	$15,000	
Less depreciation	1,750	
	13,250	
Plus land	3,000	
		16,250
Taxable gain		$ 4,900
Taxes (assume)	$ 1,225	
Proceeds of sale		
Net price	$21,150	
Less mortgage	13,550	
Pretax proceeds	$ 7,600	
Less income taxes	1,225	
After-tax proceeds		$6,375
Less seller's initial		
down payment		3,000
Net profit, after taxes, aside		
from cash flow		3,375
After-tax proceeds		
Carry-back second mortgage	$ 2,500	
Cash	$ 3,875	
		$ 6,375

SMALL APARTMENT BUILDINGS: DUPLEXES, TRIPLEXES, FOUR- AND SIX-UNIT BUILDINGS

One of the disadvantages of owning several or more rental houses is the time it takes to go to each of the properties. An investor finds it much easier if the several properties are located in the same neighborhood, preferably on the same block.

If the rental houses are next to each other or on the same lot, you have a management situation similar to having a duplex (two-unit building), triplex (three units), or even a six-unit building. Many investors own rental duplexes or four-family flats and thereby cluster the location of their rental units.

A popular way of avoiding the problem of being away from the rental property is to have a property with one unit for the owner and the others for tenants. Many of the two-, three-, and four-unit buildings have a resident owner. Some of the newer buildings are even designed to have a more spacious owner's unit. There are also a few larger apartment buildings containing eight or more units that have an owner's apartment.

There are some advantages to this type of investment. The investor-manager lives on the premises, and does not lose any time traveling to the rental units. When needed on the premises to rent it, it just means staying home. Gardening and other maintenance is almost as though it were for a single-family home, except there is more of it.

There are some disadvantages. For one thing living next door to a tenant makes the owner quite accessible for requests for service. Also the dual role of landlord and neighbor sometimes provides discomfort in personal relationships.

The investment characteristics of a two-to-six-unit building differ, depending on whether the owner resides on the premises or elsewhere. When the owner lives in one unit, there is the assurance that at least one unit is occupied. When the owner lives on the premises, there are some efficiencies in management. On the other hand absentee ownership is similar to owning a cluster of rental houses.

BENEFITS

Ownership of real estate is prestigious. Ownership of high-rent property is very prestigious. It is only the ownership of slum property that has negative amenities.

Most investors find their pride of ownership increased if others know that they own property and if they own a little more property than their friends and neighbors do. Thus being a resident owner of a small apartment building has status in that neighborhood. It may mean little elsewhere, but it is an amentity that is worth something to many prople.

The pride of ownership also exists in absentee ownership of property. The owner's status is then related to the quality of the property and/or tenancy. Frequently the greater the pride of ownership, the lower the financial returns. This is so because status properties cost more to buy and to maintain. However when the time to sell arrives, there are seemingly more buyers for the "better" properties.

Another benefit is the opportunity to practice nepotism. A relative may be favored by being given the position of resident manager. Ownership of real estate requires spending money—much of it for jobs that you could have some relative do. Such help can be especially convenient in buildings with many apartments.

Cash flow benefits would be small, in typically financed situations, if the owners paid for all property-management and maintenance services. Since in most cases the owner performs these services himself, the cash flow may be substantial. There is no point in computing a COD ratio if the owner is performing these services. The COD is meaningful if you deduct an imputed value of the services. The COD computed as though you paid for all services in cash would be lower, maybe 6 or

7% on a typically financed property by historical standards. At today's prices it could be 4 or 5%.

The tax shelter benefit to be derived from owning a
small apartment house is good. Generally the more apartment units you have, the more value there is in the
building, rather than in the land. Since you can
depreciate the building and not the land, you would for
tax shelter purposes prefer to have most of the investment in a depreciable asset, such as a building. Furthermore if you furnish the apartments, you can depreciate
the furniture over a short period of time and thus obtain
high depreciation allowances.

Resident-owners frequently obtain relatively high
loans on their smaller apartment houses. If the property
is heavily financed, the tax shelter may be quite attractive. The proceeds of sale are frequently a major benefit.
The market for these smaller properties is generally quite
wide. Thus if your timing and financing are right, you can
sell to optimistic purchasers at prices much higher than
the buyer would be justified in paying on a long-term investment basis. One indication of appropriate timing is illustrated in the rents. If the rental market has been
strong and rising, the price you could obtain should be
high. If on the other hand the general level of rents is not
rising, prices will not rise. If you are faced with rising
taxes and replacements of equipment, your potential cash
flow will be impaired and your proceeds of sale will be
low because of the low price.

Real estate taxes are a substantial portion of the expenses on a real estate investment—and the property
taxes have been rising. If your locality shows little
responsibility in fiscal matters, you may find rising taxes
burdensome.

As for replacement expenses, they do happen. The
AMAD side of the pyramid (Chapter 6) described how
deterioration and obsolescence occur as the property
ages. In estimating your cash flow you probably did not

include the cost of major replacements—you hoped the next owner would pay for them. When the time comes, you will either have to make these replacements or the need for them will be reflected in the sales price, thus lowering the proceeds of sale.

SELECTING THE PROPERTY

Resident-owners should select a property the way they would select a home. The price that they are justified in paying is another matter, but the characteristics should reflect their own needs and preferences in a residence.

The space and facilities of the owner's unit are a usual place to start. The number of bedrooms and bathrooms is of prime importance. So are the size of the kitchen, the eating area, and the service facilities since you may rightly expect many of the amenities of a house. The basic requirement should be sufficient for six to eight years, unless you plan to become an absentee owner. In some markets you could sell your house every four years, but your commitments in income property should be based on a longer period of time.

In selecting small apartment buildings in which you will occupy one unit, you are also selecting tenants and neighbors. If you would not be satisfied with the tenants as neighbors, do not buy the building. You could change the tenants—but it is expensive and you cannot be sure that the new tenants will be any better.

The neighborhood is equally important. Your biggest benefit may be proceeds of sale—if you select the right neighborhood. If the neighborhood seems to be on the way down, forget it. Look for a location that is attractive to you and has accessibility to schools, shopping facilities, transportation, or whatever community facilities you need for a suitable residence.

If you will be an absentee owner, you should use the

standards of the typical occupant. It will pay you to talk to tenants in similar properties in order to get an idea of their standards.

LOCATION AND DESIGN

As we have seen much of the cash benefit in property ownership derives from the owner doing his own property management and maintenance. Substantial tax shelter benefits can occur, but you must have a winner, or the depreciation you took may turn out to have been real—in the economic sense.

To obtain the most benefits you need the proceeds of sale and that means you need a good market. Aside from the general timing of sale and sale financing, you must have a design that is attractive and will remain attractive so that you will have a strong market. But most importantly, you need location.

If you find a location in the direction of the city's growth, a location that is being upgraded or is developing, you will have an opportunity to make large profits because your rents will rise and your property will increase in value. In the selection of an income-property investment, start by looking for the "right" location.

FINANCING

Owner occupants of single-family houses get the best mortgage terms because they can repay the loan out of their income and the property is an added security. Owner-occupants of several rental units on a single parcel of land can still obtain good mortgage terms as long as their ability to pay is strong relative to the obligation. Loans on duplexes, triplexes, and four-family flats are evaluated in much the same way as loans on single-family residences. However when there are very many units, the owner's ability to pay becomes much less important than the income-producing ability of the real estate.

With a high loan-to-value ratio, you can obtain the leverage necessary to get the maximum tax shelter for each dollar invested and hopefully high proceeds of sale relative to your initial investment. Realizing this brokers have convinced sellers to carry back a second mortgage or trust so that the purchase can be made with as little as a 10% down payment. To avoid a very small, or negative, cash flow, the seller may agree to interest only for five years and then a balloon payment (the unpaid balance becomes due and payable). This type of financing has too much risk for someone who wants to buy a home with a few rental units, unless ready cash reserves are available to make the balloon payment when it comes due.

For the investor who wants high leverage, a fully amortizing second mortgage as well as a fully amortizing first mortgage is more suitable. The payments on the second trust may be at a 12% annual constant, but the hazard of the balloon is gone.

The operating statement that you will usually see is woefully inadequate. It tends to omit fees for management and makes little, if any, allowance for maintenance and repairs. Expenses are likely to be higher than anticipated in the operating statement. Unless given careful study, highly leveraged properties may show negative cash flows very quickly. Even with conservatively financed property, there is the hazard of underestimated expenses. Make some reasonable allowances for variations in income and expense and then consider the debt service. You should have enough cash left over to carry the property with substantial variation in income and expense. If you are able to carry the property until the mortgages are paid off, you will have a profitable investment.

The ability to carry the property until you decide it is time to sell is heavily determined by:

1. Rental income associated with variations in the market.

2. Expenses, which are related to quality and condition of the building.
3. Debt service, which is related to the amount of the loan and terms of repayment.

If you borrow too much, but can eventually repay it, you will be safe. But if you borrow too much because you paid too high a price and then cannot service the debt, you could obviously have difficulty.

CONCLUSIONS

Smaller apartment buildings, although not the most profitable investments, are attractive first ventures, especially for those who will live in one of the apartments. It is a good way to get started in real estate investing.

Many of the more experienced advanced investors buy garden-apartment projects that have a greater number of rental units per project. The advantages of these larger rental properties are discussed in the next chapter.

12 GARDEN APARTMENTS

Residential income property is the most popular type of real estate investment for the individual investor. This popularity is assisted by the rules of the IRS which permit accelerated depreciation. More importantly however, the vast majority of real estate investors find that residential income property has the kinds of risks and rewards that best meet their investment objectives.

You have probably made an investment in at least one residential income property or are planning such an investment. You will probably be comfortable with an investment in the kind of real estate with which you already have some familiarity. Since we all use housing and have made housing decisions, we know something about it. But we also know that providing housing for others is a business.

A typical garden apartment structure would be a two-story building of frame and stucco or brick construction. The floors would be supported by wood joists, except possibly for a concrete slab on the ground floor. The apartments would have outside entrances and there would be no elevator. Only a small part of the land area would be covered with buildings, so that there would be a considerable amount of open space. There are many properties that by the strictest of definitions would not qualify as garden apartments, but have similar investment characteristics.

In varying degrees our discussion of garden apartments includes one-, three-, and even four-story structures; masonry and concrete structures; and buildings with hallway entrances. The discussion even covers buildings in a high-density land-use pattern with less open space. For simplicity apartment buildings are being divided into two groups: garden apartments and high-rise apartments. Any hybrids and variations are discussed as special cases of either of these categories.

Families need a place in which to live and they spend a large part of their income for housing and related amenities. Housing is expensive because land in urban areas is expensive and construction costs are high. The easiest way to reduce land costs per housing unit is to put more housing units on a parcel of land. As far as construction costs are concerned, this works fine until the only way left to put more housing units on the land is to stack them higher. If they are stacked more than a few stories high, the type of construction has to change and the construction cost rises sharply. The second easiest way to reduce per unit housing cost is to put a few units together, using common walls as in row houses; to build a second floor; or both. Thus town houses, the modern version of the old row house, reduce per unit land costs and some construction costs by using one or two common walls. A garden-apartment type of construction is an even better way of keeping housing costs low.

The fact that garden-apartments can provide more housing per dollar of cost than the other types of rental housing (such as single-family dwellings or high-rise buildings) is important to the investor because it means that the rental market for garden apartments is very broad. In real estate, as in other investments, the broader the market for the product or service, the safer the market. The so-called "bread and butter" investments will always rent, because at modest rental levels there are many tenants in need of housing. It is important to be in a well-located neighborhood and in a growing city. Under these circumstances the demand keeps getting stronger.

Another reason why garden apartments are popular

among investors is that they generally afford substantial depreciation in relation to the total cost or purchase price of the investment. This is so because the land costs or values (which *cannot* be depreciated) are generally low in relation to the cost of the improvements (which are depreciable). For example the construction of a development of 100 garden apartments in a suburban area might cost approximately $24,000 per unit. The land cost would be approximately $4000 per unit. Both costs combined would amount to approximately $28,000, for a total cost of $2.8 million. The *ratio* of improvements (the building) to land would be $24,000 to $4,000, or 6 to 1. An office building in the same area might show a maximum ratio of 3 to 1, and a medium-size shopping center a ratio of 2 to 1. The higher the ratio of improvements to land, the more depreciation is possible. Thus it is no wonder that many investors who seek tax shelter prefer investing in garden apartments.

The market for property services, that is the rental market, being strong, and the market for garden-apartment investments also being strong, it is understandable that investors bid up the price of such properties. The prices get bid up so high that the profits here are lower than in most other real estate investments. You may nevertheless be interested in garden apartments because they have the kinds of risks you are prepared to take and still offer sufficient benefits.

Occasionally you will see what is called a "medium-rise" apartment. This has many of the features of a garden apartment, but is usually from four to six stories tall. It may have many of the same construction features, such as wood-joist construction, but is equipped with an elevator. These apartments have somewhat higher rents than the garden apartment, but do not generally cater to a significantly different market from that using comparable space in garden apartments. As a result maintenance costs are equally high and frequently higher. The type of elevators used generally are not the same as in high-rise buildings. They are mostly of the hydraulic type, which are quite slow, and most are hor-rendously noisy compared to their speedier and quieter counterparts in much taller buildings.

Medium-rise apartments appear in some areas where a higher density of land use is permitted by the local authorities. Yet land-use restrictions as to setbacks of front and rear as well as side yard requirements force the developers to go up instead of sideways, and thus these hybrids appear. The medium-rise elevators beats climbing stairs, which is a major objection to garden apartments of the three-story type.

The medium-rise buildings tend to create a greater pride of ownership in a new investor and they somehow seem to have a "better look" than most of the typical garden apartments. Economic benefits of ownership may be as good or better in these units as in comparable garden apartments in the same area, although the risks are higher.

MANAGEMENT

The first job of management is to sell the use of space and keep it sold. This means renting apartments and keeping them rented. If you are going to buy an apartment building, or an interest in one, you want to know how dif-ficult this job is going to be. If there are plenty of apart-ments standing vacant, forget it. That is no time to go into business, unless you have some very special condi-tions.

If the apartment building has a good occupancy ex-perience, then you could be interested. Good occupancy means that the rents collected amount to 95% of the scheduled gross income. Vacancy and collection losses might be less than 5% in some prime properties in very good markets or where management has failed to raise rents to keep them in line with the rising rents of the com-petition. A vacancy and collection loss of 10% might not be too bad at the right time. For example a purchase in the mid-sixties at prices that reflect high vacancies coupled with ensuing tight money, which choked off competition, provided some excellent results. It is necessary however to have the conditions that in fact reduce the vacancies and increase the rents.

You should review the rental records of the apartment building or otherwise assure yourself that satisfactory rents will be forthcoming. It is a relatively simple matter to shop the market by going to see the vacant apartments of the competition and making discreet inquiries of the resident managers.

The resident manager takes care of the day-to-day operation of the property, which includes showing apartments to prospective tenants. Professional property management is the top administrative level and provides supervision of the resident managers. You will find that checking the market with a knowledgable professional property manager will help you to evaluate the property's rental potential and will facilitate your subsequent investment decision.

Many real estate investors act as property managers for the property they own. In some parts of the country there are many garden apartment properties, with 12 to 20 units, in which the owner is the property manager, sometimes also the resident manager.

Some investors own a number of separate smaller (12 to 20 units) garden-apartment properties and spend a large portion of their time taking care of their investments. A few investors put the bulk of their real estate investment funds in a single large garden-apartment property and spend their time managing that investment as their business.

The trend toward large-scale projects (50 to 100 units or more) has stimulated the use of professional property managers. Some developers put together a syndicate to build garden-apartment projects (large and small) and retain the right to manage it until sold. They could, when the time came, sell small projects to buyers who would want to take over the management themselves. There are a great many such investors for the 12-to-20-unit building because there are a lot of people that have $20,000, $30,000, and even $50,000 or more to invest in real estate. But with the trend toward large projects, professional management of residential real estate takes on an increase in its relative role. Most of these developments are managed by professional property managers under the supervision of an individual who has been awarded the CPM designation by the Institute of Real Estate Management.

Providing the services to the tenant to keep him as a tenant and keeping the expenses in line require a high degree of professional competence. A CPM, or other competent property manager, can help you in evaluating the potential income and expenses and can provide some guidance in ascertaining the quality of the building. Although you can get equally good advice from well-qualified appraisers and other professionals in the field, your decision to invest in garden apartments may be heavily predicted on the cash flow you believe competent management will produce.

The professional property manager knows how to advertise your property as well as what services you will have to provide to keep your property rented. These may include facilities for laundering clothes and recreation (including swimming) as well as the usual hall cleaning, trash removal, exterminating, repairs, painting, and grounds-keeping services. These are by no means all the services ownership is required to render in order to remain competitive. You or your manager need to know comparable rent structures and changes in other apartment projects in order to strike that delicate balance between maximum occupancy and minimum turnover. There is no doubt that the quality of management shows both in the physical appearance of the property and in the cash flow statement.

So diverse are management services that management organizations frequently have large staffs with individual specialists among them. In large projects it is fairly rare for an owner to perform management services himself. The rates charged for professional management vary widely among localities. Some management firms charge as little as 2.5% of the gross income, others charge up to 7%. Most firms vary the amount charged, depending on the number of units in a single development and on the rentals charged.

If you employ a property management firm, the professional property manager will supervise the resident manager as well as take care of the other activities. Property managers can be more efficient if they have several properties to supervise in one general area. Thus field time is limited to a little over one half of their working day. the remainder of their time is spent in the central office—buying, answering complaints, solving problems, reviewing bills, approving payrolls, and occasionally conferring with the owners.

With only a part of their time available for field work, their travel time to each project is an important consideration. Your property will cost more to supervise if it is not reasonably close to other properties being supervised by the manager. It follows that the property may be more effectively supervised if it has more units. Supervision of a 50-unit project is not much different from supervision of a 200-unit project.

Central office bookkeeping is frequently broken down by unit cost. Whether by hand posting, bookkeeping machines, or computer, the costs are generally computed by rental unit. If the average monthly rental in an apartment development is $100 and the central office monthly cost of supervision, record keeping, and reports to owners is $5, the project will be a breakeven proposition to the management company at 5%. Naturally no management company can make a profit on this basis. This is why smaller units with lower monthly rentals can sometimes cost as much as 7% or more of the gross income to manage.

Assuming a unit cost to management of $5 monthly, a large building of 400 units can be profitably managed by professional management at only 3% of rents if the average rentals are $200 monthly. Management can earn $1 each for each apartment managed if its commissions are $6 monthly and its costs are $5.

It is important to remember that the larger properties with higher average rents can be professionally managed at a lower unit cost, which means more cash flow to the owners. Some owners of smaller properties do not understand the "unit" cost accounting system employed by most professional management firms and believe there is an inequity in fees charged by management companies. The simple fact is that the owner of smaller projects buys himself a management job. In some areas the smaller projects are managed at cost or below cost rates because of heavy competition for the related brokerage business.

It is traditional in the real estate management industry to charge fees on a percentage of rents charged. A more recent practice, which is gaining popularity, is to charge a fixed fee on a per unit basis, rather than a fixed percentage of rents collected. In larger cities professional management of large low-income properties is frequently contracted on a fixed annual charge without relation to gross income or percentage fees. There may be a boom ahead in moderate income housing. If you invest in it you may well be contracting for management on the fixed fee basis. When buying any property, large or small, it is wise to determine in advance who is going to manage it and at what fee.

BENEFITS

Cash Flow

Cash flows are probably lowest in apartment projects, compared to office buildings, shopping-centers, or industrial and special-purpose income-producing real estate. However assuming a reasonable equity, a loan of not more than 75% of value (loan-to-value ratio), and reasonably sound construction, apartment ownership acquired at the proper place in the pyramid will produce a substantially more stable cash flow than other forms of realty ownership. You get less cash flow in garden apartments than in other investment property because everyone wants the stable cash flow and the market price for properties is bid up accordingly.

The large projects may produce large cash flows because the markets are not so wide in the larger projects as in the smaller ones. Also the per unit operating costs are lower because of the economies of scale in operating the property. You can for example double the number of units without doubling the maintenance or management costs.

Large apartments frequently have some built-in competitive advantages. Many amenities found in the larger projects are not available to tenants in smaller units, as their initial cost or lack of space preclude their inclusion in smaller developments. Swimming pools; tennis courts; putting greens; well equipped playgrounds; recreation rooms featuring table tennis, billiards, and soda bars; and staffed nursery schools are simply out of the question for the smaller apartment projects. These facilities and a lower per unit construction cost make large projects relatively more profitable to build and operate. The result is that the larger the project, the more cash flow you can reasonably expect.

With the obvious advantages of owning larger projects, do small investors have a chance in apartments? They have excellent opportunities. But they must be willing to assume the burden of professional management and must sometimes act as resident managers with the associated responsibilities of doing some maintenance themselves, or at least providing the supervision. Many owners, otherwise professionally occupied, employ their sons or other relatives in many management and maintenance functions. Some owners invest in numerous small projects and thereby develop substantial business opportunities for themselves, their relatives, and their friends.

What about small investors who have neither the time nor the inclination to perform management services, but still want the safety associated with apartment ownership? They can buy small projects and pay for these services, but the cash flow will be low. Or they can buy an interest in large projects that are professionally managed. Later chapters discuss group ownership and getting into larger investments.

The smaller garden apartment projects provide excellent opportunities for short-term investments. So some investors trade in the market and move up. They are willing to accept the lower cash flow and use the investment as an excellent way to build up equity while gaining investment experience.

Tax Shelter

As already mentioned, since considerably more of the cost or value is in the building than in the land, the tax shelter is normally greater in garden apartments than in other types of income-producing property. Therefore investment in garden-apartment projects offers excellent tax shelter opportunities.

If you are the original owner or part of a group who is the initial owner of a newly constructed residential property, you can under the law that exists at this writing use the double declining (200%) method of depreciation. This enhances your tax shelter possibilities substantially. If the project has been previously owned, the 125% declining balance method of depreciation is available as long as property has a useful life of 20 years or more.

As in all forms of realty depreciation, the amounts of annual depreciation taken must be related to the "useful life" of the structure. If you cannot be the original owner, the maximum depreciation can be obtained by acquiring older properties with shorter useful economic lives.

Older properties have greater risks (see Chapter 6), but the rewards, especially relating to tax shelter, are rather attractive. Financing and refinancing of older properties is much more difficult and frequently more expensive compared to newer properties. This may have a tendency to diminish some of the tax shelter because lenders normally expect (and get) faster amortization from loans on older properties.

For income tax purposes a generally safe way to allocate the cost of the purchase between land and building is to use the same ratio as does the local tax assessor. Since the tax assessor is not concerned with what you are doing in calculating your income tax, his appraisal may be taken as objective.

A frequent trap fallen into by even some highly sophisticated investors is to become overly enamored with depreciation and tax shelter. They "need depreciation," they say. All the taxation gymnastics available, and there are many, cannot succeed without a solid evaluation of the property and its present and future profit-making potential. Yet upon discovering the fact that depreciation in a garden development may not only develop cash flow that is not immediately taxable, but also may even develop losses to offset their other income, they sometimes go strangely berserk. They think they have discovered love!

There is a fine market for the sale and resale of apartment projects. Because this is so and the depreciation rewards seem so attractive, many have overpaid for properties that not only failed to produce the expected cash flow, but also were losers because of poor location, shoddy construction, or both. The tax shelter so desperately sought at the outset has developed into an economic nightmare for many of the "smart money boys."

Some of these investors used every taxation device

conceivable including questionable devices of their own, only to develop serious financial losses because of the reasons stated. On top of that the use of unusually high leverage magnified the problem and the investor never really had a chance.

Any property that needs to be better than 90% occupied to break even is mighty risky. Do not be mesmerized by tax gimmicks; they are just that. Soundly conceived and financed investments produce enough rewards, including tax shelter, to satisfy reasonable investors if they will only select the right kind of property with the right form of ownership and the right financing.

Table 14 shows how an apartment building worth about $150,000 and financed with a $100,000 first mortgage produces a $4000 cash flow. The tax flow shows a taxable income of $1600 without taking accelerated depreciation and $500 if the 125% declining balance method is used.

A $25,000 second mortgage at 8% interest with monthly payments of $250 including interest would have the effects shown in Table 15.

The tax loss of $1500 on a $25,000 investment plus the modest cash flow and the expected proceeds of sale would prompt most buyers to pay more than the $150,000 the property is worth. The second mortgage may be worth a premium of $5000 and the tax shelter may be quite appealing. There are many ways in which the property can be presented and the financing arranged to make the tax shelter especially attractive to someone who just wrote a big check to Uncle Sam. For example you might obtain the information given in Table 16 and form the opinion shown there.

If eager enough, one might believe the $18,000 income before mortgage and depreciation. Then with the $100,000 mortgage payable at $9200 for the year, the cash flow would be $5800. The seller might be asking $175,000 for the property (a mere 7 times gross income). You could pay $160,000 and get almost 10% cash on the

Table 14 Apartment Investment

		Cash Flow	Tax Flow
Scheduled gross income		$24,000	
Less vacancy allowance		$1,800	
Effective gross income		$22,200	$22,200
Expenses			
Property taxes	$ 2,500		
Insurance	300		
Utilities	1,000		
Maintenance and replacement	2,000		
Management	1,200		
Other expenses	2,200		
Total operating expenses		$ 9,200	$9,200
Interest payments		7,000	7,000
Amortization		2,000	
Depreciation (straight line)			4,400
		18,200	20,600

(Book value

Land $ 40,000

Building 110,000

$150,000)

Estimated remaining life
on building
25 years; depreciation rate 4%
(0.04)($110,000) = $4400

Cash flow		$ 4,000	
Taxable income			$ 1,600

Note: If accelerated depreciation were used,
expenses would be;

Operating expenses	$ 9,200
Interest expense	7,000
Depreciation	5,500

(0.05)($110,000)

21,700

Tax flow would be as follows:

Income	$22,200
Expenses	21,700
Taxable income	$ 500

Table 15   Leveraged Apartment Investment

	Cash Flow		Tax Flow
Gross income		$22,200	$22,200
Expenses			
Operating	$ 9,200		$ 9,200
Interest, first mortgage	$ 7,000		7,000
Amortization, First mortgage	2,000		
Interest, second mortgage	1,000		
Depreciation			5,500
		21,200	23,700
		$ 1,000 Cash flow	($1,500) Taxable income
The new cash flow would be		$ 1,000	(loss)
The new tax loss would be			($1,500)

---

down payment. But suppose you get the idea that it can be bought for $35,000 down and a $35,000 second mortgage with you taking over the $100,000 existing mortgage (paying a total price of $170,000). The second mortgage is at 8% with payments of $350 a month, including interest. Then you have the situation shown in Table 17.

Table 16 Evaluation of Income and Expenses

	What They Say	What You Believe
Gross income Apartment rentals should produce $25,000 year; are producing if full $24,000	$25,000	$24,000
Allowance for vacancy Never a vacancy but allow 4% (what would you believe?)	1,000 (4%)	1,800 (7.5%)
Effective gross income	$24,000	$22,200
Expenses		
Property taxes	$2,500	$2,500
Insurance	300	300
Utilities	1,000	1,000
Other expenses	2,200	5,400
	6,000	9,200
Income before mortgage and depreciation	$18,000	$13,000

Thus you would "get" a $1800 fully tax-sheltered cash flow plus a $600 tax loss. Furthermore if you arrange the second mortgage to be payable interest only, the cash flow is up to $3200 ($1800 + $1400), which is in addition to the $600 tax loss. And if one really needs the tax loss, borrow the down payment, remembering that the interest is deductible. The only problem is that the cash flow will be negligible or negative. Overpaying by 10% or more need not be disastrous if you can wait for the property value to catch up with what you paid for it—if it does. It is not just the optimistic cash flow expectation that leads to overpaying; it is the gimmickry that makes the tax shelter too good to be true. And if it looks too good to be true, it might indeed be.

Proceeds of Sale

The proceeds of sale from garden apartments have provided many investors with exceptional profits. This has been in addition to some fairly good cash flows, largely tax-sheltered.

Table 17   Estimated Cash Flow and Tax Flow

	Cash Flow	Tax Flow
Income before mortgage and depreciation	$15,000	$15,000
Interest, first mortgage	$7,000	$7,000
Amortization, first mortgage	2,000	
Interest, second mortgage	2,800	2,800
Amortization, second mortgage	1,400	
Depreciation		7,200
Cost		
Land　　　　　$ 50,000		
Building　　$120,000		
Remaining life 25 years		
Straight-line rate 4%		
125% of straight-line rate		
$(1.25)(0.04) = 0.05$		
$(0.05)($120,000) = 6000		
Total "expense"	$13,200	$15,600
Cash flow	$ 1,800	
Tax loss		($ 600)

Sometimes the proceeds of sale are attractive even after the investor has refinanced more than once. Much of the profit develops simply because of the timing of the sale, aided by rising costs. Proceeds of sale have not always proved the investment to be profitable, but mostly because investors paid too much at the wrong time for poorly located and shoddily constructed properties and then failed to hold on long enough.

If you can only hold on during difficult times, the amortization will build an equity, so that eventually you will own the project relatively free of debt. The overall value may have declined, but you will be able to get substantial proceeds of sale because of the consistent reduction in debt.

Proceeds of sale are very attractive when you "get" the amortization *and* the price rise. Although the building must eventually wear out, the replacement costs can rise sharply over a decade and the land value can increase so rapidly that a purchase with a modest down payment can provide outstanding returns, even though risky at the outset. The higher price results because the rents rise, *and this is the key.*

If you invest in apartments where the rents can rise, you are virtually assured a substantial profit. Inflationary conditions tend to help the rent rise if not offset by overbuilding, which can result in fierce competition. But property located in areas on the upgrade rise more rapidly in rent than the average. Well-designed and well-managed projects also do better because rent increases are more acceptable and the tenants alternatives to do better elsewhere are sharply restricted.

Since rents are the key to profits, astute investors watch rents carefully. They not only keep informed on what the competition is doing, but periodically test the market to see if they can get higher rents. Frequently they rent their apartments at higher prices as they become available. If rents rise rapidly or a large discrepancy between new and old rates developes, investors or their managers will raise all the rents to a competitive level, except of course those that are fixed by a lease agreement.

You can get your best price by selling out when the market expectations seem to be the highest in terms of future rents increases. You should also note that the larger the property, the fewer the buyers—and therein lies an element of risk. With less of a market, a great deal of care should be taken in the selection and ultimate purchase of a property of the larger type. You may own it a long, long time.

SELECTION

Selecting a property means choosing one that will rent well and will offer some potential for the future. Of course you may expect to stay with the investment for a long time, perhaps 8 to 12 years, but if you want to sell, the question is to whom? Investors who like to get in and out *fast* are generally "clobbered" in the real estate apartment market.

All that has been said about desirable locations for rental houses applies also to garden apartments, only more so. Because renters of such apartments frequently are one-car owners, they will seek good transportation facilities. Depending on their needs, they will look for proximity to good schools, churches, shopping areas, recreational facilities, employment, and similar activities. Investment in an apartment project should be analyzed by evaluating, among other things, the needs and desires of prospective tenants.

Rents as well as other prices have been rising sharply in recent years. Residential rents however are prices that somehow get singled out for control. Thus investors should be wary of investing in areas where rents will rise too rapidly and where rent controls are likely. Rent controls are most likely of course in jurisdictictions in which most of the voters are renters.

Rent Control

When citizens of a community, county, or state become annoyed enough by anything that affects their pockets, be assured that changes will occur. The startling and overwhelming effect of the votes on California's *Proposition 13*, which mandates a reduction of 57% on that state's real property taxes, has caused immediate (and numerous) government reactions. While this new California law captured headlines and everyone is aware of it, no one is yet certain what effect it will have on local and state services to taxpayers.

Rent controls on the other hand have been tried and for the most part have been ingloriously removed, New York being the major exception. The New York case has been disastrous. The more recent cases, such as in Washington, D.C., will take time to prove. As an indication of what to expect, however, consider that from 1973 through 1978 over one-half of all rentable apartments in the District of Columbia have *disappeared* from the market. This has been due to condominium conversions and abandonment.

This disastrous consequence is causing such controls to be reexamined even by political rent control advocates. The process is as follows: shortages of rental apartments occur and local legislators, mostly elected to office for two-year terms, respond to an outcry from the citizens and enact *long-term* rent controls. In a political climate such as this there is no incentive to maintain the property since the owners cannot pass on the increased expenses to their tenants. Thus deferred maintenance becomes the rule. This has the deleterious effect of putting many properties in the "marginal" column, which is a short step from abandonment. If you can't sell the property, how long would you continue sustaining economic losses? When abandonment starts escalating, the total inventory of rental housing shrinks and finding decent housing becomes increasingly difficult.

Once rent controls are put on the existing inventory, most developers are reluctant to construct new rental housing. The reasons are twofold. The first is that while rent controls have artifically held down rents, escalating costs have made it necessary to price rents in newly constructed projects very high. The old rents, when compared to new properties, look like a real bargain. New apartments cannot economically compete if anything is available in the existing rental market and therefore become very risky to build. The second reason is the political risk is too high to take. Even though *new* and *future* developments are frequently exempt from rent control, they later are often controlled by the same laws from which they were initially exempt. Because of this developers and lenders are wary of any political jurisdiction that enacts rent controls on apartments. The predictable result is that the older apartments wear out before their time, and very few, new apartments, if any, are developed.

The message is that unless you have a penchant for risks, avoid any residential rental properties in political jurisdictions where there is a reasonable chance of rent controls. You lose when there are more renters than owners. Politicians respect one thing above all others, the votes of their constituents. The votes are after all the "sine qua non" of political life, even when it leads to disastrous results.

FINANCING

The financing of apartment projects is seemingly similar to that of individual homes, the major difference being the size of the loans. Because an apartment project that is located where people want to live will attract tenants if offered at the right price, apartment financing is readily available. The major insurance companies have been putting a substantial portion of their mortgage loan portfolio in apartments, usually of the garden or low-rise type. Insurance companies, savings and loan associations, mutual savings banks, and larger commercial banks that offer permanent financing of single-family homes have become very interested in the financing of apartment projects. What makes the smaller apartment building so attractive to investors is the ease with which they can frequently borrow with the property as security. It is readily financed because the amount of the loan is not great and its sources are numerous and competitive.

When you move from the realm of smaller-unit projects into those of 100 units and up, the sources of primary financing begin rapidly to diminish since there are fewer institutional lenders capable of large loans. This is partially influenced by the policies of the Federal Home Loan Bank Board which requires that the maximum loan of a member association be tied to the assets of the association. A loan of $10 million on an 850-unit apartment development is capable of being financed by relatively few lenders. Some developers in the Washington, D.C., area estimated that no more than 20 lenders in the entire country could possibly make such a permanent loan—the nation's top 14 insurance companies, 3 of the largest commercial banks, 2 mutual savings banks, and 1 savings and loan institution. This estimate might be questioned, but it serves to point up the scarcity of lenders for the largest loans.

Some apartments qualify for long-term government- insured loans. These loans are available for institutional lenders, largely through mortgage bankers and mortgagae brokers.

Many sellers of apartment buildings will take back secondary financing, and the leverage that can be obtained on some purchases is amazing, The lowest down payments, sometimes only 5%, can be used in acquiring apartment projects. When the cash flow is good and appears to be stable, many private lenders will offer secondary financing. Any large city has many real estate practitioners who own dozens and even hundreds of smaller apartments and maintain large staffs of personnel to perform all the management functions. The ease of acquisition and the ease of selling such smaller units, aided by relative ease of financing, make this phase of the business a very active one.

Unlike the financing of homes, when making loans on large apartment buildings, lenders seldom demand personal liability on the part of the borrower, but look solely to the property for their security. As an investor you should ascertain that the mortgage or deed of trust contains an exculpatory clause specifically absolving you of any personal liability in the repayment of the loan. Naturally if you do not insist on a sole security clause, it is not likely to be found, because most lenders will take all the security they can obtain. In an investment however you should insist on limiting your liability to the down payment. Many things can happen, and you should not, and need not, take on the added risk of personal liability to repay the loan. Sometimes you cannot be free of that risk if you are the borrower. Your choice is to accept the risk, which could be nominal, or seek limited partnerships or other group-ownership arrangements.

When buying an apartment building and using secondary financing, you should be especially careful about signing notes that may involve personal liability. It is in this secondary financing area that the best known firms are not active, and indeed are forbidden to lend money by regulation. Insurance companies, banks, savings and loan associations, and mutual savings banks ordinarily may not make secondary loans out of their own institutional funds.

Part of the secondary financing available to owners of apartment projects may come in the personal property area. Some investors have discovered for instance that their rental market caters to relatively short-term tenants. They have furnished some or all of their apartment units with furniture purchased by use of chattel mortgages (mortgages on personal property). The repayment structure can be less than the added rent attributable to the furniture, thus increasing the cash flow and enhancing the depreciation. Furniture qualifies for rapid depreciation because of its relatively short economic life.

Others have leased furniture, outdoor playgrounds, and even permanent swimming pools, all with the idea of obtaining greater leverage. The majority of leasing arrangements appear to be most beneficial if the owner has the option to buy at a reasonable price at some future date when cash is more available. Without such a provision the risk is great, because when you go to sell, either owners or lenders may not for example like the idea of a leased swimming pool.

MAINTENANCE

Getting the most from the benefits of investing in apartments calls for a careful analysis to determine the level of maintenance and the level of rents as well as the extent of major improvements. Errors in judgment in these areas, especially among new investors, seem to abound. Many properties are overmaintained. Like homemakers, some property owners seem to have a fetish about cleanliness. Of course cleanliness is a highly desired feature by all tenants, but some apartment projects seem not to have a blade of grass out of place and their halls seem to be scrubbed twice daily. Conversely poorly maintained apartments have difficulty in attracting and keeping good tenants. Some of the best maintained apartments seem to have the least turnover and the lowest scale of rents. You may have heard owners say, "I've never had a vacancy."

You may be sure that in such cases the rents are too low, the property is overmaintained, or both.

Most practitioners in the management field strive for cleanliness and a small but reasonable turnover. They constantly "test" the market by inching up rents until they find the resistance causing more than a modest turnover.

Trying to save money by undermaintaining ("milking") properties is equally foolish. All increases in cash flow will be short-term at best. Since most of the profit is make by refinancing and ultimately selling the property, it is foolish to put too much emphasis on cash flow. Lenders are bullish on good-looking, well-maintained properites, and so are buyers. You should remember that the sale at the end is where the best chance for big profit lies.

CONCLUSIONS

Investing in garden apartments produces substantial benefits in cash flow, tax shelter, and proceeds of sale. The risks are low because well-designed and well-located properties rent well, and even mediocre properties are rentable in weak markets, albeit at reduced rates. The risk is comparatively low because apartment space is the most economical type of housing and most people want better housing.

It is relatively easy for owners themselves to manage smaller projects, and they can economically obtain professional help for the larger projects. Managing and maintaining one's own property provide some additional benefits. Projects that are not overly financed will produce an attractive cash flow, but the competition among potential investors, especially in the smaller projects, pushes up the price to a point where the cash on the down payment is not the major benefit.

The tax shelter is attractive because most of the value is in the building, rather than in the land, and the building is depreciable. The big benefits however are in proceeds of sale, that is when the investment is a winner. Although larger investments have some economic advantages, there are ample opportunities for successful investments in properties of all sizes. You should look for neighborhoods that are going to improve and you should get in before the area is overbuilt. The right location and timing will produce winners.

You should be able to evaluate the property in part from the experience that you have already developed in your housing decisions. Of course you can magnify your gains by using lots of borrowed money. But do not become overly enamored with the high-leveraged situation that produces a tax loss and not enough cash flow to absorb the shock of tougher markets. Garden apartments may not be the most profitable real estate investments, but with their minimal risks they can certainly be attractive.

If you seek somewhat higher returns than are available in garden apartments, you will be interested in high-rise projects. The next chapter explains how your risks and rewards increase when you invest in high-rise apartments as compared to garden apartments.

13 HIGH-RISE APARTMENTS

History obscures which came first—the elevator or the need for it. Perhaps the need created the product. The unwillingness of people to endlessly climb stairs, contrasted with the desire to live, work, or vacation in a specific location, created a need for vertical transportation.

With the demand for land continually increasing, especially in certain very desirable locations, there is a continuing need to create a greater intensity of land use. Before the advent of mechanical ventilating and air- conditioning systems this meant constructing buildings upward; today they can go up and down, but there is no room to go sideways.

What physically characterizes a high-rise building is its vertical look. In some metropolitan areas laws and regulations limit the height of the buildings, while in others the only limiting factor is economics. As buildings reach higher and higher skyward, costs to cope with the problems of height become disproportionate to the possible advantages of gaining more rentable space. Buildings that really soar, all the way up to 1000 feet are tremendously expensive to construct. Provisions to "hold" all the weight resting on the lowest level become extremely costly and involve complicated engineering techniques at the outset. The force of the wind at higher levels needs to be dealt with because all buildings of extreme height actually "move" in heavy winds.

234

The psychological forces playing on the tenant who lives or works in the upper floors of skyscrapers are fascinating and occasionally weird. Imagine living on the 90th floor. On a clear day the view is magnificent, on a cloudy day you may be above the clouds and unable to see the ground. On a windy day you may be bothered by the sway of the building and the noise of the wind against the glass windows. On a calm day the simple task of opening a window may be avoided because of a fear of heights. People living or working at extreme heights sometimes worry about how they can "escape" from an imaginary fire. Others are bothered by extremely high-speed elevators, which cause rapid pressure changes that may affect the ears of sensitive persons and induce, in rare instances, considerable pain. Yet others enjoy the "thrill" of a high-speed thousand-foot ride.

Whatever your personal opinions about living or working in high-rise buildings, such buildings are being created with increasing frequency in the major metropolitan areas of the country. Land costs are increasing endlessly in the most desirable areas, and underuse of such land does not make good economic sense. The trend is strongly up, up, and away; and with parking facilities having become a modern necessity, many high-rise buildings are also being built down, down, and under.

So valuable is the land in some areas that buildings are being constructed *over* railroad tracks and stations, or over public roads. This has created a new owning concept in the realty and construction industry known as "air-rights." The high-rise building owner has a long-term lease on the rights to use all the "air" above a parcel of ground, which already has some use that requires little space, such as a railroad track or a railway station.

In addition to the benefits of prestige and accessibility, there is the benefit of soundproofing for those who live in high-rise apartments, which comes as a by-product of the method of construction.

CONSTRUCTION CHARACTERISTICS

Of necessity high-rise apartments have concrete floors, of varying degrees of thickness. In buildings of "reinforced concrete construction" floors have steel rods that are embedded in the concrete. Thus tenants can rarely produce enough noise to disturb their vertical neighbors above or below. Unlike wood-joist construction, which transmits noise, concrete is a sound deadener.

Steel buildings also deaden noise. Instead of thick columns being used to help tie the floors together, I-beam steel is first assembled, much like an erector set. The weight of the concrete floors is held not so much by the vertical columns as by the horizontal I-beams. The end result with respect to soundproofing is virtually the same—noise transmission in high-rise apartments traditionally occurs through the integrated ventilating systems and through the vertical partitions separating apartments on the same floor if they are not adequately soundproofed.

The systems used to air-condition and heat high-rise apartments are highly sophisticated compared to those in garden apartments, especially the garden apartment that employs individual, rather than central, heating and cooling systems. As a consequence a more highly trained, hence more expensive, licensed stationary engineer is employed. The licensing requirements vary among political jurisdictions, but they tend to require more specially trained technical personnel in high-rise buildings, The resident engineers are basically rated on their ability to service and maintain the mechanical systems (heating, air conditioning, and plumbing), with special emphasis on the size of the air-conditioning load. The "tonnage" of air conditioning required to service the New York Hilton or the Americana Hotel in New York is phenomenal and costs millions. You may be sure that their chief resident engineers know their jobs.

AMENITIES

Because it costs much more to build, operate, and maintain high-rise apartments than garden apartments, rents are necessarily higher. Although not originally intended to cater to a more elite market, the economics of the situation make them so. Developers and owners of high-rise apartments frequently include amenities not found in garden apartments. They do this because *all* costs (both construction and owning) are higher on a square-foot basis, hence they must attract higher-income tenants. Many owners are forced to provide extra amenities in order to remain competitive, Others strive to create an elegant atmosphere and thus give the building and its occupants greater status.

These amenities frequently include doormen, indoor parking, secretarial (switchboard) service, mail and package receiving rooms, sauna baths, swimming pools, health clubs or exercise rooms, hospitality rooms, and where zoning permits, such commercial services as beauty and barber shops, food stores, and laundry and dry cleaning establishments. All of this is reflected in the rentals.

RISKS

The major risk in the development and ownership of high-rise apartments lies in attracting tenants in a "soft" rental market. Assume that you own a garden apartment building in which you are offering a two-bedroom apartment at a monthly rental of $250. Although the apartment is attractively maintained and well located, you are having difficulty in renting it. Common sense dictates a rental reduction. You decide that you would rather have full occupancy at 10% less rents than 80% occupancy at current rents. You would then also avoid the high costs of advertising and redecorating on a more or less continuous basis. You now offer the same apartment at $225 monthly. Any response? Probably yes.

In most metropolitan areas there are always many families who need better housing. The major deterrent is the amount of rent charged for such housing. There seems to be an endless supply of families at the next lower economic level ready, willing, and able to occupy your apartments. The lowering of the rent by 10% is assurance of attracting more tenants.

Now suppose that you own a high-rise apartment building in which a two-bedroom apartment rents for $560 monthly: a 10% rent reduction would place the apartment on the market at $504 monthly. Would you be able to fill the vacancies at this rental rate? Probably not. And here lies the greatest risk in owning high-rise apartments. The prospective tenants for high-rises no doubt want value, but their reasons for wanting to live there are not heavily tied to the rent structure. They are searching for amenities, not the least of which is status. The pragmatics of renting high-rise apartments bear this out. A person who can afford a $504 monthly rental can probably pay $560 equally well. Price *alone* will neither attract nor deter him, although the price must be competitive. To cover a $504 monthly rental, his income must be such that the additional $56 per month is a small percentage of his uncommitted income. The 10% reduction in a garden apartment is important however when you consider the relationship of this reduction to the spendable income of the typical garden-apartment tenant.

A Manhattan management specialist in high-rise apartments recently told a group of fellow Realtors that when faced with vacancies in the 10% range, he *increases* the rent and has splendid rental results. Although this method may sound farfetched to the layperson, many Realtors in the audience nodded approval. Most property managers claim that their prime sales attraction in high- rise apartments is the "atmosphere." Because they are catering to the upper-middle-income group (and in many cases, the highest-income group), the rentals charged, if not grossly out of line, are *not* the specific key to the ability of the apartments to rent.

Since there is little difference in the cost of building high-rise apartments in the central city and the surrounding suburbs, the investor should first seek a well- designed building with good apartment layouts in a *location* that has the best chance of becoming highly desirable. Older, well-established, high-class locations catering to an elite market are unquestionably a good choice. An even better choice is a location that has a chance of *becoming* an unparalleled status location. You can develop or acquire such a winner at a considerably lower costs than you would have to pay for those that are already winners. The reason why a building can command higher and higher rents is its location.

Look for trends toward a posh environment. Remember that square-foot operating costs are greater in high-rise buildings than in garden apartments. To make the most profit you need a location that can constantly absorb increases in rents, If you miss the market (Heaven forbid!) or if there is a shift away from your location, ownership of such an apartment building can be a devastating experience.

Here are some pointers that may be valuable as an aid to selection of a winning high-rise location and some comments on building amenities and equipment. You are cautioned that these aids are based on empiric observations. Truly representative data are not available since they would require expensive research. Some of these observations are funny and even weird, but they are rooted in reality.

In most major cities the successful locations seem to be those that are found on the major north or northwest streets, heading to and extending through the suburbs. One explanation offered is that in bygone days the better homes were built northward and westward to avoid the smoke and soot of city factories. Since the prevailing winds are from west to east, they would carry smoke away from homes in the northernmost or westernmost areas.

Exceptions do arise. The theory explodes so to speak when the location offers a fine view, especially of a river, lake, or ocean, or is at a considerably higher elevation than the surrounding areas. The sector theory of city growth identifies the factors of high ground and open space for expansion as forces pulling high-income development to a particular section of the city. Aside from such factors however most high-rise apartments seem to do better if they are located on the northerly or westerly main roads out of the central city. What about south or east? We do not really know why the southern and eastern areas seem to do less well. Streets that bisect the main routes can be attractive and many buildings have fared well, but you should not move against the main trend in locating your property without some attractive amenities that compellingly affect this disadvantage. It seems also that the more visible the high-rise to the most traffic, the greater the appeal.

Buildings of dark-colored brick do not seem to do so well as buildings of a light color. There are plenty of exceptions of course, but why not go along with the odds in your favor? Dark-bricked buildings with light spandrels or white vertical columns, which brighten the appearance, are satisfactory, but dark-looking buildings should be avoided.

Buildings that are somehow "activated" seem to do better. There are only two major ways to get action into a high-rise—by use of water, such as fountains, and by use of fire, such as torches—and both amenities should be considered as assets.

Avoid buildings with little or no inside parking. First, higher-paying tenants want to be out of the weather when they leave or enter their cars, especially when it is extremely windy or cold or when it is raining or snowing. Second, a building that has much outside parking space will need large areas of monotonous concrete or asphalt, making attractive landscaping very difficult or nearly impossible.

Avoid buildings where the elevators are insufficient to do the job. Everybody hates waiting. Most modern elevators require regular shutdowns for service; this can paralyze a one-or two-elevator building. One hundred units to each elevator is adequate. Seventy-five is an outstanding ratio.

If the only way to move furniture in and out of the building is through the lobby, you have an unfavorable arrangement. Tenants become annoyed when they and their guests are inconvenienced by hard-working, perspiring movers standing about the lobby elevators. Separate service elevators are very desirable, but passenger elevators are satisfactory provided that loading is done below the lobby floor or perhaps behind the lobby through rear-opening doors. A further annoyance are elevators that are too low. For some reason, many owners and developers buy and install elevators of 8 or 8½ feet in height, floor to ceiling. Imagine the inconvenience when moving 9 or 10 foot sofas. Elevators must then be manually operated, usually by a factory serviceman at high hourly rates, who either partially removes the elevator ceiling or supervises placing furniture on top of the elevator cab. It scares the movers half to death to ride an elevator in an open shaft, while holding on to an unwieldy sofa on top of a cab, and in many instances they refuse to do so.

REWARDS

Who enjoys more status, in your opinion—the owner of a gas station under lease to a major oil company or the owner of the finest high-rise apartment in your town? The consensus appears to be that high-rise owners have more status than gas-station or even garden-apartment owners. A sociologist of psychiatrist might be able to explain the cultural and psychological reasons for this. One psychiatrist said that some of these reasons seem to be related to the importance of being the landlord to a large number of high-income tenants.

Cash Flow

Whether fact or fiction, most high-rise tenants assume that owners are "loaded." The truth is that they potentially have a stable cash flow if they are enjoying good occupancy. This is so because their tenancies are more stable. There is considerably less turnover of apartments in high-rise buildings than in garden apartments. While this is undoubtedly related to the costs of furnishing the better apartments, the fact that the housing needs of families with small children are more subject to change also has bearing. Families tend to grow and their schooling needs change. Most heads of households in high-rise apartments are older and have fewer young children. Many parents feel that a high-rise apartment with high-speed elevators and limited play facilities is not the milieu in which to raise children. Quite a few high-rise tenants are older couples who have sold their homes to free themselves from the responsibility incident to maintaining a home. Young married couples seeking companionable neighbors tend to gravitate to garden apartments, which cater to other couples with young and growing children. Personal contact seems more frequent in the spatial arrangement of garden apartments. Many who can afford it buy homes in new areas because their neighbors then are in the same general age group and have young children.

Any high-rise apartment owner will attest to the fact that his tenants are far less destructive than tenants with small children living in garden apartments.

The amount of financing and the terms of repayment are a major consideration in determining the cash flow. Since the loans generally available have a smaller loan-to-value ratio, high-rise buildings have high cash requirements and cash flow is then not so sensitive to fluctuation in gross income. In addition tenant turnover is not high, so that the cash flow is relatively stable.

Intelligent investors not overly enamored with maximum leverage seem quite willing to put more cash in a high-rise building and get more stable cash flow.

Tax Shelter

The tax shelter can be quite favorable in a high-rise building. Tax results are comparable to those found in a garden development. The ratio of building cost to land value is much higher than in a garden apartment, but much of this benefit is nullified because of the longer life of the structure. The high-rise steel and concrete construction lasts longer than frame with stucco or brick. Thus the actual rate of depreciation is lower. The component method of depreciation will help with the tax shelter, but the shell of the structure has a long life and is a large part of the cost.

Proceeds of Sale

If you have a winner in a high-rise that you either developed or acquired, the results can be spectacular. Rising rent levels not accompanied by an equal cost of operating the building can drive the price of the building up considerably over even the most optimistic expectations at the time of acquiring or developing it.

A brisk demand for units in a high-rise is more specific and often not genuinely related to a shortage of housing. In an era of increasing personal incomes, the search for the better life is interpreted by many to mean a more elite form of living. Aside from a large home or estate, the next best status move is into a plush high-rise. The financial rewards are great for those who own a winner, which can be earmarked by a large waiting list of persons wishing to occupy a certain building. Owners experienced in the ways of our modern society go to great lengths to create an atmosphere that will command better rents and longer waiting lists. Large plush lobbies with doormen attired in expensive uniforms are again amenities not related to the actual comfort of the residents. Posh reception desks staffed by bright and attractive personnel also add to the atmosphere of a status building. Well-landscaped areas with attractive gardens are surely indicia of the "better" atmosphere.

Creating better atmospheres in periods of rising opportunities is an effective way of competing for the consumer's dollar. High-rise apartments are more in a luxury market than in a shelter market. As new ways are found to respond to the increased ability of the populace to pay for its needs, more profit is made. High-rise apartments have been demonstrating that potential.

CONCLUSIONS

High-rise apartments are more desirable and more costly than garden apartments. They also require higher down payments. Generally the result is a more stable short-run cash flow than is available in garden apartments.

The long-term risks in high-rises are somewhat greater than in garden apartments because the lowering of rents in times of market softness does not necessarily mean you will rent more successfully.

In selecting your investment in a high-rise, do not buck the main trends: make certain that the building has good visual qualities; is located on a main thoroughfare, preferably north or west out of the central downtown area; is architecturally appealing; is light in color; is "activated" (water or fire); has sufficient elevators; and is designed so that tenants do not "move in" through the lobby.

Your tax shelter will be favorable—not so great as in garden apartments, but quite acceptable.

If you have a winner in a growing area, your proceeds of sale can be highly rewarding, much more favorable than in a winning garden development.

Are there better investment opportunities in other classes of real estate? Many investors think so. Let us now examine the investment possibilities in office buildings.

14 OFFICE BUILDINGS

Office buildings house the administrative and clerical employees of governmental agencies of every kind and office staffs of most of the major corporations in our society. They also house most of the lawyers, accountants, advertising agencies, and engineering staffs that provide professional services to government, privately owned institutions, and individuals. In large cities office buildings tend to become specialized with regard to the type of tenancies. Some buildings house nothing but medical and dental personnel and their staffs and supporting services. Such buildings are developed with emphasis on the special plumbing facilities that are normal requirements for the medical occupants, but would not be necessary for lawyer's offices. An office building for lawyers might have the special facility of a central law library.

The physical requirements and amenities built into office buildings can vary widely in response to the types of tenancies involved. The location of office buildings that must attract special types of tenancies is of prime importance. Professionals tend to gather together, even though one would think that since their services are often competitive, this would not be the case.

Investing in buildings that house offices is different from investing in residential buildings. The risks of not renting the space are greater in office buildings than in residential buildings, the services expected by the

246

tenants are generally more expensive, and there is a higher risk of obsolescence. The risks in location and timing are greater for offices than for apartments, but so are the rewards. This chapter explains the risks inherent in office-building investments and of course identifies the rewards.

RISKS IN RENTING SPACE

The demand for office space varies widely over time. While there is always someone willing, if the price is right, to move up in housing accomodations, users of office space are not sensitive to bargain prices, unless they have some other reason for seeking new quarters. Office space users do upgrade, but it is accommodation and location not price, that determine the move. In the older sections of many downtown metropolitan areas you can observe stores on the ground floor and what used to be office space on the upper floors. Many of the upper floors are boarded up or bricked in—sad testimony to the fact that enough rent cannot be commanded to attain a breakeven point in operating expense.

Office space demand is related to the needs of the business and professional community and, even more important, to *modern* needs. Status locations will bring higher rents for identical space with identical amenities. Thus the owner of an office building that is out of the location stream of other and better office buildings has some incurable economic problems. Unlike a high-rise apartment building, the repairing, remodeling, or upgrading of an office building, (all combined with a reduction in rents) may still result in finally having to abandon the project altogether. Lowering the rents from, say $5.50 to $4.50 per square foot per annum in an undesirable location usually produces a few more prospects, usually of questionable credit, who do not solve any of the owner's problems. On the other hand well-located buildings in the general vicinity of other fine office buildings that have virtually 100% occupancy can do extremely well financially, in fact much better than even the very successful high-rise apartment project.

The risk in unleased or short-term-leased office buildings is greater than the risk in high-rise apartments, but the successful ventures make it more than worthwhile. The modern office building, aside from its "in" location, must offer good elevator service, excellent char service, carpeted corridors, and, above all, an excellent and dependable heating and air-conditioning system. Property managers and developers who have extensive experience in the operation of office buildings will tell you that the reasons why business firms move to other locations (aside from needing more space) are related to poor elevator service, poor char service, a poor system of heating and air-conditioning, or a combination of all of these factors. Add to this the catalytic agent of prosperity and it becomes obvious that people not only want but also can get something better.

Initially attracting tenants is related to the status of the location and to the personal and specific business needs of the tenant. Association executives want to be near other association executives and feel that their association deserves at least as good a building as do those of their fellow counterparts. Lawyers specializing in administrative law, who do not need to be near courthouses, feel that their clients will evaluate them, among other factors, on the location and character of their offices. Can you imagine the Washington representatives of the largest oil companies in the world working in substandard space, while their friends in other companies enjoy prestigious offices? Hardly. And so it goes. The best locations, with well-planned buildings, attract the best tenants. Best in this sense means the economic best. The tenants are companies whose credit is absolutely unquestioned. While the leases of major corporations are frequently negotiated by real estate officers or their staffs, the local representatives generally make the first and second choices regarding the preferred locations. The real estate officers who specialize in negotiating space are not only very knowledgable about planning the space, but are also very much aware of the amenities necessary in a first-class building. They are very concerned about the comfort of their fellow corporate officers. In today's rental market a building in which the heat and air- conditioning cannot be turned off or on in each separate executive office is almost obsolete. This room-by-room control that enables you to heat one room while air- conditioning another is frequently accomplished by what is called a four pipe system. In the "traditional" two-pipe system you can obtain heat by turning on the convector in the room if the main system has hot water heating the pipes; of if the central system has chilled water in the pipes, then you can obtain air-conditioning. In the four-pipe system both hot and cold water are being constantly circulated, so that the system can produce either heat or air conditioning, as the tenant desires.

There are some variations, such as a three-pipe systems or electric air-conditioning in the convector that does not depend on chilled water, but the most popular is the four-pipe system. In cities where the weather is not subject to extreme fluctuations-the crabgrass belt where summer grasses do well for only two or three months and the cool-weather grasses do well only during the coldest spells—a four-pipe system for new buildings is virtually a must. If the building owner cannot turn on the air- conditioning or the heat when the weather turns unseasonably warm in March and April or cold in September and October, he may face a steady outflow of tenants at lease-renewal time.

The four-pipe system, although still a superluxury in even the finest high-rise luxury apartments, is virtually a must in today's modern office buildings. When you consider that there are changing levels of demand for office space as well as increasing desire for amenities, it is obvious that the risks in renting office space are substantially higher than those in renting apartment space.

There are some important economies in scale in office buildings. The largest have an economic edge over the smaller buildings. This is so because the core of a building is unrentable, consisting mainly of elevators, lavatories, staircases, and large ventilating shafts. In a smaller building this unrentable core can be as much as 40%; in larger buildings the area can be as small as 8%. The size and shape of the building lot as well as the size of the building influence the amount of rentable space for each expended construction dollar.

The costs of staff needed to service a larger building are lower per square foot than the costs for smaller buildings. The mechanical system may require an engineer. It is more economical to service one 350,000 square-foot building than to service ten 35,000 square-foot buildings. The skills required are somewhat higher for the larger buildings, but the average cost per square foot per year is much lower.

Inasmuch as most functions are virtually automated in an office building, relatively little personnel is needed, except for the char force that comes into the building during the evening to pick up trash in the wastebaskets, empty ashtrays, and occasionally dust furniture and vacuum the floors.

Business tenants have come to expect other amenities as well from the finer buildings. In-the-building parking is almost a must. Most executives do not want to go out in the weather to reach their automobiles. On rainy or snowy days, businesspersons silently cuss the landlord who has not provided in-the-building parking. On such days the importance of luncheon facilities on the premises also becomes obvious, and the building without such facilities will not remain competitive very long.

Office building leases are usually of a much longer term than residential leases. They can run for up to 20 years, but the national average seems to be 5 to 10 years. The data available on this subject on a national basis are insufficient for an accurate estimate, However if most of the tenants move into a building when it is new and have, say five-year leases, and the building owner and management do not provide sufficient services, or the amenities are missing because of poor design, many tenants can vacate at approximately the same time. This can produce a serious economic loss for two major reasons. First, there is loss of income. Second, unlike apartment dwellers, office tenants are not likely to fit into pre-designed offices. Thus expensive remodeling to accommodate the needs of a new tenant can be expected. To the uninformed the thought of large expenditures for remodeling a five-year-old building may be shocking, but such are the facts in many buildings that experience turnover because of faulty design or lack of amenities.

Office building owners and managers experienced a boom in most major cities after World War II. By the end of the war much of the inventory of office buildings consisted of 25 year-old edifices—those that had been built during the great office-building boom in the twenties. This boom had created excess space; the Depression eroded much of the demand that had existed. Then during the forties demand grew. Space was scarce and, as the economy continued to expand after the war, it became even scarcer. New downtown office buildings for financial and business centers were constructed during the late fifties to meet the demand, and office space in outlying suburban areas began to spring up, following the boom in suburban shopping centers. And as prices for prime downtown space rose higher and higher, some office buildings were constructed for special tenants who had no compelling need to be downtown. By the early sixties the office-building boom was flourishing.

Of course in some cities there is really no need to concentrate on a downtown area. For example Los Angeles has many fine office buildings concentrated in various locations other than downtown. Wilshire, Beverly Hills, Century City, International Airport, and other locations in the Los Angeles area all boast new and modern office buildings housing many tenants who, if located in New York or Washington, would prefer to be "downtown."

To meet the needs of the many residents who moved to suburbia after World War II, smaller office buildings to house the offices of local dentists, doctors, and lawyers have been built. Many accountants and other professionals have good practices in the suburbs, hence not only need not to be downtown, but definitely prefer to practice near the clients and their homes.

Many professionals have moved into shopping centers or small free-standing buildings near such centers. Others have moved into former residential houses that found themselves in the commercial stream and were converted to offices. To this inventory you must add the many smaller office buildings erected and occupied by the owners themselves. Many branch offices of large insurance companies occupy such smaller office buildings, as do branch offices of many national organizations.

RISKS IN LOCATION

The increased use of air travel and the suburban-exurban movement has increased the number and size of clusters of nondowntown office buildings. These newer locations, although riskier, can be very profitable. There is a wide variation in the cost per square foot of land between suburban locations and downtown locations in most of the larger metropolitan areas. For example office building land in 1969 could be purchased for as little as $4 a square foot in suburban areas around Washington, D.C.; the price per square foot of land in the best locations in the central city was as high as $175 a square foot. Inasmuch as it costs approximately the same to build an office building in suburban parts of the Washington metropolitan area as it does to build one downtown, the main difference in total cost is in the cost of the land and its density of use. This difference of course is reflected when the finished product comes upon the market. In 1969 office space in the finest locations of the District of Columbia would rent for approximately $7 per square foot per annum, while in a fine suburban location the rent would approach $5 per square foot.

A decade later office-building land could be bought in the suburban areas for approximately $16 to $20 a square foot; the price per square foot of land in the best locations in the central city was as high as $350 and $400. The land costs were reflected in the price of space. New finished space in the suburban areas would be leased at $10 per square foot, while office space in the finest locations of downtown Washington would rent for $13.50 per square foot. Both areas had substantial increases, but obviously the riskier suburban locations paid off handsomely.

Poorly located office space will frequently not bring in enough rents to cover operating costs. Such buildings, however well designed and planned, will encounter difficulty because there is no need for the kind of building and location. As previously inferred people do not go into business just because rent is inexpensive, nor do they move to different locations at high moving costs just to get cheaper rent. Office building tenants are not so mobile as apartment-house renters, who will quickly upgrade themselves if they feel they are getting a real bargain. Some apartment dwellers will move rather than put up with the mess of repainting. A reduction in the rent will not be helpful in leasing a poorly located office building, which makes for a tremendous risk in selecting a location.

On the other hand good office-building locations seem to attract numerous other good office buildings. Those who build early in good locations find that the locations are strengthened by the magnetism of their own building and the quality of their tenants, which in turn gives impetus to the construction of even newer buildings by others, which again attract financially sound tenants. Good locations just seem to get better with the addition of newer and competitive office buildings in the same general area. An important axiom in the real estate industry is that desirability of location is judged, in part, by the character of the surrounding properties. The desirability of location is highly dramatized, and highly magnified, with respect to office buildings. If you pick a location that is going to get better, the rewards can be fantastic.

RISKS IN TENANCY IN NEW BUILDINGS

In the development of new office buildings, financing is not readily available, unless all or a substantial part of the building is leased in advance to tenants of high credit. Such is the practice generally followed by most lenders who commit first mortgages on office buildings. Life insurance companies finance most new office buildings, especially those in the $2 million and higher cost range. Their lending policies vary from city to city, but rarely will they lend on a long-term mortgage without evidence of sound leases in advance of their commitment. This should serve as a guide to you in assessing the risks of office-building ownership. The stability of the income from ownership of an office building is tied to the length of the lease and the financial stability of the tenant.

In the few special situations where unleased office buildings may be built, there are holdbacks of a certain portion of the permanent mortgage until satisfactory leasing up to a certain agreed-on amount has been attained, Since insurance companies do not usually make the construction loans, the developers are limited to the lower amount committed by the insurance company in that this amount is usually the maximum the developer can borrow from the construction lender, often a commercial bank. This spread between the full loan, based on satisfactory leasing, and the lower loan, which is committed regardless of leasing, makes developing a new and modern office building highly speculative. It also calls for a clear understanding of where the funds are coming from to complete the building in the event the leasing amounts specified cannot be obtained before the closing of the permanent loan. The major insurance companies rarely will allow more than 30 months from the date of their commitment until loan closing, so that leasing to obtain the maximum loan amount can be almost frenetic for the owners. The spread between the guaranteed loan amount and the full loan based on satisfactory leasing can be enormous, usually falling between 40 and 20% *less* than the higher loan amount. On a $4 million loan this could amount to over $1.5 million, which can frighten even a multimillionaire.

Costs of developing a new office building that is not leased prior to construction can be only guessed. Most experienced builders or contractors can estimate the cost of the structure itself, but this estimate is not closely related to the final cost until the tenants' needs are known, which may not occur until *after* the basic structure is completed. Costs of building the tenants' interior layouts frequently amount to approximately 30% of the total cost of the building, and if you do not know who the tenants will be, there is no way of knowing their partitioning and other interior requirements. You could rely on accepted standards relating to partitioning, lighting, interior decorating, and occasional special requirements, such as special bathrooms for executives, but this is like throwing darts at a board. The financially acceptable tenant is not really very interested in *your* standards; he has standards of *his* own. In a buyers market, you may be sure, *his* standards will be applied.

Another scary factor in the development of new and unleased office buildings is the fact that between the day of land purchase and the day the building is completed there may be a time-lapse of 1½ to 2 years or more. This time-lapse can make an objective and analytical businessperson act like a fortune-teller, complete with crystal ball. If the economy slows down and they have over estimated the need for office space, they can easily become clobbered. If however their timing is superb and they come onto the market with space for which there is relatively little competition and great demand, they can hold out for the highest rentals, the longest leases, and the best tenants. The latter situation *has* happened, and when you are fortunate enough to be an investor in an office building where all the economic forces are favorable, the winnings are among the highest attainable in any form of real estate investment.

Some buildings serve a select market by specializing in the type of tenancy. For example some buildings cater exclusively to medical doctors or dentists. On occassion some of the future tenants turn out to have been investors in the building from the outset. Such investment can be attractive to professionals inasmuch as rent is a deductible item in the cost of performing their services, and yet in a sense they could be paying the income to themselves if they represent a part of the ownership group. Occasionally large-space users, such as large trade associations or other large institutions, will lease buildings in which they have some ownership interest—again to accomplish the same goals of deducting rent and yet having income through an ownership position.

Multitenanted buildings of a general-purpose nature, which will house all types of business tenancies, are sound investments provided that the tenancies have high-quality credit and the leases are for reasonably long terms. Obviously the stronger the financial ability of the tenant, the smaller the risks to the owners. The stability of the income is also affected not only by the length of the lease, but also by the inclusion of escalation clauses in the lease itself. These provide for automatic increases in the rent based on either average increases in operating costs to the owners or at least an increase in the property taxes or insurance to the owner throughout the life of the lease.

In new structures the laying out of partitions and wiring and generally tailoring space to the needs of new incoming tenants is a job usually performed by a leasing agent in concert with the architect representing the ownership. The cost of tailoring the space varies widely, depending on the quality of the tenant and the amount of rentals charged. The cost of such tailoring is quite variable of course, depending on individual needs of tenants, which vary widely. Thus some tenants require large open spaces, while others, such as those occupying the building for medical practice, require a large number of small partitioned rooms as well as an unusual amount of plumbing.

The cost of remodeling space when one tenant vacates to meet the needs of another tenant is frequently higher than the cost of tailoring the space in the initial instance. This is so because a dual job is required—first the tearing down of existing facilities and the cleaning of the area to be remodeled followed by the actual remodeling of the area to accommodate the new tenant.

As indicated before office space is not readily absorbed in the market by reducing the price. One effect of general price reductions, when a large amount of attractive space is being offered at the same time, is that more and better space is used, which means that owners of older buildings will find their market quite soft; in fact they might find their market nonexistent because their old space has been made obsolete.

Tenants are not responsive to price when they are satisfied and have adequate space, and a builder owner who stays competitive not only in price but also in the quality of service offered will suffer less than the owner of a new building who is developing space for a market that in fact is nonexistent.

The task of negotiating office space is ordinarily left in the hands of a leasing specialist who usually works for a management firm. In recent years however there is a trend toward companies that do nothing but specialize in the actual leasing of space. Although it would seem not quite believable to most people who are not familiar with the kinds of negotiations that take place in leasing space in office buildings, rentals sometimes vary quite widely among tenants in the same building. These variations come about because the largest users with the strongest credit are in a position to command a better price, and often do. Their willingness to accept a longer-term lease, which smaller tenants dare not do in limited or modest financial circumstances, has a bearing on the price the tenant is paying for each square foot of occupied space. Such variations in cost per square foot among the various tenants within a building is a rather accepted fact in the business community; complaints about variances in rental are rather infrequent.

BENEFITS

Cash Flow

Successful office buildings produce a substantial cash flow. In rising markets this cash flow can increase substantially. Thus after a successful building has been held for five to seven years, there may be excellent opportunities for refinancing. These opportunities are very attractive in times when money is generally easy. The lenders look at the length of the leases, the escalation clauses for taxes and other expenses, and the quality of the tenants. In many cases, because of the unusually high cash flow, an owner can support a substantially higher mortgage than he originally obtained; for this reason, many have retrieved their original cash out of the buildings, and then some.

Tax Shelter

In the downtown areas of most major metropolitan cities the ratio of cost improvements to land is not very high, rarely in excess of 4 or 5 to 1, especially in buildings of 16 stories or less. Because of the low ratio and the long useful life, there is very little tax shelter in the development of a new and modern office building in downtown locations. Additionally depreciation is limited to 150% declining balance, as it is for all *new* nonresidential property. As you will recall, investors acquiring *used* nonresidential property are limited to straight-line depreciation.

The ratio of cost of improvements to land is relatively higher in suburban office buildings. Using construction other than concrete and steel will result in a shorter useful life of the structure, and consequently more depreciation can be obtained. This type of construction is often limited to two-story suburban office buildings. These properties offer some tax shelter. The net result of ownership in office buildings is that the depreciation allowance is quite small when compared to apartments of similar construction.

If you need tax shelter, then a low-rise suburban building on relatively low-price land may be of interest to you. The financial risks of developing or acquiring an office building that is unleased in a suburban location are such that novice investors would be well advised to stay out of this type of investment and seek the tax shelter that they can obtain more safely in either garden or high-rise apartment developments. Owner-users have a different risk position and may find substantial tax shelter in investing in office space that they use. Physicians, attorneys, and accountants who wish to invest would do well to explore suburban office-building space if that is where they need offices and if they can use much of the space themselves.

Proceeds of Sale

The proceeds of sale may be substantial for the winners, especially those who came in on the upside of the pyramid. Investors who buy buildings that turn out to be well located and who find themselves in a rising market can capitalize on this location benefit either by new financing or by selling and obtaining the proceeds of sale. However all post-1975 excess depreciation over straight line depreciation is fully recaptured as ordinary income regardless of how long the property has been held.

Obtaining the benefits of proceeds of sale are frequently deferred because office buildings, especially those that are 100% occupied, are relatively easy to own. The contact between tenants and owners is infrequent, and sophisticated management techniques are not required. The most irritating facet is that of providing decent char service. Usually the char service is contracted out to firms that specialize in this type of activity. Nevertheless those who own successful office buildings consider such investments superior to those in other types of real estate, because office buildings are profitable and easy to own.

The owning costs however are high. The main reason is service. But contributing to the high owning cost in office buildings is the practice of spreading the cost of the leasing fees over the life of the lease. This expense may not be deducted for tax purposes under current law, even if paid in full and in advance. Sometimes the owners will find themselves involved in the buying out of old leases to accommodate larger tenants who seek expansion in the same building. The costs of tailoring space are high, so that turnover of tenants is unusually expensive.

You should carefully weigh the difficulty and cost of renting the space. You should carefully evaluate the leases, thoroughly analyze the market, try to forecast what the market will be, and consider the financial strength of the tenants. All of these factors will surely be considered by the buyer to whom one day you will attempt to sell your office building and will thus influence your proceeds of sale.

FINANCING

Many of the loans are so large that lenders frequently go along with variations in financing not found in the ordinary financing of apartment buildings. Often lenders will purchase the land and lease it back to the developer. This is a way of getting tax shelter out of office buildings and of increasing leverage. Sometimes lenders will give amortization terms that run as high as 27½ years with the unpaid balance being due and payable at the end of the twentieth year. Investors thus get an annual constant based on a 27½-year loan, which of course helps their cash flow. Lenders may also make long-term leases of the land with an option to the building owner to buy the land at some later date. The lenders, mostly insurance companies, will frequently "lock in" an office building loan from 10 to 15 years, when interest rates are high and they want to protect themselves from borrowers refinancing for lower interest rates.

In 1966 as a result of the tight-money market, many lenders started to make loans on office buildings, provided that a fixed percentage of gross or net income went to the lender. The arrangements are sometimes called "participations," although they are participations without the lender putting up equity funds. They may make loans for a higher amount, a lower rate, or a longer term. These participations are a device to increase the earnings on the first mortgage and are colloquially referred to as "a piece of the action." The piece-of-the-action philosophy has become popular with many of the lenders for a wide variety of investment-type property. In the late sixties, with money tightening, the lenders became especially innovative in finding ways to participate in the benefits usually reserved for investors. Thus investors must explore their timing very carefully and must choose their lender wisely. The correct choices, frequently made with the help of a mortgage banker, will give them the best opportunity to negotiate the type of financing they can live with.

CONCLUSIONS

One of the most important characteristics of an office building, which differs sharply from residential buildings, is that rarely will price alone—that is, lowering the rent—help to keep an office building rented. Therefore a quality location is the single most important factor in selecting an office building investment.

Businesspersons demand fast elevator service, good char service, and dependable room-by-room air-conditioning and heating. Because of these demands, services to tenants in an office building are not only more costly than those in a high-rise residential building, but also *initial amenities* built in the structure must be acceptable (besides location) in terms of these demands.

Smaller office buildings are at a disadvantage in competing with the larger ones because of the obvious economies of scale. The best place for smaller office buildings is in suburbia.

Turnover of tenants has a very high cost in office building investments. Remodeling suites to accommodate new tenants is inordinately expensive. Yet cash flows are appreciably greater in office buildings than residential buildings because of the higher risks in location, leasing, and servicing tenants.

The cash flows are even higher in successful shopping centers and stores. We will now examine the risks and rewards in owning shopping centers and stores.

15 SHOPPING CENTERS AND STORES

Stores, in one form or another, seem to have been with urban society almost from the beginning. Both those shops that sold almost everything that people in a community needed and those that were very specialized have had in common the tendency to group together, forming a marketplace. A recent force that has had a profound effect on the nature of the marketplace is the use of the automobile to do shopping.

Investors in stores or shopping centers can more readily see their trading area than can investors in office buildings. Also the owners of retail property do not have to wait for lease renewal time to see what is happening to the value of their space. Typically the lease in retail property has some percentage arrangement, making the rental income dependent on the volume of business done in the store. The percentage lease feature and the market competition are key features of such investments.

This chapter points out that the risks of investing in shopping centers and stores are higher than those in other types of income-producing real estate. As always the risks could be low if there were a long-term lease providing an assured income. The typical arrangement however is for the owner of the real estate to get more or less rent, depending on the sales volume of the store. Thus cash flow can be the big reward.

RISKS

Investments in stores or shopping centers tend to be exposed to greater hazards than investments in office buildings for several reasons: variability of rents based on store sales; possible devastating effects of competition; and dependency on tenants other than those of the highest credit for the best cash flow.

It is common practice for store leases to call for minimum rents. Higher rents are payable depending on a certain volume of business, with percentages of gross sales above the minimum volumes payable to owners of the real estate. Thus the real estate owners are rewarded when the business of their tenants is superb, usually do well when it is average, but can suffer severe financial losses when it is poor.

Before the advent of the shopping center phenomenon in the suburbs, the best store locations, producing the highest volume of business, were downtown. Such locations were called "100% locations." Streetcars, buses, and other forms of public transportation generally converged on these locations. Land in downtown areas has always been scarce, especially near the 100% location. The easily identifiable commercial district, which exists in every city and indeed in every town, has its best location—a Main Street—and in the past there was fierce competition among the stores for the prime location. Getting "the" location was important and there were no equally desirable locations. Thus a new store—a prospective competitor—had a difficult time in getting a foothold, except at a less desirable location where it would do less business and pay less rent.

Shopping Centers

Shopping facilities follow the people and the movement of people has been to the suburbs. The first shops that moved from the city formed rather small neighborhood centers. They were built on relatively inexpensive land and often did extremely well, earning huge profits for the shopping center owners. To attract high-credit tenants, such as established drug and foodstore chains, inexpensive minimum rents were offered, with higher rents based on a percentage of the gross volume of business above a certain predetermined level. Both the owners and the institutional lenders took some substantial risks, as at times triple A tenants (those with top-quality credit ratings) barely produced enough rents to cover the mortgage payments and collectively sometimes not enough. The owner was then dependent on local shops (such as hardware and delicatessen stores) or service-type establishments (such as barber shops, cleaners, shoe-repair shops) to obtain the rents that would help in carrying the mortgage, pay local property taxes, and hopefully produce an adequate cash flow.

Landowners, seeing a local neighborhood center doing well, emulated and often improved on the original centers by offering better parking, larger variety of stores, and many other attractions to woo local business to their centers. It was easy to build too many stores. Absorbing extra stores is more difficult than absorbing extra apartments. You could lower rents to $1 a year, but tenants would not lease stores if they could not make a living because of a lack of customers.

In a given trading area, better centers can destroy the profitability of a smaller and less appealing center. The shopping habits of suburban residents are constrained by time and distance, so that no matter how enticing a center is in terms of quality shops, parking facilities, decor, and customer convenience, it competes at a local level. Shopping centers, created in what is a proved market, usually have to pay more for land, which seems to go up in price endlessly. Rising costs of construction also make the new center cost more per square foot of retail space. Naturally these two factors tend to hinder the profitability of such investments. Well-located modern centers with a growing population in a well-defined trading area do very well, but what can be devastating is the effect of a brand new shopping center close by, especially if it does a better job.

Shopping centers may be classified into three categories: neighborhood, community, and regional. The neighborhood center is just that, catering to the neighborhood needs of a small area and confined to necessities. It is usually of a "strip nature" with a drugstore at one end, a grocery at the other end, and smaller stores between the two. It is the modern version of the traditional neighborhood strip commercial development where customers could walk to the store.

Community centers cater to a large trading area. They are generally much larger and attract shoe chains; may even have a suburban branch of a local department store; provide bank and post office facilities; usually have a national variety store; and may also include both groceries and drugstores. These are modern versions of the local business districts that were relatively easy to get to. Buying there could save you a trip downtown.

Regional centers usually have two or more department stores and such other major tenants as J.C.Penney; Montgomery Ward; and Sears, Roebuck and Company. The newest feature enclosed malls. They all have many specialty stores, such as apparel, shoes, sporting goods, and restaurants, as well as the type of stores found both in the neighborhood and smaller community centers. The largest regional centers are significant rivals to the downtown shopping districts. They are also developing into centers of community activity and are increasing the range of services offered.

In evaluating ownership risks, you should consider the availability of nearby land that might be zoned for another center and thus develop into devastating competition. Unlike an office building or an apartment house, both of which tend to help when built near others of their kind, new shopping facilities almost always hurt a center that is already operating. Adding more apartments or offices increases the magnetism of the area. Adding more stores of different kinds in a center will help, but not a new center that duplicates many stores and provides no increase in trade area, but only a new division of the existing market. The risks vary among the different kinds of stores and centers, but the risk from new competition is constant in retail real estate.

There are many forms of strategy for protecting your investments from undue risk. For example large scale developers select their shopping center sites from among the potential residential sites and then build up all the land. Another device is to prohibit competition by having all potential competing shopping center sites zoned residential and then lead in the opposition of any attempt to rezone.

Strip Stores

A strip store in the city may be quite risky because the tenants are not ordinarily those with high credit. If there is a lot of strip-store land available, competition can destroy the profits. You may have observed how some strip stores have attracted a lower quality of occupancy with each succeeding tenant. Some are converted for use by light manufacturing businesses, printing shops, and repair stores. Others are used for storage, and still others have uses that can best be described as "seedy". Yet some strip stores can be good investments. A strip store leased to Safeway the A & P, or other national high-credit tenants, with long leases will, however provide good-quality investments. Other stores that are free-standing, have adequate parking, and are rented to strong tenants that are put to interim uses, when you are in effect holding the land for an ultimate profit, can also be profitable. If the land develops into high-priced office-building land for example, just holding a strip store with enough income to help pay the land taxes until the

ultimate land sale is consummated can be very rewarding. In the 1920s many one-story buildings were built for
an interim land use, while being held for a radical upward price change. These are called "taxpayers." Some
have had about that amount of success. Others turned out
to be so well located that the profits were outstanding.

If you purchase a strip store for investment without a
long-term lease, from a nationally rated tenant, consider
that you really are engaging in a form of speculation and
that you have a high-risk investment. Hopefully this type
of investment should produce a better-than-average cash
flow because of these risks.

Evaluating a Shopping center

Neighborhood shopping centers usually have one or two
major tenants in the form of a supermarket and a
drugstore. The strength of your center is determined in
part by the strength of the tenants and also by the basic
size of your trading area. The financing of these centers
is not too difficult, but you will have to rely on the service
stores for your cash flow. The rents from the major
tenants is what the lender is relying on for repayment of
money. If you are satisfied with cash flow that will
primarily be generated from a dry cleaner, barber, beauty shop, or other tenants of this type, do not hesitate.
Many investors however cannot live with this type of risk.
The lenders are also reluctant and may be willing to lend
only with strong credit of the borrower and personal
liability.

Here is an area where you could get reliable help in
developing reasonable data before making a decision.
Most cities have at least one real estate consultant and
market researcher who can provide you with economic
data and analysis on which you can reasonably rely.
These professionals can give you foot traffic counts,
automobile counts, population data, income levels of the
residents of your trading area, and much better data than

you could obtain for example in a study of possible future office-building tenants. This is so because data for making determinations about trading areas for retail purposes are much more easily obtained than data for use in decision-making for most other kinds of nonresidential income-producing property.

Considerations relating to investments in community centers or regional centers are much more complicated and sophisticated. Aside from location, which is most important, and the size of the trading area, other considerations will include the layout of the center, facilities for parking, methods of promoting the center to the public (the owner's responsibility), and plans for maintaining the center and servicing the tenants. The larger the center, the more important are these largely technical matters. Most regional centers are owned by professionals in the business, often developers who have a specific experience in the field. Since the leasing in the original instance, often long before the center is built, is the key factor of the ultimate success of the center, only persons who have national chain-store contracts and access to the largest financial institutions are prone to develop the large regional centers.

The financial reward of the regional shopping center to the investor has probably been greater than in any other field of real estate development. Where the land was originally bought at residential prices and subsequently rezoned for commercial use, the successful projects, with such innovations as the enclosed air- conditioned shopping mall, have reaped and are still receiving phenomenal financial benefits. Not only has the increase in value of land from residential to shopping-center use brought profit, but extra payments have come from the high-credit tenancies on long-term leases in which percentage leases produced overage payments. Some developers have recovered their entire cash investment shortly after the center was completed and occupied. At a high-level conference between a large life insurance company and a developer of one of the largest regional shopping centers of the Eastern Seaboard, a foreign exchange student, upon learning of the absence of any cash investment on the part of the developer, exclaimed, "Why, your rate of return is infinite!"

Although the rewards for the development of a large regional center can be splendid, you must consider the high speculative risk that accompanies the original purchase of a huge tract of acreage. If successful zoning is not obtained and aggressive leasing does not attract tenants with high financial ratings, the owner is left holding a large tract of land that can be used only for the building of houses. The original cost of the land then becomes very high when you add the costs of the economic studies, of holding land (especially if heavily mortgaged), of attorneys' and architects' fees, and of service charges of all those engaged in the predevelopment process. The end result can be nothing more than the ownership of a large tract of land zoned residential, which the owner then must sell at a substantial financial loss to a developer who can put only houses on it, hence will pay only residential prices.

BENEFITS

Cash Flow

In the real estate ownership of a store or shopping center the rental income is usually determined on the basis of a minimum amount of rent plus a percentage of the gross income from sales above that amount which would ordinarily be required to pay the minimum rent. These percentages vary in accordance with the type of establishment. The Urban Land Institute publishes a list of typical rates, which shows the average percentage of gross incomes that stores of different kinds can be reasonably expected to pay. The percentages vary from as little as 1.25% for high-volume food stores to 12% of the gross income for some elegant restaurants. As an investor you certainly would not want to purchase any store or shopping center whose leases do not stipulate a fixed minimum that the tenant must pay. One owner did and found that 8% of nothing is nothing, the volume in a vacant store is very low indeed. Some shopping centers' leases control the business hours of its tenants and other business activities to assure the proper amount of rent. If you choose not to have a percentage lease, then your rent is limited for the duration of the lease. It is reasonable to assume that taxes will rise, the cost of living will rise, and consequently the price of the goods or services sold by the tenant will also rise. With a percentage of the gross sales for such goods and services, it makes good sense to be in an ownership position with such percentages forthcoming. A recently negotiated lease for a banking institution called for a minimum rent and annual increase based on the percentage increase in both demand and time deposits. A major benefit from these investments is overage rental.

Minimum rents are of exceptional importance to potential lenders who want to know that their loan will be serviced from minimum rentals. The amount of the loan depends largely on the income from minimum rents, less expenses. Also the quality of the tenants and the length of the lease will influence the amount of the loan. In shopping centers where the majority of tenants are of the triple A category, as is usual in the larger community and regional shopping centers, the lending institution is making the loan largely on the credit of the tenants over the life of their long-term leases. A very successful leasing program enables the developer of a center to have little or no cash invested after the center is initially tenanted. Although lenders relate the loan to the cost of construction of the improvements and the value of the land, lenders also want to know how they will be repaid. When the majority of tenants are those with excellent national credit and are on long-term leases, lenders make their loans on the basis of the credit of the tenants, rather than the value of the real estate.

In general the longer the lease, the longer the loan. Because the loan will be longer, the amortization per period is less, hence the annual constant will be less. Naturally the longer loans permit a higher cash flow.

Investors try to borrow as much as possible, thereby reducing the amount of cash they have to put in. This high borrowing reduces the amount of cash flow. Thus the cash flow is quite sensitive to changing sales volume. It rises sharply if the center does well and diminishes rapidly if it does poorly. The amount of cash flow thus depends on the volume of business done by the center.

Tax Shelter

Most of the value of a shopping center is in the land itself. Land in good locations is very expensive. Thus under ordinary financial arrangements there is very little, if any, tax shelter in owning stores or shopping centers. Generally a very small portion of the land is used for the buildings, and the balance of the land is used for parking. Since most of the value is in the land (and the land is not depreciable), and very little of the value is in the building (and the maximum rate of depreciation for new shopping centers is 150% declining balance), the tax shelter is practically nonexistent.

Tax shelter may be developed when the investor leases the land. The lease payments are of course deductible as an expense. Since the improvements are depreciable and the loan is on the value of the improvements, which are largely determined by the tenancy and term, it may be possible to develop substantial tax shelter. However the investor, if he holds the property long enough, will give up most of the proceeds of sale that result in the increase of the value of land if he uses leased land. The longer he holds the leased land, the less the time left on his lease.

Naturally the benefit from the favorable lease diminishes and the lease expiration approaches.

Unless the land is leased for an extremely long period of time, say 99 years, and the lease terms are favorable, that is fixed at a low rate over this entire period of time, it may be a mistake to build a center on leased land. All the tax shelter in the world can never be so beneficial as the rewards that can be obtained from proceeds of sale when the land has gone up in value from, say $1 to $10 per square foot.

Another reason why there is very little (if any) tax shelter in owning a store or shopping center is that the amortization on the loan is generally high. The loan terms are usually shorter for shopping centers than for office buildings and sometimes for apartments. Since store leases are not frequently for periods of more than 5 to 10 years, except in the large regional centers where some stores are on leases for as long as 20 years, the result is generally a short-term loan with high amortization. Because the depreciation is small and the amortization is high, there is very little tax shelter, and whatever tax shelter exists at the beginning diminishes quite rapidly. Stores and shopping centers are generally not suited to investors who are tax-shelter-oriented.

Proceeds of Sale

Proceeds of sale are a major benefit to the winners because an investor will buy an expected cash flow even if it is variable. Of course for the losers there is little or no cash flow and the proceeds of sale can be less than the cash invested. The quality of the property and its location to serve its market are of prime importance. Your risk is reduced through leases to high-quality tenants. Since your lower-quality tenants account for the bulk of the variation in cash flow, their success is critical to your success.

If excessive competition erodes the sales volume of a center, the proceeds of sale can be very small or nonexistent. If the cash flow diminishes, an investor would have to wait a long time to get a substantial benefit. The longer you have to wait to get the money, the less it is worth. Buyers will pay more for demonstrated cash flows than for those that they are "assured" will be forthcoming. Because of excessive competition some shopping centers have deteriorated. Some stores are leased to lower-quality tenants and some, though relatively new, are torn down and the land put to some other use. The obsolescence of the center is the great risk.

Successful centers, by producing very high cash flows, provide a highly successful profit at sale. Investors are looking for potential increases in sales volume and will pay for it, but at rates that reflect the risk. Thus the cash flow must be the major benefit because if it is not high, there will be little or no proceeds of sale.

Owning stores, particularly strip stores, is similar in management to owning rental houses and apartments, but does not require the same frequent activity. It certainly is less aggravating and time-consuming to collect rents from one or two tenants than it is to collect the same amount of rent from many tenants, as in an apartment house. The disadvantage of owning one store is the same as in owning one house, only more so. When the store is vacant, you have a vacancy loss of 100%. Renting a vacant store typically takes longer than renting a vacant house. The market is "thinner."

Even though owning store property is more risky than owning apartments, the competition to acquire a smaller shopping center or a store is not quite so keen as that which exists in the marketplace for smaller apartments. It is therefore possible for an astute investor, who can properly assess the risk, to develop a much higher cash flow than would be possible in an apartment project. Since the larger neighborhood centers, community centers, and regional centers are developed by professionals in the real estate business, you would be generally in association with a developer if you were to get in on the upside of the pyramid. You can get in on an existing shopping center, but it would be on the downside of the pyramid, and unless you have good leases, the risk is high.

SELECTION

In selecting an appropriate investment in a store property, location must be the most important consideration. You have to be assured that not only is there a demand for store services at that location, but also that the demand will be growing. Try to determine what area the store will serve. Carefully evaluate other buildings in the area and concern yourself with what competition can do to take away the market that you feel exists in the area. You must carefully evaluate your tenant or prospective tenant and be concerned with the terms of the lease. You must also concern yourself with the physical and functional characteristics of the property. Inexperienced investors generally do not evaluate some items, which can amount to fairly expensive errors in the selection of a store. Aside from location, the most expensive error can be in buying a store with an air-conditioning and heating facility that has either worn out or will wear out soon, requiring total replacement. Another error frequently made is in failing to evaluate the quality and adequacy of the plumbing facilities. Care should also be exercised to determine that the roof is in sound condition, and if it is not, to have an estimate made of the cost of its replacement. Most store leases are written so that the owner is responsible for "structural" repairs, while the tenant is responsible for decorating. All three of the items mentioned fall into the category of "structural" repairs.

In acquiring a shopping center you have to be concerned about the same questions as in buying stores, but you generally need (and can relatively easily obtain) a professional market research study. You should have the valuable data necessary to help you make your decision. Few investors jump into the ownership of major shopping centers or engage in major shopping-center development without the company of professionals in the business. Even with the expertise being provided for you, it is incumbent on you to ask the same questions and to examine the performance record of the professional with whom you choose to invest.

In addition to the factors just cited, remember that obsolescence in shopping centers is high, with styles and modes of development continually changing. You must convince yourself that the shopping center will be able to compete for quite a while and that the trade area is large enough not only to support the center but also to enhance it in terms of a growing population. The safety of the investment is inherent in the location. The lease is a form of insurance that cash will be generated. If you have neither, forget it, If you have both, the rewards can be attractive.

FINANCING

The financing for stores and shopping centers is quite limited as compared to apartments and office buildings. This is so because they are more risky. As already mentioned, amortization is high because of the relatively short term of the loans, and there is an increasing trend, because of the risks involved, for lenders to take a portion of either the gross or the net income received by the owner from the operation of the property. Because of the short-term leases, there is a possibilty that little or no cash flow could be developed. It is necessary therefore to find a lender who is willing to set the amortization rate for a longer term, such as 20 or 25 years, even though he may require a balloon payment at the end of 10 or 15 years. It is increasingly difficult to do this without offering the lender either a very high interest rate or participation in the cash flow. And you had better be right about the center and its location, because refinancing when the balloon payment becomes due depends heavily on your leases. With the added risk of changing mortgage markets, you would be well advised to use a sole security clause to protect yourself from personal liability.

The investor who is considering the purchase of stores or shopping centers will no doubt conclude that the risks and the rewards are higher than in office buildings and apartments. A new investor might invest in a store or even two, but it is not recommended that he invest in a shopping center until he has either an apartment development or an office building in his real estate investment portfolio. This is so because it is hardly the type of investment someone could buy for retirement income, unless of course it is a single store, such as a free- standing grocery store leased to a very high-quality tenant for at least 20 years. The chance for profits is excellent if the location is good, but most investors who have done extremely well in shopping center investments have done so because of their association with a large-scale developer who has all the elements necessary for success.

CONCLUSIONS

When investing in a shopping center still to be built, it makes good sense to evaluate the developer, the kinds of percentage leases that bind the owner, and the type and quality of tenants. These influence the cash flow during ownership and the proceeds of sale later. The proceeds of sale will be the greatest when the original cash flow based on minimum rents has considerably increased because of consistent rental overages (rental payments in excess on minimum, as required in a percentage lease).

Seasoned developers will know what percentage they can get on the lease and will be aware of the devastating effects of competition. Hopefully they would have examined the possibilities of other shopping centers inside their trading area and selected a favorable location and time.

Because the tax shelter is relatively small, the cash flow must be adequate, without even considering overages. If the cash flow is not high, you will be taking inordinate risks. You can get excellent rewards from owning shopping centers, but you have to depend on the overages.

Some investors prefer special-purchase property: hotels, motels, and industrial buildings. These can give rewards comparable to those of owning shopping centers. The risks and rewards generally found in special-purpose properties are discussed in the next chapter.

16 INDUSTRIAL, MOTEL, HOTEL, AND OTHER SPECIAL-PURPOSE PROPERTY

Industrial and special-purpose property is more hetero-geneous as a group than any of the previously discussed kinds of real estate. The group is so diverse because of the physical differences among the various properties that fall into the classification and because the rental markets vary quite widely.

Some industrial and special-purpose property is owner-occupied and is not available to the real estate in-vesting public. The only way you could participate in the benefits from the investments in the owner-occupied pro-perty is by being the owner-occupant. This is frequently done in the case of small family-owned companies. They have the assurances of a tenant as long as they have the business and as long as the property is suited to the business. If you own a business, you might consider own-ing the real estate you use.

If you invest in the stock market, you may be par-ticipating in the benefits of owner-occupied real estate if the company in which you have a share owns rather than rents. Many companies rent or lease because they do not want the risks of ownership or prefer to use their capital in other ways. Some firms aggressively seek investment opportunities for the real estate they use in their business and may make substantial profit from these "side operations." For example food chains and some department store companies go into shopping center development.

There is also industrial and special-purpose real estate that is leased for the life of the building. The user of the space does not want to tie up his capital in real estate, but is willing to make a long-term commitment to pay for the use of the property. The investor prefers to have the guaranteed cash flow (provided that the credit of the tenant is good) and the benefits of tax shelter and proceeds of sale.

Some industrial and special-purpose property competes in a space market where at some point in time there is a vacant building available for lease. Markets for this kind of space can be very "thin," that is there are few buyers and few sellers. This chapter emphasizes risks and rewards in investing in properties with these "thin" markets for space.

Motels and hotels are also special-purpose property. They have been called "transient residential." More recently they are sometimes referred to as being in the hospitality and convention business. Operating a motel or hotel is more of a business than operating other kinds of real estate investments; the management techniques also differ. In most income-producing property the investor sells space, generally to the same party for a long period of time. With motels and hotels, the duration of the stay is short, and frequently the convention-support services, recreation, or such other services as food is what the "tenant" is buying. These properties are more of a real estate investment when they are leased to motel and hotel operators. They thus have characteristics similar to other special-purpose property. Unleased motels and hotels may well fit into your investment portfolio, but only if you want to own a real estate used in your business: that is owning such real estate will put you into the motel or hotel business.

RISKS

If the property is leased for the life of the building or even just a very long term, then the risk is very closely related to the credit of the tenant and the terms of the lease. If the property is repeatedly exposed to the market for leasing, then the risk is closely related to the breadth of the market. Properties with strong leases and broad markets are low-risk investments. Properties with weak leases and thin markets are quite risky.

Industrial space used for research and development-type facilities may resemble office-building space not only in physical appearance, but also in risks. Industrial space in industrial parks are a type of facility that can, within reason, adapt to numerous users and therefore need not stand vacant long because there are tenants who are continually coming into the market. Under normal circumstances, a steady stream of tenants are entering the market.

Problems arise when there are few potential users coming into the market for the space and not only is the frequency low, but also the timing is erratic. Under those circumstances a property could sit vacant for a long time.

It might not be difficult to find a tenant for an inductrial project of modest size when there is a basic structure of four walls, a floor, and a roof with high adaptability to many uses. But there could be a problem in finding tenants if a prospective tenant required one or more of the following:

1. Floor of high-load-bearing qualities, as for printing or other heavy machinery.
2. A vibration-free structure for some type of delicate electronic work.

3. Sound, temperature, and humidity control for electronic data-processing equipment.

4. High electric power capability for machinery use.

5. Pure and consistent water supply for beverage manufacture.

6. Elaborate and ample office space for unusually large office staff.

7. Raised dock facilities for shipping by truck.

8. Rail spur for rail transportation and storage.

9. Exceptionally high ceilings for movement of large objects.

10. Minimum shelter from the elements, permitting a low-cost facility.

With such special requirements, particular tenants may find that many available buildings do not meet their needs. Sometimes the buildings could not be brought up to these standards even if the tenants or the owners were willing to make an additional investment. The available space may have features that were expensive to install, but are of little, if any, use to the prospective tenant. They would therefore be unwilling to pay for them, and owners would be unwilling to rent for less than what they consider to be a fair market price. The difficulty is that the market for space of particular physical characteristics is very limited.

Theaters and bowling alleys are examples of special-purpose properties with the same type of problem. When movie attendance was down, some old theaters were gutted and put to a lower use. The capital loss was substantial, but in many cases it was the best available choice. Currently movie theaters are being built in shopping centers and will have some more adaptability, but the adaptability is expensive.

Bowling alleys may not adapt so easily if the structure is a free-standing building. The risk of competition in bowling alleys was very high during the boom. One bowling alley could do quite well. When a second opened near-by, both went broke.

There are varying characteristics that influence the adaptability of special-purpose property and the element of risk. Generally the more that is spent on specialized design and facilities, the thinner the market and the greater the risk. The longer you have to wait to recover the extra cost, the greater the risk.

The larger number of potential uses for specialized space without major alterations, the less the risk. The greater the strength of the lease *and* the tenant, the smaller the risk.

The location is always important. When the lease is over, the factor of location may be critical. If the area has deteriorated, a prospective tenant for the same kind of use would be difficult to find even with a sacrifice in rent-al. If however the area is upgraded so that higher and bet-ter uses are available to the land, there is a substantial reduction in risk. The vacant building does not have to be razed to get a benefit from the improved location. rather, additional investment to adapt the building to a needed use may well be warranted. When that building is ob-solete, the land may be cleared for another use.

If the property is leased for the economic life of the building, or the building is leased to a series of tenants long enough, the risk is fairly low. A big benefit may result from appreciation of the land. If the land is appreciating because the location is getting better, the risk is low. If not, you had better get your benefits while the building is leased.

Rewards

The rewards will vary by the kinds of risks that you take. Property leased for a long period of time will provide modest, but steady cash flow. The big variable will be proceeds of sale. Property with space that is repeatedly exposed to the market will provide high cash return on the down payment (COD) when leased. The relative benefit of tax shelter will vary with the land value. A well-leased building on cheap land in the middle of no place will provide great shelter. Property with high-valued land will provide little tax shelter.

Cash Flow

The cash flow on leased properties is readily determinable if the lease is "net net net," which means that the tenant pays all the expenses except perhaps for preserving the structure of walls and roof. Under the terms of such a lease, tenants would pay real property taxes and would pay any increases in taxes. Investors would know how many dollars they would receive.

The investor might be uncertain as to the purchasing power of those dollars and would therefore seek to get some protection from inflation in the lease. Sometimes an index lease is used. Under this arrangement the rent changes periodically in the same proportion as the price index. Any price index could be used—wholesale price index, retail price index, or construction cost index. None of these however is necessarily an accurate reflection of the changing rental value of the property. Sometimes a reappraisal lease is employed. Under this arrangement the property is periodically reappraised to determine its fair rental value, which then becomes the new rent. Typically the lessor and the lessee would each select an independent appraiser and the two appraisers would select a third. the three appraisers would then agree on a fair rental value, which would be the new rental under the lease.

The investor may choose between properties that are leased for a long period of time and those that repeatedly come up for lease renewal. There are substantial market risks in short-term leases, hence the allowance for vacancies must be high, as must the expense ratios. If the market is strong and getting stronger, the cash flow will be exceptionally good. The cash on the down payment could turn out to be 15 to 20%. On the other hand prolonged vacancies and expensive remodeling could reduce cash flow to negative amounts for substantial periods of time. The average cash on the down payment (COD) would be very small, if any.

Many investors desire a stable cash flow and accept as little as 7 or 8% or even less when the tenant and the lease are strong. This may be the major reward when there are few depreciable assets and the lease is for a long term.

Tax Shelter

The amount of tax shelter is determined by the excess of depreciation over amortization. One determinant of depreciation is the distribution of value between land and building. An investor bought a warehouse located in a remote area on cheap land. The ratio of building to land was about 10 to 1, so that most of the cost was depreciable.

Another determinant of depreciation is the remaining life of the building. In the case of a 20-year lease on a building that has no expected use after the 20 years, the rate of depreciation would be 5% per year on a straight-line basis. Using accelerated depreciation at 150% of the straight-line rate (available only to first owners), it would be higher in the early years.

If the loan were amortized over the life of the building, say the 20 years of the lease, the amortization in the early years would be very low. Thus the combination of an accelerated depreciation and a long-term loan could give a substantial tax shelter in the early years. Most industrial or special-purpose properties however do not have this extremely favorable set of tax shelter conditions, so that tax shelter, though it may be obtained in varying degrees, is not the typical major benefit.

Proceeds of Sale

There are investors who bought cheap, sold dear, and reaped big profits in a short period of time. This can be done in a "thin" market by finding something underpriced and then selling it to the "right buyer." Doing so is a business, not investing. In fact the IRS would classify such a so-called investor as a "dealer" and attempt to tax the "capital gains" as ordinary income.

Although it is possible to make such transactions occasionally and still preserve the investor status along with the long-term capital gains, they are not recommended for investors. The risks of loss of time and money in trying to make a profit from someone else's lack of knowledge about current conditions and opportunities are very high because you would have to buy "under" market. It is difficult enough to find a suitable investment at market price without the risks of taking a bargain. When it looks too good to be true, watch out.

A Strategy

Investors should seek situations with which they can live for a long time. If you want to make short-term profits from proceeds of sale, then pick situations where some underlying forces for change are at work, causing the value to change. Under these circumstances you can get the profits from the rise in value when the market recognizes what you "knew" all along.

If you are going to deal in a market, you should know that market, We suggested earlier that investors in rental homes had opportunities for short-term profits. The house market is an active market and one with which any investor can develop familiarity. As you move to thinner markets, the knowledge about events affecting current conditions becomes more difficuly to come by and the cost of error much higher. You would therefore do well in markets in which you have more expertise—and the thinner the market, the more difficult it is to acquire expertise. There are relatively few speculators in industrial and special-purpose property. To paraphrase a saying of aircraft pilots, there are old speculators and there are bold speculators, but there are no old bold speculators.

There are types of investors about whom we hear little. They are not the type talked about at social affairs. This is in contrast to the social conversation among and about business and professional people who invest in real estate as an avocation and who discuss opportunities and results as though they were talking about baseball, the stock market, or other "game" activities.

The very wealthy have to keep their money invested. And unless someone is operating their investments for them, they would welcome staying with an investment a long time, if only because finding a suitable investment is time-consuming and expensive.

Such investors do not sell frequently because replacing the investment with a better investment is very difficult. They do not refinance properties to draw out the cash because they would only have to find some other place for it. Saving the interest expense seems to be earnings enough. They do not use accelerated depreciation because they do not wish to hasten the day when amortization exceeds depreciation. They hold some properties so long that they are mortgage free, or close to it. The cash flow is a major benefit. It is true that they could obtain substantial benefit from proceeds of sale, if they were to sell, but they like their position in the property. Such investors find a place for well-leased industrial and special-purpose property in their portfolio.

The message that we are sending in various ways is that it is important to know not just how to get into the investment, but also how to get out of it. Of all types of property, the industrial and special-purpose type is the most difficult to get out of. Therefore timing is of exceptional importance.

You should time the sale for a favorable market. You, the investor, must choose when. And if you do, the proceeds of sale may produce very high profits.

You may wish to sell when the demand for the property is strong. In the case of leased property, if a few years are still left in the lease, there may be some problem about the uncertainty of the event several years hence. Sale to a user at the time of availability could produce a favorable price or sale to an investor shortly after leasing for a long term could provide an attractive price from an investor who wants the cash flow.

Usually there is a catalyst for a sale. It can be a lease expiration. It can be the pressure of vanishing tax shelter or the presence of some other opportunity. The best pressure is that of an investment plan that suggests the right timing for all of the investment portfolio considerations. Under those circumstances the trade could be a very helpful device.

SELECTION

Selection of location is always important. When you are ready to sell, what has happened to the location may be the biggest single factor in determining the profit.

Selection of the tenant or the tenant-property combination is also of great importance. With the right tenant and length of lease, the location is irrelevant. The selection process then requires the choice of risk combinations of location and tenant.

In looking at property you will want to consider its physical characteristics and marketability. The selection process is influenced by picking the right characteristics of the property, with such leases as it has, for your purposes.

FINANCING

Financing special-purpose property is more difficult than financing other kinds of real estate. Generally the rates are higher and the repayment period is shorter. This is so because the property is less marketable. Strong leases change the picture. If the lease is strong enough, the loan may be made on the strength of the lease rather than the security of the real estate.

Frequently the seller provides some financing. If you want a highly leveraged investment, you need a seller who will carry back a mortgage. When you go to sell and want top price, you may find yourself holding the mortgage, which may fit into your portfolio quite well.

Industrial and special-purpose property is not the place to start your real estate investing. As your portfolio grows however you may be prepared for some of the risks and find the rewards attractive.

The increased rewards may well be the high cash flow and some element of diversification. You would also have an investment that requires little of your time to manage. You may become interested in such property at the right time in developing your real estate investment portfolio.

CONCLUSIONS

Unless you have an unusual situation—a very high-quality tenant under a long-term lease—you are dealing in a very "thin" marketplace.

The result is a very high risk at the time of sale of special-purpose property. Because of this market risk, the cash flow should be substantially higher than for properites that have broader markets, such as apartments, shopping centers, and office buildings.

By now you may have formed an opinion of the basic types of properties you would consider as an investment. Your strategy has shaped itself to accommodate one or more choices among all the classes: rental houses, small apartments, office buildings, garden and medium-rise apartments, high-rise apartments, shopping centers and stores, and perhaps motels, hotels, and other special-purpose buildings.

Before you learn how to "get in" on real estate investments, perhaps your strategy should include an assessment of the advantages and disadvantages of the various methods of ownership. In the remaining chapters we examine the various forms of ownership and focus on how best to "get in."

PART FIVE

GETTING IN ON INVESTMENT PROFITS

17 SELECTING THE FORM OF INVESTMENT

When you are ready to make your first real estate investment and have made all the decisions so far discussed, you still must decide on the *method of ownership.* The right decision will assure you of equitable federal and state income tax treatment as well as give you the control you need.

Should you own the real estate solely; with your spouse, brother, or sister; or perhaps a parent or child? Should your ownership be in partnersip with friends, or strangers?

What about stocks or securities of real estate builders or investors?

What kind of evidence of ownership should you have?

The answers to these questions are not purely legal or tax oriented. Although a lawyer should be consulted when a decision to buy is imminent, other considerations—financial, social, and even philosophical—are present. These considerations should be part of your investment strategy. They should be made in advance of your purchase.

The easiest way to get in on real estate investments is to respond to a few selected advertisements in the Sunday newspaper, inspect an array of property that seems to fit your needs, and, after making some comparisons, buy.

This is the way many investors originally get into real estate. But it is not necessarily the best way.

For some people the most convenient way of getting in on real estate investment is to join others by investing in a real estate syndicate, which may be offered by a developer or through his attorney or accountant. Another way to get into these syndicates is through friends and colleagues who know the principal who is developing or acquiring the property.

If you do not want to go it alone and do not have the comfort of the company of your friends or colleagues, you could seek out any of several well-known real estate development companies or real estate investment trusts that are listed on the major stock exchanges. You are then in the stock market, having to make such an investment through a securities broker. Some of the major industrial companies listed on the New York Stock Exchange are into real estate, so that if you happen to buy stock in Gulf Oil, U.S. Steel, ITT, or Chrysler, you are indirectly investing in real estate.

You can get into real estate by any or all of the foregoing ways. The difference lies in what you want to own, how much control you want over your investment, whose expertise you will rely on, and the kinds of risks and rewards you seek. This chapter provides a guide to getting into the form of real estate investment best suited to your investment objectives.

DIRECT OWNERSHIP

The most popular form of real estate ownership in this country is direct ownership. By direct ownership we mean that one or more persons own the "fee," which means having title to the real estate.

Having title means possessing various rights to the property, such as the right to use and to exclude others from using as well as the right to lease to others and to get possession back at the end of the lease. Other rights include pledging the property as security for a debt, as with borrowing under a mortgage.

Owning all the rights to a parcel of real estate means having a "fee simple" interest. This is as complete an ownership as is possible under our system. Within certain limits you can do whatever you want with your property. The use that you make of it may be limited by zoning and building regulations, which are derived from the state's police power. You may be forced to sell your property to make the land available for another purpose, such as highways or schools, in the interest of the community. This right to take private property for public use, with just compensation, is called eminent domain. Your rights are also economically limited by property taxation in that if the property taxes are not paid, the property may be sold by the taxing authorities to pay the taxes.

Your ownership and control when you own the "fee" may be quite complete except for the limitations of police power, eminent domain, and taxation. You also have the right to convey the property during your lifetime or you may devise it (leave it by will). Property not passed by will goes to heirs according to the laws of the state. Where there is neither provision for passing ownership nor heirs, the state claims title by "escheat".

Owning the property in fee means that you have the residential claim. You or the previous owner or his predecessor could have encumbered the property—by borrowing on it, by being behind in taxes which become a lien on the property, by having an obligation to contractors or subcontractors for work performed on the property for which mechanics' liens have been filed, by having given someone the right to make limited use of the property without taking possession such as by granting an easement for a pipeline or driveway. You could also have leased the property for a long term, giving the tenants most of the rights, with you retaining the right to collect the rent called for by the lease and the right to get possession and use of the property at the end of the lease.

As one person, you could have all of the rights of ownership (less those that you may have contracted away). In the case of a husband and wife owning their residence, some states provide for a form of ownership called "tenancy by the entirety." This form of ownership views the husband and wife as one person under the law. Thus title remains vested in the survivor. In many states husband and wife take title to property as joint tenants with right of survivorship. Joint tenancy means that the surviving spouse becomes the sole owner. It may be used for investment property not only by husband and wife, but also by any two or more people of very close relationship who wish the survivor to become the owner.

When two people own the property together, but want the right to dispose of their undivided one-half interests separately, they take title as "tenants in common." They share the benefits equally and have, in combination with each other, control over the property. A tenancy in common may be held by more than two people and they may hold equal or unequal shares. But in combination all the owners have control of the property.

You may desire some form of direct ownership of real estate in order to have the complete ownership and control. You will have to rely on your own expertise and judgment, using any expertise you can hire, You then bear all the risks that go with sole ownership and you get all the benefits.

CONDOMINIUMS AGAIN

The condominium is a form of direct ownership (see p. 196). It is direct ownership of a unit that occupies horizontal and vertical space in a complex (apartments, office, or other). Thus there are other direct owners of somewhat similar property with some common interests.

Aside from any generally similar interests, the various condominium owners jointly own the common property. Usually this includes the land on which the building is built. Almost always there is a set of common spaces, such as central hallways, lobbies, swimming pool, and the like.

Investing in condominiums thus involves a special kind of group ownership. That is group ownership of common facilities. Investors who choose to utilize this form of investment will find that the control over the property is limited by the rules and regulations which govern all members of the group of which each condominium owner is a member.

GROUP OWNERSHIP

If you want to join with others for the purpose of investing in real estate, you might become a member of a syndicate or joint venture. Simply stated, a syndicate is a group of investors. Syndication of real estate merely means obtaining a group of investors to own the property together.

They each have an undivided interest in the whole. Properly organized and operated syndicates and joint ventures *pay no federal income taxes.* Only the members pay taxes. Consequently losses generated by depreciation flow directly to the members or individuals. Sometimes the syndicate takes the form of a general partnership. Title would be held in the name of the partnership and each of the partners can act for the partnership. This means that you will be bound by what your partner does. You would own an interest in the partnership and have a strong element of control—but so would your partner.

If what you really want to do is to get together with some other investors for a single investment, you could participate in a joint venture. Under the joint venture arrangement you and your associates would designate some member or members of the group to act as trustee or trustees. The trustee would hold title for the benefit of the participants and would manage the affairs of the joint venture. This form of ownership is used in jurisdictions not having a limited partnership act.

When you enter into a general partnership or a joint venture, you can decide with your associates on the rights and liabilities of each partner. You have a great deal of freedom as to what you agree to among your selves. The public however will deal with your organization, solely relying on a partner to represent the partnership and a trustee to represent a joint venture. The law attempts to protect innocent third parties, so that you may find yourself bound to others by the commitments made by your associates.

Frequently a syndicate is put together by an investor, developer, broker, or other real estate specialist with the idea that he or she will manage the affairs of the syndicate. The syndicator will exercise complete control over the operation of the investment, as provided in the partnership agreement. A limited partnership is formed to effect such an arrangement.

The syndicator usually becomes the general partner. He manages the investment because he is vested with control of the property. He assumes the liability ordinarily held by partners in a regular partnership. He may put in money, or services, or both. And he of course shares in the benefits.

The limited partners are the other investors. They put up their money. The amount of loss they could sustain is limited by the amount of money they put up. The limited partner does not actively participate in management. Such control as he has is set forth in the limited partnership agreement.

The limited partnership has become very popular for the passive investor. One reason is that many states have adopted a uniform limited partnership statute that is generally well understood in the investment community. It is popular with those who wish to rely on the expertise of others and who do not want the responsibility of management nor the liability of a general partner. The economic benefits of ownership remain the same except as modified by the agreement.

As you would expect the general partner is compensated for his services. Infrequently the compensation is paid at the beginning. Usually the general partner enjoys his benefits during ownership and at the time of sale.

The major disadvantage of investing in any syndicate is the lack of liquidity. Selling a syndicate interest is frequently more difficult than selling the entire property, as in direct ownership. What you would have to sell is an interest in an investment, and the market for such an interest can be very limited. Furthermore the partnership agreement usually places certain restrictions on transferability.

If you invest in small groups, you may use a buy-sell type of agreement. Under such an arrangement you would offer to buy out your partner(s), but give them the option to buy you out. Sometimes you can sell your interest to other people. One limitation may be found in the terms of the agreement, while another may be the lack of marketability of your interest.

If the syndicate is a private syndicate—a few friends, acquaintances, or business associates who got together to make an investment—then the SEC does not regulate the initial offering of interests to your associates. However if the interests are offered to a larger, diversified group, the syndication becomes a public offering and is subject to SEC regulation. If you own an interest in a private syndicate, you can look around for someone to buy you out, but it is almost always financially more rewarding to be prepared to wait until the property is ultimately sold and the syndicate is dissolved.

Public syndicates may have a large number of owners and the interests may be widely traded. How widely they are traded depends on a number of factors: the size of ownership units, the number of investors in the venture, how successful it is, and the presence (or absence) of a securities dealer who may be maintaining a market. Sometimes you may have as much liquidity as you would in an over-the-counter common stock.

While the real estate owned by an investment group may have spectacular increases in value over the short term, you will usually have to wait until refinancing or sale of the property to get the full benefit. This occurs in group ownership because all you can sell is your interest in the property, and the market for that interest may bring you a lower price than your proportionate share of the value of the real estate.

REAL ESTATE CORPORATIONS

The need for liquidity in group ownership of real estate may be met by use of the corporate device. Title to the real estate is held by the corporation, and the affairs of the corporation are managed by its officers. Investors own stock in these corporations much as they would own stock in any other corporation. Naturally the wider the market for the stock, the more liquid the investment.

The disadvantage of the corporate entity for real estate is that the corporation has to pay corporate income taxes. The dividends paid to the stockholders are taxable to the stockholder. Thus the income earned by the real estate is taxed twice—once when received by the corporation and once when received by the stockholders. This disadvantage can be offset by having investments that produce only tax-sheltered income. The tax-sheltered income that is distributed to the stockholders is considered to be a return of capital rather than a dividend, for federal income tax purposes. In this instance the cash flow is not taxable. The cost basis of the stock is however reduced; hence when the stock is sold, a capital gains tax has to be paid. However for taxable years beginning after June 30, 1972, dividends can no longer be sheltered by the excess of accelerated depreciation over straight-line depreciation.

A major reason for using a corporation is the limited liability for all investors. Some of this advantage may be offset by the fact that some lenders require guarantees by the principals of the corporation if the financial strength of the corporation in inadequate for the loan.

Frequently a real estate corporation is involved in developing investment property for its own account. Thus the firm is a hybrid—part developer and part investor. Some real estate corporations make their profit by developing and selling, frequently giving up the possibility of making capital gains because the IRS considers them as "dealers." A few diversified large corporations, whose shares are widely held and traded on the New York Stock Exchange, have sought further diversification and have entered the real estate development and investment business.

REAL ESTATE INVESTMENT TRUSTS

When the business of the organization is passively holding real estate for investment, the device of a real estate investment trust may be used. Under the real estate investment trust arrangement, the trust must distribute 90% of its taxable income if it wishes to be exempt from paying income taxes on the distributed amounts.

As an investor in a real estate investment trust (REIT) that qualifies under the real estate investment trust provisions of the *Internal Revenue Code,* if the REIT distributes all (instead of 90%) of its taxable income, you pay taxes while the trust pays none. Undistributed capital gains however are payable by the trust itself. The trustees of a REIT manage the investments, so that you have no control over the investment policy. You own a beneficial interest, which is marketable. Some are even listed on one of the stock exchanges.

It is frequently difficult to know what the real estate owned by a trust is worth. Traditional accounting methods when applied over long periods of time to income- producing real estate do a very poor job of reflecting earnings and values. A depreciation allowance is calculated and book values are kept. But there is no way to reflect changes in land value or changes in building value brought about by urban growth, inflation, and higher building costs. The public finds it very difficult to evaluate the real estate assets of a REIT by reading its financial statements.

Appraisers could help you judge the assets of the trust, but in the last analysis, owners of shares benefit from cash distributions and possible future capital-gains taxation combined with possible profit of the sale of trust shares. The price you receive from the sale of your trust shares is as much a reflection of the securities market as it is of the underlying real estate values. Thus when you buy into a REIT, you are buying a *security* whose assets are predominately in real estate.

There are two basic types of real estate investment trusts—*equity trusts* and *mortgage trusts*. They differ in the type of investments they make.

The equity trusts have most of their investments in the form of equity (fee title) in real estate. They buy residential, commercial, and/or industrial real estate for long-term investment. Frequently they finance the purchases by use of long-term amortizing mortgages. The trusts distribute all of the taxable income, so that only the investor (not the trust) pays tax on the rental income.

The mortgage trusts have most of their investments in the form of real estate mortgages or trust deeds. Some of the investments are in permanent (long-term) mortgages on income-producing real estate and owner-occupied housing. The more profitable business in the early 1970s was in interim loans that provide money for construction. The mortgage trust lends money as a construction loan (on the upside of the pyramid) and has its loan paid off with the proceeds of a permanent lòan. Since construction loans are expensive, these trusts earn attractive rates of return. These earnings are enhanced by the use of borrowed money. Many of these trusts got into great difficulty by lending on projects which should never have been built. The adverse consequences of these bad loans were magnified because the trusts themselves were heavy borrowers. Some borrowed so much that the banks which lent to them also got into trouble.

The equity trusts are for investors who want:

1. The long-term benefits of real estate investment.
2. A passive position in their investment.
3. The liquidity of the real estate investment trust shares.

The mortgage trusts, particularly those that specialize in interim financing, are for persons who prefer the high returns that go with the development process on the up-side of the pyramid. In recent years these trusts have run into the problems noted and the survivors are taking a new look into their future.

FINDING THE INVESTMENT

Finding a suitable investment is not an easy task. The market is sufficiently disorganized so that you can spend a good deal of time looking for the suitable investment even if you know the right place to look. Looking in the wrong place will of course make it even more difficult, if not impossible, to find a suitable investment.

The difficulties in finding a particular type of invest-ment are part of the consideration in selecting the type of investment. Thus you will want to consider the time in-volved in the searching process when you decide what kind of real eatate investment is best for you.

Direct Ownership

If you want to invest through direct ownership, you must seek out the property. You could start looking for the property directly or you could look for a real estate agent, preferably a Realtor, to help you.

If you have decided on the location, which is frequently the case, you can select a Realtor by finding out who is active in the general location. One way to do this is to drive through the neighborhoods that interest you, searching for the "For Sale" and "Sold" signs. If you are looking for single-family houses or small apartment buildings or land, you may be able to find the property directly. If you are looking for larger investment properties, this method will not work because this type of property does not usually have a "For Sale" sign on it.

If you are undecided about the location and class of real estate, you may want to explore various locations. The classified ads are a good place to start. By following through on various ads you will discover areas of the city in which there is some sales activity. Clues will include what is being advertised as well as what the brokers and salesmen show you and tell you. Listening is one of the best forms of gathering market information, especially if you ask questions that let people show you how much they know about what is happening in real estate.

When responding to ads it is well to remember that most real estate ads are designed to find buyers, not to sell a specific parcel of property. While it is true that an ad is meant to help sell the advertised property, it should also be obvious that a real estate agent with fifty properties cannot consistently afford to advertise all of them and so will spend the ad money in order to get prospects. He advertises what he thinks will get the most calls from prospective buyers and he sells whatever the buyer will buy, advertised or not.

When you call in response to an ad, you should ask a few pertinent questions to help you decide whether to make an appointment. The questions are usually about the property in an attempt to "qualify" it, that is to see whether it is worth pursuing. You might rule it out because it is in the wrong location, too big or too small, old or new, or excessively overpriced. One thing about income-producing property is that it pays for itself, and most property available is not on the market to be sold at the best obtainable price within a given period of time as is frequently the case with a house. As a result you could spend a lot of time looking at property that can be bought only if you are willing to overpay.

What you really want to do in your call in response to an ad is qualify the property and the sales agents. If they are novices, they will more often than not wind up wasting your time, and theirs. If they know their business, they will be able to provide you with the help you need.

When you call, astute salespersons will qualify you only to the extent of finding out whether you should meet. They will answer whatever question they can in the process of making an appointment. The person who knows the business will seek to establish a relationship quickly without scaring the caller away. Since you need a qualified salesperson, you should play the game, making appointments only with those who do their job properly.

There are frequently easier ways to find a good salesperson and a good firm. Personal recommendations from your friends and acquaintances can be helpful. They may know of qualified Realtors because they have been doing business with them. Your accountant, attorney, or banker may know who can help you. If you do not have such a reference, you could seek out the local real estate board.

Most local real estate boards are affiliates of the National Association of Realtors (NAR). This trade association seeks to increase the professional competence of its members and the industry as a whole. It also has a code of ethics and self-polices its membership. Members who belong to the affiliate professional associations are also likely to have achieved high levels of professional competence.

The man or woman to see at the local board is the chief executive officer. The title is frequently executive vice president or executive secretary. In any event he or she usually is the highest-paid full-time staff person, knows who does a good job, and will gladly give you a few names from which to choose.

The real estate editors of local newspapers also know who is active in various specialties. You can check with them or at least watch the real estate section of the newspaper to see who is most active in the areas in which you have an interest.

Simply stated you have to find the right people in order to find the right real estate investment. You need someone who knows what is for sale and, unless you are prepared for some agonizing time wasting, you should look for a qualified man or woman.

You may find that working with two or three salespersons suits your needs. In essence they will build a profile of what they believe you would buy. They will look through their own listings to match available properties with your needs. They will look to competition to cooperate in a sale and will list properties as they become available. You may portray slightly different profiles to different salesmen.

Unless you enjoy spending lots of time looking at property, you should sort out the kinds of property you will consider. There are various ways to sort, depending on your objectives.

Typically you will determine a price range and a down payment range. You will also determine a general class of property, such as apartments, stores, or shopping centers. Sometimes the category would be very specific, such as a 12-to 20 unit apartment building. you might also select age or other characteristics. You will have some location preferences. Once you have found an image of the most important standards, you can decide what to look at.

Overpriced property is a problem. You can develop "gross income multipliers" to help you decide what is worth exploring. A gross income multiplier, as you know, is the ratio of sales price to gross income. Once you look at a number of properties of the same general type, You can have an idea of typical gross income multipliers. A reliable gross income multiplier needs to be based on sales prices, not asking prices. It also needs to consider rent levels, vacancies, and expenses, as well as building age and land value. The gross income multiplier is only a rough guide, unless it is backed up with facts that are amenable to analysis.

If you know the seller's reason for selling and the various circumstances surrounding the sale, seemingly overpriced properties may well be worth inspecting. If a seller has a compelling emotional (divorce or partnership disagreement) or economic (no more tax shelter, severe business losses) reason to sell, forget the price. It is traditional to ask prices that are higher than the property will bring. The seller does not make the market; you and he *together* determine the price. After carefully examining a number of well-selected properties, you should know what is available.

Group Ownership

Finding investments under group ownership is different from finding investments under direct ownership in that you look for others who will invest or have invested in your kind of property, rather than for the property; you look for the people who will locate others like you, rather than for the salesperson who will find you your property.

Finding the right group also means selecting the right form of ownership.

If you choose a private syndicate, then obviously you will be investing with friends, relatives, colleagues, business associates, or acquaintances. That list is so wide that it really does not give much of a clue. Yet you might inquire of those who you think are in real estate investments with others. If they are, you will want to meet the general partner, developer, or promoter.

Another approach is to check with an accountant, attorney or banker whom, if you intend to invest in real estate, you will need to provide professional services for you. They can frequently provide considered recommendations.

If you have difficulty getting access to private syndicates, ask your local real estate board to recommend someone who occasionally needs investment capital to either develop or acquire income-producing properties. The practioners in group ownership are known to the industry in our major metropolitan areas. While the local Board of Realtors can supply you with names, your investigation of the practitioners' policies and practices as well as their integrity should be excruciatingly thorough.

Real Estate Corporations

Real estate corporations issue stock that you can buy through stockbrockers. They can provide financial information about the corporation's past operations.

Real estate accounting can be very misleading because accountants record history, not current events. Thus the accountant will show what was paid for real estate, how much depreciation was taken, what the mortgage was and is, but not what the property is worth. You may find it especially difficult to evaluate real estate securities. You should select a stockbroker who not only understands securities, but also who is knowledgable about real estate.

Real Estate Investment Trusts

Getting into real estate investment trusts is similar to getting into owning stock in real estate corporations. The usual procedure is to go through your securities broker.

If the trust is in an equity trust, you will have the usual problem of evaluating the worth of the real estate and you will need a securities broker who knows something about real estate. If the trust is a mortgage trust, you may evaluate its earnings on the same basis on which you might evaluate earnings of other financial-type institutions. You could select the trust that you thought would perform best in increases in future earnings relative to current price.

MAKING THE INVESTMENT COMMITMENT

If your stockbroker provides you with information on a real estate security and you decide to buy it through her or him, the process is very simple. If you do not have an account, you fill out a card and obtain the account. If you want to buy, you may telephone the stockbroker and indicate how much you want to buy and the stockbroker will execute your order, if it is possible. You may bind yourself and the stockbroker, that is his firm, by unwritten instructions. It is very easy to buy and sell. Remember that in order to obtain liquidity in real estate, you generally have to give up something else, usually some of the cash flow for professional management and some of the other benefits of ownership, such as tax shelter and some of the benefits or proceeds of sale. Nonetheless real estate securities may be a very rewarding investment as compared to other securities.

You could buy into a limited partnership or other syndicate type of arrangement by signing partnership or joint venture agreements. Now there are many syndicate opportunities whose securities are requires to be registered by the SEC. These may be obtained through your securities broker or sometimes directly from the issuer as in smaller syndicates.

You should obtain legal counsel in any real estate venture to be sure you have the kind of legal protection you need. If you want direct ownership, then instead of owning a security, which is *personal property*, you own real estate, which is *real property*. Your evidence of ownership in real estate is a deed that is given to you by the seller. You transfer title by a deed when you sell. There are various kinds of deeds and they provide different protection to the purchaser.

Once the deed is delivered, you own the property. If you want to buy a property, you must submit a written offer to purchase. A verbal offer is not binding. When the seller accepts the written offer, both parties are bound.

It is customary to offer a deposit on the purchase price when making an offer. This "earnest money" provides the seller with an indication of your interest. It may also provide him with a quick way of collecting damages if you fail to complete the contract. This happens because the deposit receipt usually calls for the seller to be able to retain the deposit as a forfeiture in the event you do not complete your part of the bargain. He may still have other remedies at law, so that if you are not sure of all the legal ramifications, you should protect yourself by consulting a lawyer well versed in real estate transactions.

You may use contingencies if you are uncertain about the loan you will be able to get, zoning restrictions, or a multitude of other factors that affect your decision. When you offer to purchase and put up a deposit, after your offer is accepted, you are bound by those terms.

You may use various contingencies to gve you a way out, but unless they are legitimate, you may find yourself bound. If you want an option, you should use an option to buy, rather than a contract that obligates you to purchase.

Most properties are sold for price and terms that differ from the price and terms offered. It is therefore customary for the buyer to make the offer, usually at a price lower than the asking price. Since the seller cannot count on you to back up your verbal offer, you will be writing checks and signing contracts when you make bids on properties. You should therefore be comfortable with your decision when you make the offer, since it usually is not revocable without financial loss. Besides, sellers do accept offers and you will want an investment you can live with.

SUMMARY

When you alone own the fee, your ownership of real estate gives you exclusive control subject to some limitations. The limitations include police power, eminent domain, and taxation. Once you decide on a different form of ownership, you decide on lesser control over your investment.

In considering group ownership of any kind, the critical condition for you to identify is that the policies of the group are compatible with *your* strategy. After acquiring ownership, the decisions will not be yours alone; hence you should find out what your "partners" intend to do before you bind your investment to theirs.

You can get corporate-type investment by investing in stocks of real estate *investing* companies. But the corporation pays income taxes and so will you. A real estate investment trust, under most circumstances, relieves this double taxation problem. You can find out the kinds of policies pursued by publicly held real estate companies and real estate investment trusts by getting information through your securities broker.

Because of the nature of the real estate market, getting in on worthwhile real estate investments of any kind requires some *positive* action on your part, *You* must initiate the action. Do not be afraid to consult a Realtor, to answer ads in the local newspapers, and to inquire of your local real estate board as to which Realtors are most active in the location and class of property that fits your strategy.

Real estate market activity is best known to your local Realtor. The *securities* of real estate companies engaged in real estate investing are best known to certain stockbrokers. Since the real estate securities are not always well understood by all stockbrokers, the National Association of Securities Dealers located in Washington, D.C., can supply you with the names of brokers who tend to specialize in this type of security. If you have a liquid real estate investment (a stock or an investment trust certificate), you will have given up some other economic advantage.

You and the seller of real estate "make the market," not the broker. If you like a certain property, try to determine if there is a compelling economic reason for the seller to sell. If there is, start negotiating through the Realtor. Forget the asking price—make your offer based on your own knowledge of the risks, be sure that the rewards are adequate based on the guidelines you have acquired either in this book or through your own practical experience.

18 YOUR INVESTMENT STRATEGY

Your investment strategy is a personal matter that depends on the risks you are prepared to take and the rewards you seek. Each of us seeks a combination of risk and reward that has the proper balance for us. This chapter provides you with a step-by-step guide to developing such a personal real estate investment strategy.

LIQUIDITY

You must first determine how much cash you are prepared to invest, knowing that your investment is illiquid. The amount of cash you have for investment may well be what is left over after you have met your liquidity needs. What is best for you depends on your circumstances and preferences. The point in developing the strategy is for you to evaluate your own circumstances and preferences and then to realize that the cash you put into the investment will stay invested for a while.

Using *borrowed* money for a down payment naturally puts a strain on future liquidity. High-income professionals sometimes borrow money knowing they may be pinched for cash at a future date. Most of them feel they may be helped if the tax shelter from the investment is so great as to provide an offset against ordinary income. The risk is that the debt will have to be repaid irrespective of fluctuations in rental income or personal income.

MORTGAGE LOANS

In addition to the amount of cash available for a down payment, you will probably use some mortgage money to finance a purchase. If you wish to have the least risk of a negative cash flow, you will not borrow any money. You will not make as much profit, but the risk of losing the property will be negligible. And while you will make less profit, the worst that is likely to happen is that you will have a lower rate of return on your investment. You can lose some money if you try to sell a loser, but the loss will be relatively small. Most investors are not so conservative as to buy with all cash.

Many real estate investors will borrow what is generally available on a first mortgage and pay the balance of the purchase price in cash. Some take over the existing first-mortgage loan, especially in periods of tight money. In either case using a single amortizing first mortgage (in an amount ordinarily available from a mortgage-lending institution) will usually be safe enough for most investors. The prudent lender wants to be sure that the rental income (after deducting all operating expenses) is enough to cover the mortgage payments. He lends only that for which he believes he can be repaid out of the income of the property less a safety factor. Thus properties with such loans should produce a positive cash flow even if vacancies or expenses tend to rise.

Some less conservative investors will use as much borrowed money as they can, frequently taking the highest loan available, even though the interest rate is more than they would have to pay for a smaller loan. Although they look for the lowest annual constant in order to get the highest COD (cash on the down payment) they seek to control as much property as possible. Obviously this is risky. But when they have winners, they have big winners.

Those who need a stable cash flow stick with a single mortgage. The stability you expect of the cash flow and the price you are prepared to pay for borrowed money will determine how much you will seek to borrow. You can tailor your down payment to the risks you can readily accept. If you are speculatively inclined and can stand the risks, borrow to the hilt. You may be able to buy with as little as 10% down. If you are a middle-of-the-roader, pay about 25% down. If you are a conservative, seek the lowest interest rate and invest a greater amount in cash. Your down payment could be 35% or more. It would be rare for even the most cautious of investors to pay more than 50% down. Prudently using borrowed money enhances the benefit of investing in real estate, and most real estate investors find the risk of some borrowed money quite acceptable.

DIVERSIFICATION

Your cash payment and the amount you borrow determine the total price you can pay. Since real estate comes in large economic units, it takes a great deal of money to diversify by acquiring many different properties.

The investor with $5000 to $15,000 to invest can diversify best by acquiring shares of beneficial interest in one or more real estate investment trusts. Or you might acquire several limited partnership interests. But the smaller the amount of money to invest, the more difficult it is to diversify.

Most real estate investors make their initial real estate investment without any immediate concern about diversification. They do not put all their cash in real estate, but start with one property. As time goes on, they add other real estate investments to their portfolio.

If you start by selecting the property and financing that has the kind of risk you can live with, then you can get your diversification later. You can build your strategy by deciding on the risks you will take to get started. You can later adjust your portfolio to accommodate the need for diversification.

FORMS OF OWNERSHIP

If you are among the many investors who wish to actively manage their investments, you will prefer direct ownership. If your preferences do not require that you exercise control over the operation of the investment you will want to consider group ownership as well as direct ownership. If you are ready to stay in a very long time, you may consider some form of joint venture. If however, you want the liquidity of a traded security you will consider an investment in one of the investment trusts. Your preferences on risk, control, liquidity, and size of investment will guide your selection of the type of investment.

The type of investment becomes important in your strategy because the different types have different risks. Once you have set these constraints of risk, you will be ready to select the type of property.

TYPE OF PROPERTY

Your strategy will involve some policy as to the type or types of property you seek, In multitenanted properties, ordinarily the safest is residential income property. Depending on how much risk you will take in order to make more money, you can move to select riskier properties.

You may continue to build your strategy by selecting the kinds of property with which you are comfortable. The more experience you acquire, the more specialized the type of property you will be willing to consider for investment.

If you need or have a preference for tax shelter, that may influence the kind of property you seek to acquire. Generally, *the more of value in the building (instead of the land), the greater the allowable depreciation.* In addition, *greater depreciation is allowed for tax purposes in the case of residential rental property.* You will be naturally doing some mental gymnastics as you trade off between tax shelter and risk as well as among tax shelter and the other benefits of investing.

BENEFITS OF INVESTING

Ultimately the strategy must get the benefit you seek. If you are looking for retirement income, then obviously your strategy will call for properties with relatively high cash flow and minimum risk. You might even plan on acquiring a property with the idea of having most of the purchase price paid by the time of retirement.

If you are getting clobbered with income taxes, you might be buying property with 10% down—and borrowing that on personal, business or professional credit. You will pay less taxes, and though risky, it might turn out to be a very profitable real estate investment.

Other investors are seeking to accumulate wealth. They may acquire property with little tax shelter and little or no cash flow. But the value of the real estate will be increasing.

THE MAJOR OBJECTIVE

The objective of investing is to make money. But you may care a great deal about *when* you get the money, how it will be taxed, and the risks you have to take at the outset. So you can best develop your strategy by deciding what risks and rewards are for you. You have the guidelines for developing your strategy and for making your decisions. Now it is up to you. We hope you develop an *inbalance* real estate investment strategy because it will put you in the winner's circle.

Good-luck!

THE INVESTOR'S BOOKSHELF

An Annotated Bibliography
of Selected References
for Real Estate Investors

Compiled by Carol Culp, and John Kokus, Jr., Ph. D.
Real Estate Consultant Washington, D.C. 1978

REAL ESTATE INVESTMENT

Anderson, Gordon J. *How to Compete Successfully in Real Estate Investing.* New York: Exposition Press, 1973. 191 pp.

Stressing the importance of specialized knowledge to the real estate investor, the author discusses the economics of the metropolitan area and economic and technological change as factors in value. The characteristics of the real estate market are explained and the significance of location and human behavior patterns is examined.

Beaton, Willian R., and Terry Robertson. *Real Estate Investment.* Englewood Cliffs, N.J. : Prentice-Hall, 1977. 358 pp.

In addition to chapters on basic investment fundamentals, forms of ownership, and financing, the book contains a comprehensive section on income tax considerations and a chapter on investment mathematics. Sophisticated analysis techniques are explained and excellent case examples are presented to identify investment characteristics of land, industrial space, shopping centers, office space, and residential real estate, including mobile home parks. This is a good reference for students and investors.

Henry, Rene A., Jr. *How to Profitably Buy and Sell Land.* New York: John Wiley, 1977. 203 pp.

Written for real estate professionals and sophisticated investors, the book provides an up-to-date survey of land as an investment, with detailed explanations of techniques of finding and acquiring land. Stress is placed on the radically changed climate of land investment due to direct and indirect public land-use controls. Chapters are included on real estate accounting practices and tax considerations and on foreign investment opportunities. (This is a book in the "Real Estate for Professional Practitioners Series.")

Mader, Chris. *The Dow Jones-Irwin Guide to Real Estate Investing.* Homewood, Ill.: Dow-Jones-Irwin, 1975. 236 pp.

This is an aid for the investor offering suggestions for strategy, explanations of the investment characteristics of different types of real estate, and analysis techniques, including methods that reflect the effects of inflation. By assuming a certain level of inflation and applying this percentage to income, expenses, and sale price for each year of the holding period, overall rate of return is much higher and, according to the author, a more realistic picture of the investment's profitability is revealed. The final section of the book is devoted to tables analyzing the profitability of residential and commercial property as well as land and the personal residence.

Maisel, Sherman J., and Stephen E. Roulac. *Real Estate Investment and Finance.* New York/San Francisco: McGraw-Hill 1976. pp.

Designed as both a classroom text and a reference, the book presents an extremely thorough coverage of financing, forms of ownership, risk evaluation, and strategy, stressing the importance of careful analysis of real estate investments in the 1970s. The role of government in financing and tax considerations are explored. A few case examples are presented, as both debt and equity positions are examined.

Messner, Stephen D., Byrl N. Boyce, Harold G. Trimble, and Robert L. Ward *Analyzing Real Estate Opportunities.* Chicago: Realtors National Marketing Institute 1977. 319 pp.

The book is a guide to conducting market and feasibility studies. It is also an aid to the user of such studies and especially real estate brokers specializing in investment property.

Seldin, Maury. *Land Investment.* Homewood, Ill.: Dow Jones-Irwin, 1975. 242 pp.

Written primarily as an aid to decision-making for the investor, this book is not too technical for the general reader who seeks to understand the forces of land use change. The first section of the book deals with the risks and rewards of land as an investment. The second section discusses the forces of urbanization, suburbanization, and interurbanization; monetary and fiscal policy; demographic patterns; and local development forces. The third section discusses land conversion, and the final section explains locating, financing, and negotiating the purchase of land.

Temple, Douglas M. *Making Money in Real Estate.* Chicago: Henry Regnery, 1976. 314 pp.

This guide is intended as an aid to enable the beginning real estate investor to understand the investment process and to identify risks and evaluate rewards. Stressing careful analysis, the book discusses the general economy, leverage, financing, and tax considerations. In addition to chapters on land, income property, and passive investments, a large section is devoted to the home as an investment.

Wiley, Robert J. *Real Estate Investment: Analysis and Strategy.* New York: Ronald, 1977. 347 pp.

After identifying the basic data necessary for making real estate decisions, the author explores methods of analysis from traditional techniques to the most sophisticated, including discounted cash flow and risk/return analysis. Strategy, as related to the investor's goals, is discussed with a focus on available options in the form of ownership, financing, holding period, and disposition of the property. The characteristics of various property types are explained; the final sections of the book deal with property development.

VALUATION

American Institute of Real Estate Appraisers. *The Appraisal of Real Estate.* Chicago: American Institute of Real Estate Appraisers, 1973. 596 pp.

This is the sixth edition of the Institute's basic textbook on the fundamental concepts of real estate valuation. Among the areas covered are: economic trends, depreciation, the approaches to value, functional utility, capitalization techniques, and the appraisal report. Compound Interest tables are included.

Rams, Edwin M. *Rams Real Estate Appraising Handbook.* Englewood Cliffs, N.J.: Prentice-Hall, 1975. 636 pp.

In addition to discussing appraisal techniques, the author devotes a large part of the book to urban growth and development and demand-supply analysis. Value impact and environmental impact studies are covered, as is appraisal of different kinds of real estate, including special-purpose property. A chapter is included on rehabilitation for profit.

Ratcliff, Richard U. *Valuation for Real Estate Decisions.* Santa Cruz, Cal.: Democrat Press, 1972. 346 pp.

A product of the "New School" of appraisal thought, the book stresses the appraisal as an investor's tool in the decision-making process. To this end topics explored are: the establishment of market price; valuation of single-family homes, of income property, of land, of industrial real estate; and appraisal for condemnation.

Ring, Alfred A. *The Valuation of Real Estate.* Englewood Cliffs, N.J.: Prentice-Hall, 1970. 660 pp.

Written as a training and teaching guide for persons seeking professional appraiser status, the book begins with a good deal of theory: political, social, economic, and urban forces that influence value are discussed. Chapters are then focused on neighborhood characteristics, site analysis, land valuation, market approach to value, building construction and plan reading, and building costs and depreciation. Income and expense analysis, capitalization rates, and valuation mathematics are then explained. Final chapters cover the income approach to value, leaseholds, and condemnation appraisals. The Appendix includes demonstration appraisals and present value, capitalization, and amortization tables.

Robinson, Peter C. *Complete Guide to Appraising Commercial and Industrial Properties.* Englewood Cliffs, N.J.: Prentice-Hall, 1977. 364 pp.

The author clearly outlines the appraisal process, illustrating the cost, income, and market approaches as well as mortgage-equity analysis. The text consists in large part of model appraisals, thoroughly covering the determination of value of office plazas, apartment houses, shopping centers, leasehold estates, and special-purpose properties.

Society of Real Estate Appraisers. *Real Estate Appraisal: Principals and Terminology.* Chicago: Society of Real Estate Appraisers, 1971. 131 pp.

A second edition, updated to reflect changes in investment analysis and appraisal, the book lists alphabetically, and describes clearly, real estate appraisal and construction terms. Also included are the standards of conduct of the Society and a brief section of architectural drawings to aid in the identification of construction features.

Wendt, Paul F. *Real Estate Appraisal Review and Outlook.* Athens, Ga.: University of Georgia, 1974. 268 pp.

Perceiving the real estate appraiser as essentially an economist, the author includes discussions of economic base analysis and urban growth theories, in addition to explanations of gross-rent multipliers, market comparison, income capitalization, and replacement cost methods. The book is directed to the professional appraiser and the college-level student, and emphasis is on new techniques.

REAL ESTATE TRANSACTIONS

Estes, Jack C., and John Kokus, Jr. *Real Estate License Preparation Course for the Uniform Examinations for Salespersons and Brokers.* New York: McGraw-Hill, 1976 246 pp.

Written as both a home-study guide and for classroom use, the authors discuss the essentials of real estate to prepare applicants to pass the state licensing examinations. All-inclusive, especially useful are questions and answers and complete sets of forms, such as listings, offer-to-purchase agreements, and settlement statements. Includes closing cost calculations and math assistance.

Gettel, Ronald E. *Real Estate Guidelines and Rules of Thumb.* New York: McGraw Hill, 1976. 234 pp.

The author argues for the informed use of rules of thumb, but points out exceptions and inaccuracies in many that are widely used. Topics covered are site planning, lot sizes and shapes, houses and condominiums, and income property. A miscellaneous chapter is included. Numerous charts and tables appear for quick reference. Among them are guides to number of lots per acre, development cost of land, annual constants, debt coverage ratios, and operating ratios for income properties. This book should prove useful to developers, investors, and brokers.

Gross, Jerome S. *Encyclopedia of Real Estate Forms.* Englewood Cliffs, N.J.: Prentice-Hall, 1973. 458 pp.

As the title suggests this is a compendium of sample forms used in conducting real estate business. Alternative clauses and forms appear in each category. In addition to the more common documents, such as sales contracts, mortgages, and deeds, less familiar forms appear, including exchange agreements, assignments, affidavits, construction contracts, and options. This is a fine reference for the real estate professional.

IBP Research and Editorial Staff. *Real Estate Forms Desk Book.* Englewood Cliffs, N.J.: Institute for Business Planning, 1976. 477 pp.

Compiled for lawyers as well as others in the real estate business, the book, in Part I, contains checklists of important considerations in various transactions. Part II consists of numerous sample contracts, including those of sale, option, exchange, lease, brokerage, management, and limited partnership. All contract clauses are separately indexed. This is an excellent reference for aid in writing or evaluating agreements.

Reilly, John W. *The Language of Real Estate,* Chicago: Real Estate Education Co., 1977. 585 pp.

This is a dictionary of real estate terms that goes far beyond simple definitions. Several paragraphs may appear after an entry to clarify, explain the applicable law, or give an illustration of the term. Contracts, brokerage, financing, and real estate law are topics represented and separate glossaries of abbreviations and building terms appear. Sample forms are also included.

THE DEVELOPMENT PROCESS

Applebaum, William. *Shopping Center Strategy.* New York: International Council of Shopping Centers, 1970. 202 pp.

Shopping Center Strategy is a case study of the development of a regional shopping center, Del Monte Center in California, with particular emphasis on the market analysis prepared for the project. An attempt is made to identify and evaluate the key decisions made during the development process for the benefit of developers, and projections are made with regard to the future outlook for the center.

McKeever, J. Ross. *Apartment Development: A Strategy for Successful*

Decision-Making. Washington, D.C.: The Urban Land Institute, 1974. 58 pp.

This publication looks at multifamily development in the face of ever-increasing costs, rent controls, and land-use regulation. After explaining the demographic factors that influence demand for apartments, the author summarizes the development process, discussing market analysis, project feasibility, site selection, design, financing, marketing, and management. Checklists of steps for the developer to follow are presented throughout.

McKeever, J. Ross, Nathaniel M. Griffin, Frank H. Spink, Jr., and the Commercial and Office Development Council of ULI. *Shopping Center Development Handbook.* Washington, D.C.: The Urban Land Institute, 1977. 290 pp.

This may be everything you always wanted to know about shopping centers, but were afraid to ask. The book, for the developer and the student, is clearly written and, after discussing the types and characteristics of centers, follows the development process from market analysis and site selection and acquisition through physical planning, financing, parking considerations, and leasing. Tenant mix and management are also discussed. Nine case studies are presented which include the Mercado in California, Tall Oaks Village Center in Reston, and the Citadel in Colorado. The final chapter is devoted to future trends that will shape shopping-center demand and development in years to come.

McMahan, John. *Property Development.* New York/St. Louis/San Francisco: McGraw-Hill, 1976. 432 pp.

This clearly written, well-organized book explains the process by which real estate values are created. Its purpose is to facilitate decision- making in these uncertain times by providing an understanding of the fundamentals of the development process: marketing, finance, planning and design, construction, merchandising, and property management. Comprehensive chapters on market analysis for residential, retail, office, industrial, and transient commercial uses are included.

O'Mara, W. Paul. *Residential Development Handbook.* Washington, D.C.: The Urban Land Institute, 1978. 338 pp.

This handbook really constitutes a comprehensive text on the residential development process, discussing at length all facets of project feasibility, design, marketing, and maintenance. Alternative forms of residential development are described and a chapter is devoted to rehabilitation. The book concludes with an analysis of future trends—demographic, economic, regulatory, and technological.

Phillippo, Gene. *The Professional Guide to Real Estate Development.* Homewood, Ill.: Dow Jones-Irwin, 1976. 306 pp.

Intended as a step-by-step guide to successful development, funding, and investing, the book stresses timing, both external and internal, as all-important. Market, financial, and site analysis are covered, and the development of "Nine Lakes", a Kaiser-Aetna apartment project, is documented.

Urban Land Institute. *Industrial Development Handbook.* Washington, D.C.: Urban Land Institute, 1975. 256 pp.

The handbook's objective is to facilitate better planning for industrial areas and parks and planned employment centers in today's development climate, which is short on resources and long on aesthetic requirements. Culled from the experience of industrial developers, technical publications, and the authors' own experience, information is presented on land-use controls, site selection, and planning and design. A section on development strategy includes discussions of financing and feasibility analysis, The book concludes with pertinent trends and future implications.

Witherspoon, Robert E., Jon P. Abbett, and Robert M. Gladstone. *Mixed-Use Development:New Ways of Land Use.* Washington, D.C.: The Urban Land Institute, 1976. 193 pp.

For planners and developers, this is a definitive study of what is the newest and, increasingly the most important form of real estate development today—the multifunctional project. In addition to being urbane and efficient, mixed-use developments promise to play a critical role in restoring the vitality of central cities. Generously illustrated, this book discusses the development and the economics of "MXDs", as well as planning and zoning considerations. Eleven case studies are documented and the concluding section is devoted to an inventory of existing mixed-use projects, those under construction, and those in the planning stage.

REAL ESTATE FINANCE

Atteberry, William. *Modern Real Estate Finance.* Columbus, Ohio: Grid, 1972. 391 pp.

This is a clearly written and well-organized text intended to provide fundamental information about the subject and to reflect the major trends and innovations of the 1960s: REITs, condominiums, HUD, "tight money," mobile homes, pension fund involvement in real estate finance, and new government housing programs, Comnprehensive in scope, the book covers instruments of real estate finance, the rights of parties in the event of default, junior liens, coops and condos, lease financing, sale-leaseback, the mortgage market, and financing institutions. What *Modern Real Estate Finance* lacks in color, it more than compensates for in solid, understandable information.

Britton, James A., and Lewis O. Kerwood, (ed). *Financing Income-Producing Real Estate.* New York: McGraw-Hill, 707 pp.

This comprehensive text has been compiled and written in such a way that it can be used by the beginner as well as by the professional. Chapters in the first section of the book, devoted to theory, are essays by different authors on topics too numerous to list, but including investor risk analysis, tax considerations, construction financing, unusual financing techniques (Land-sale-leaseback, wrap-around), and REITs. The second section presents 11 fairly complicated case studies for analysis of their potential. Projects represented include office buildings, shopping centers, apartments, and industrial development.

Goleman, Harry A., AIA, (ed). *Financing Real Estate Development.* Englewood, N.J.: Aloray, 1974. 143 pp.

Aimed at architects the book provides an unexpectedly thorough treatment of the economics of real estate development, including not only financing sources and techniques, but also risk-reward strategy and sophisticated tax considerations. The text is illustrated throughout with diagrams and sample analyses.

Shenkel, William M. *Real Estate Finance.* USA: American Institute of Banking, Division of American Bankers Association, 1976. 421 pp.

A text for students and a reference for bankers, *Real Estate Finance* looks at the subject matter from the perspective of the commercial bank. Material in the book falls into three parts, the first of which deals with institutional arrangements: the role of credit in the allocation of real estate resources, property rights, and the mortgage instrument. In the second section financing of specific property types is discussed. In the concluding section administrative functions are explained, including credit analysis and collection policies, The final chapter deals with real estate investment yields and includes explanations of discounted cash flow and internal rate of return.

Wiedemer, John P. *Real Estate Finance.* Reston, VA.: Reston, 1974. 331 pp.

A basic book on the fundamentals of real estate finance, this could serve as a text for the beginner or reference for the professional. Clearly written and well organized, *Real Estate Finance* covers the money market, sources of mortgage money and their characteristics, secondary markets, property value, federal programs, and analysis for loan purposes of both property and borrower.

FEDERAL INCOME TAX CONSIDERATIONS

Berman, Daniel S., and Sheldon Schwartz. *Tax Saving Opportunities in Real Estate deals.* Englewood Cliffs, N.J.: Prentice-Hall, 1971. 198 pp.

Written by attorneys, the purpose of this guide is to facilitate the creative use of the income tax laws to improve real estate deals by finding tax shelters and avoiding tax traps. A key feature is a *Master Checklist* presenting questions one should ask and alternatives one should consider in structuring a real estate transaction for the most advantageous application of the tax laws. Chapters are included on the fundamentals of depreciation, tax-wise buying, selling, and mortgaging, tax-free exchanges, tax angles of leasing and managing, and tax planning. The problems of individuals, syndicates, and corporations are considered. The book is easily understood by the tax novice, but the reader is cautioned to be aware of recent changes in the tax laws.

IBP Research and Editorial Staff. *Real Estate Tax Shelter Desk Book.* Englewood Cliffs, N.J.: Institute for Business Planning, 1975. 338 pp.

The book deals comprehensively with the tax implications of real estate transactions, the understanding of which is essential to investment success. Chapter topics include: tax treatment of costs. depreciation, investment tax credit, capital-gains tax, exchanges, mortgage foreclosures, tax aspects of corporations, land development, farmland and homes. The appendix is loaded with good charts and tables on useful lives, after-tax cost of interest, and comparative depreciation that aid in determining the actual after-tax value of real estate tax shelters.

Real Estate Syndication Digest. *Tax Sheltered Investments: A Practical Introduction.* San Francisco: Real Estate Syndication Digest, 1973. 494 pp.

While oil and gas as well as cattle investments are included in this book's coverage, more than half of the text is devoted to real estate investment through partnership and syndication. Articles by contributing authors are organized in outline form and many prospectus extracts are included. Comprehensive glossaries appear in each section. In addition to explanations of tax shelter and leverage, the book contains a large section on real estate investment analysis, which includes the "payback method" and discounted cash flow. Readers should keep in mind recent changes in the tax laws that have taken place since the book was published.

HOUSING

Clurman, David, and Edna L. Hebard. *Condominiums and Cooperatives.* New York: John Wiley, 1970 395 pp.

A thorough discussion of these hybrid forms of ownership, the book examines legal structure, income tax factors, financing, and management of condos and coops. Chapters for brokers and homebuyers are included as well as a section on homeowner associations and new towns.

Schafer, Robert. *The Suburbanization of Multifamily Housing.* Lexington, Mass.: Lexington Books, 1974. 148 pp.

The author identifies the factors of supply and demand that have influenced the construction of multifamily housing and its shift to suburban areas. The effects of zoning and demographic patterns on residential location are explained and possible future trends of importance to the multifamily market are discussed.

Sumichrast, Michael, and Maury Seldin. *Housing Markets.* Homewood, Ill.: Dow Jones-Irwin, 1977. 504 pp.

This is a fine reference work that is much more than a "how-to-do-it guide for housing market analysts, although it is that too. The authors emphasize the effective use of market analysis for decision-making in order to implement building, investing, lending, or government strategy in an increasingly complex housing market. The system by which housing is produced and distributed is discussed, as are the components of supply and demand. Demographic and sociological changes are examined and some interesting predictions made. Risks, goals, and strategies of the construction firm and the financier are explored and related to analysis and evaluation of trends, demand forecasts, and location. The Appendixes include a sample market analysis and an extensive bibliography.

Melaniphy, John C., Jr. *Commercial and Industrial Condominiums.* Washington, D.C.: The Urban Land Institute, 1976. 73 pp.

This study examines nonresidential condominiums as an alternative to leasehold ownership for business operations. The physical and economic characteristics of office and industrial condominiums, as compiled from questionnaire and interview data, are presented. There is also a brief section on shopping center condominiums. Tables that compare renting to owning appear, and condo ownership consistently results in a financial advantage. Also included are short profiles of 30 commercial and 10 industrial condominium developments.

INCOME PROPERTY

Applebaum, William, and S. O, Kaylin. *Case Studies in Shopping Center Development and Operation.* New York: International Council of Shopping Centers, 1974. 280 pp.

This book contains case studies of five shopping centers, each of which deals with a different major problem confronting those involved in such projects. Analyzed are decisions on financing, tenant mix, mall enclosure, the improvement of an existing center, and the redevelopment of an old center, The centers examined are; "Southgate Mall" and "Jefferson Mall" (The identity of these two centers is disguised): Westgate Mall, Ohio; College Grove, California; and Pinellas Shopping Center, Florida.

Clurman, David. *The Business Condominium, A New Form of Business Property Ownership.* New York: John Wiley, 1973. 185 pp.

The author explores the condo as an alternative to traditional forms of leasing and ownership of real estate from business use, emphasizing the cost-cutting advantages of shared common facilities as well as the investment potential of the form. Structuring, management, financing, and appraisal of business condos are discussed as is the concept of the "sale-condoback". A section on the use of the condo form by medical practices, industries, shopping centers, multiuse facilities, and even airports is included. This book is part of the "Real Estate for Professional Practioners Series." Each book covers a fairly specific topic in a concise but thorough manner.

Downs, James C., Jr. *Principles of Real Estate Management.* Chicago: Institute of Real Estate Management, 1978. 488 pp.

This classic text stresses the importance of knowledge of the real estate market to the successful property manager. The first section of the book deals with real estate theory and topics include the money supply, the role of government, and real estate cycles. The second section discusses the marketing process, the heart of management activity. In the final section, administrative activities of the property manager are examined, such as tenant selection, collection, recordkeeping, and maintenance.

Kinnard, William N., Jr., and Stephen D. Messner. *Industrial Real Estate.* Washington , D.C.: Society of Industrial Realtors,1971. 655 pp.

A revised edition designed to reflect changes in the income tax laws and in the money market as well as increased emphasis on investment analysis, the book presents a thorough study of the economics of industrial real estate. Among topics covered are industrial property development, and sources of assistance to the industrial space developer. A particularly interesting section is included on rehabilitation and conversion of industrial properties. This should be of interest to brokers, developers, appraisers, and investors.

Lion, Edgar. *Shopping Centers: Planning, Development, and Administration.* New York: John Wiley, 1976. 198 pp.

In this reference work the author first traces the evolution of shopping centers up to the expanded role they play in contemporary life. The development process, including design and leasing, is discussed, as are the administration of shopping centers and the modernization of older centers. Numerous checklists of steps and considerations in developing and managing centers are included. Deliberately omitted are financial aspects that may vary from one locality to another or become dated.

Messner, Stephen D., Irving Schreiber and Victor Lyon. *Marketing Investment Real Estate.* Chicago: Realtor National Marketing Institute, 1975, 353 pp.

This book is concerned with fitting income property into an investment program. It emphasizes investment, finance, and taxation. Included is a section of case studies. This book is intended for investment real estate brokers and investors.

Siskind, Donald H. *Real Estate Tax and Financial Considerations.* New York: Practising Law Institute, 1975. 576 pp.

A fairly difficult law course handbook, its selected materials cover topics such as sale-leaseback, ground leases, the financing of condos and coops, and REITs. Exhibits include sample leases and agreements.

Seldin, Maury, Editor-in-Chief. *The Real Estate Handbook*, Homewood, Illinois: Dow Jones-Irwin, 1979. 1100 pp.

The most significant reference work for real estate investors. Contains chapters by leading authorities on investing in different types of real estate, sources of financing, and analyses of investment properties. Additionally, it contains chapters on real estate ownership forms, taxation, leasing, and transfer. Sixty-six chapters by industry leaders provide substantive detail to answer many questions often raised by real estate investors and practitioners.

The Urban Land Institute. *Dollars and Cents of Shopping Centers.* Washington, D.C.: The Urban Land Institute 1978. 325 pp.

A key reference in shopping center planning and design, this report analyzes income and expense data for 550 centers in the United States and Canada. (The names of centers are not disclosed.) Income, expense, net operating income, and cash flow figures are arranged by center type: Superregional, regional, community, and neighborhood: as well as geographically. Rent and sales per square foot are also included by store classification.

FORMULA INDEX

13. Taxable proceeds of sale = adjusted sales
price – adjusted book value.   49, 181-183
14. After-tax proceeds of sale = pretax
proceeds of sale – tax on proceeds of sale.   48-49, 183, 201
15. Total profit = after-tax proceeds of sale
+ after-tax cash flow (cumulative) – down
payment.   48-49, 183

INDEX

Locations, desirable, 24
 higher rents because of, 238
 one hundred percent, 264
 quality concordant with, 27
 world's worst, 96
Lock-in, 143
 office building loans, 261
Long shots, 3
Losses, real, 12
 tax, 46
Lots, 170
 subdivided, 174
Lucky, consistently, 71

M, second stage of pyramid downside, 96, 98
Maintenance, of apartments, 231
Manager, CPM, certified property
 manager, 73, 214
 executive, 69
 property, 64, 69, 72, 186, 214
 resident, 69, 72, 214
Markets, broad, 281
 real estate, 58
 realty action, 167
 sardine, 167
 thin, 280
Master plan, the, 165
Maturing process, stage of pyramid
 downside, 96
Maturity, held until, 16
Milestone, 82
Milking, undermaintaining by, 232
Mix, appropriate, 80, 81
Monetary policy, 153
Money, checkbook, 152
 in a checking account, 20
 controlling the supply of, 154
 cost and availability of borrowed,
 148
 creating, 151
 dangers in using borrowed, 108
 earnest, 309
 expansion of, 151
 as in a liquid asset, 20

long-term, 65
 making most, 10
 mortgage, 64
 other costs of, 142
 rewards of using borrowed, 128
 short-term, 65
 valves, 154, 155

Mortgage, amortizing the, 28
 as a debt, 28
 in default, 118
 first, 117
 given back, 167
 investing in, 11
 second, 117
 taking back a, 63

Mortgagee, the lender, 119
Mortgage package, developing a,
 80, 81
Mortgages, ballooned, 131
 chattel, 231
 FHA insured, 17
 purchase money, 174
Mortgage trusts, 302
Mortgaging out, 137
Motels, 280
Multipliers, gross income, 306

National Association of Realtors
 (NAR), 73, 187, 305
Needs, emergency, 11
 meeting, 9
 personal, 11
Negative cash flow, 4, 25, 108, 121,
 137, 163
Nepotism, to practice, 203
New towns, to build, 178
New York Stock Exchange, 187

Objectives, investment, 4, 8
Obsolescence, economic, 35
 functional, 35
 slowing down the rate of, 97
 varying forms of, 35

Quality, stinting on construction, 26

R's, "the three," 100
Rate, capital gains, 48
Rating, high credit, 24
Ratios, loan-to-value, 117
Ready to go, lots are, 178
Real estate, corporations, 300
  income-producing, 23
  investment trusts, 7, 107, 301-303
Realtors, 100, 303, 312
Record, "public," 62
Refinancing, benefits of, 139
  to lower the amortization, 75
  proceeds from, 23
Regulation, land use, 58
Rehabilitation, 75, 100
REIT's, real estate investment trusts, 302, 303
Remodelers, professional, 99
Remodeling, 75, 100
Renovation, 75, 100
Rents, percentage, 270
Reserve, ratios, 156
  requirements, 156
Return, rate of, 112
Rewards, discussion of, 23-53
  in owning garden apartments, 216
  in owning high-rise apartments, 241
  in owning land, 179
  in owning office buildings, 258
  in owning rental houses, 188
  in owning shopping centers and stores, 270
  in owning small apartment buildings, 202
  in owning special-purpose property, 283
  resulting, 4
Rezoned, land that may be, 165
Rezoning, land investments that depend on, 172

Risks, 4
  changes, 76
  changing the, 23
  estimate of the, 82
  financial, 11, 16, 18
  in garden apartments, 232
  in high-rise apartments, 237
  in industrial motel, hotel, and other special-purpose property, 281, 282, 283
  inflating, 18
  liquidity, 11
  in owning land, 163-173
    rental houses, 198
    shopping centers and stores, 263
    small apartments, 202
  purchasing power, 11
  in renting space, 247
  and rewards, 78
  and rewards inherent in investing, 76
  selecting, 12-22
  in tenancy of office buildings, 254
  three big, 12
  types of, 12
  of using borrowed money, 107
Roads, construction, 171
  maintenance, 171
  public improvements such as, 166
Rules, depreciation recapture, 50
  federal income tax, 44
  on deductability of prepaid interest, 175

Sale, the auction, 118
  force an unfavorable, 107
  foreclosure, 118
  proceeds of, 48
  timing the, 169
Sardine, market in, 167
Saver, obtaining his money, 20
Schedules, draw, 86
  gross income, 81

Tax Reform Act of 1976, 88
Tax shelter, 7, 23
  compute the, 114
  in garden apartments, 218
  in high-rise apartments, 218
  in industrial and special purpose
      property, 285
  limitation upon, 45
  in office buildings, 258
  on the pyramid upside, 102
  reasonable picture of, 88
  in rental houses, 190
  in shopping centers or stores, 272
Tax write-offs, 102
Tenancy, 90
  by the entirety, 297
  joint, 297
Tenants, high-quality, 25
  poor-quality, 24
Tenants in common, 297
Theaters, 282
Three-pipe system, heating and air-
      conditioning, 249
Tile, asphalt, 26
  vinyl, 26
Tilemen, 68
Timing the sale, 169
Title, pass, 61
  take, 61
  taking subject to the mortgage,
      127
Topographic map, 80
Town houses, 210
Trading, one real estate investment
      for another, 23

Triplexes, 202
Trusts, deed, 117
  deed of, 28
  equity, 7, 302
  investment, 7, 32, 301
  mortgage, 302
Turnover, in high-rise apartments,
      242
Two-pipe system, heating and air-
      conditioning, 249

Upside, of the pyramid, 83
Urban, fringe of development, 168
  growth, 165
  renewal, 76, 95
Urban Land Institute, 270

Vacancy, 100% rate, 199
Value, book, 39
  salvage, 38
Vehicle, investing, 7

Water supply, mains, 166
  public improvements such as, 166
Windfalls, 137
Wrecker, candidates for the, 76

Yield, ambiguous in terms of, 112
  nominal, 13
  not cash flow, 25
  real, 13

Zoning, authorities, 166
  regulates land use, 165
  rules of, 80